# The Idea of Monotheism

# The Idea of Monotheism

## The Evolution of a Foundational Concept

Jack Shechter

HAMILTON BOOKS
*Lanham • Boulder • New York • London*

Copyright © 2018 by The Rowman & Littlefield Publishing Group, Inc.
4501 Forbes Boulevard
Suite 200
Lanham, Maryland 20706
Hamilton Acquisitions Department (301) 459-3366

Unit A, Whitacre Mews, 26-34 Stannary Street,
London SE11 4AB, United Kingdom

*All rights reserved*
Printed in the United States of America

British Library Cataloging in Publication Information Available

**Library of Congress Cataloging-in-Publication Data**
Names: Shechter, Jack, author.
Title: The idea of monotheism : the evolution of a foundational concept / Jack Shechter.
Description: Lanham, Maryland : Hamilton Books, [2018] | Includes bibliographical references and index.
Identifiers: LCCN 2018020683 (print) | LCCN 2018023067 (ebook) | ISBN 9780761870449 (electronic) | ISBN 9780761870432 (pbk. : alk. paper)
Subjects: LCSH: God (Judaism)
Classification: LCC BM610 (ebook) | LCC BM610 .S54 2018 (print) | DDC 296.3/11—dc23
LC record available at https://lccn.loc.gov/2018020683

∞™ The paper used in this publication meets the minimum requirements of American National Standard for Information Sciences—Permanence of Paper for Printed Library Materials, ANSI Z39.48—1984

Printed in the United States of America

In Appreciation

To my grandfather,

Pinchas Schechter, z"l

who taught me the importance of faith and study.

His path to fervent belief in the One God—
the *Ribbono Shel Olam*—was manifestly
different from mine. But I hope that via the
path of this study it will become clear that
I have arrived at the same basic affirmation.

# Contents

| | |
|---|---|
| Acknowledgments | ix |
| Introduction | 1 |
| 1 The Patriarchs and Monotheism | 9 |
| 2 Moses and Monotheism | 21 |
| 3 The Prophets and Monotheism | 37 |
| 4 The Rabbis and Monotheism | 67 |
| 5 Judaism and Christianity and Monotheism | 95 |
| 6 Was Monotheism Compromised? The Divinity and the Human Being | 105 |
| 7 Why Is the Notion of the Oneness of God—the Cornerstone of Monotheism—of Such Great Importance? | 137 |
| Notes | 143 |
| Selected Bibliography | 159 |
| Index | 163 |
| About the Author | 173 |

# Acknowledgments

A key factor that has guided me in the composition of this Guide is a lesson I learned from one of my mentors, Dr. Rolf Knierim, Professor of Old Testament at the School of Theology at the Claremont Graduate School in California. During work under his guidance on my doctoral dissertation about the theology of the land of Israel, I was in search of what might be considered "new" in, or a "contribution" to, the field of study I was involved with. Dr. Knierim told me that contribution to a field of study is based on accumulating the already available data and expositions in a given field and then proceeding to bring one's own work "one rung higher"—perhaps uncovering an insight not heretofore seen, perhaps providing clarity to a murky received notion, perhaps juxtaposing data in a way that illumines the topic at hand. As the reader proceeds in this study, I do hope he/she will indeed detect a "higher rung" or two in the study of Monotheism. How truly consequential are one's mentors!

In addition to Dr. Knierim, a number of colleagues and friends have helped me in various ways in the composition of this work, and I most appreciate their constructive criticism and encouragement. In particular,

Professor Ziony Zevit, my colleague at the American Jewish University for over two decades, who read through various versions of the manuscript with great care. He made a set of specific corrections and suggestions about both content and form, which prompted me to adjust the material for greater clarity and accessibility. He also urged me to advance the various ideas argued for, by including additional works by contemporary scholars on the subject of Monotheism and related areas. I took this advice to heart, as the work will show. I am extremely grateful to him.

I much appreciate the fact that Dr. Benjamin Sommer, who today graces the faculty of the Jewish Theological Seminary, my alma mater, also critiqued the manuscript of this work with his discerning eye. More: he made suggestions that led me to refocus the last two chapters in order to integrate them with the basic thought line of the work.

There is a rabbinic dictum called *hakarat hatov*, "the recognition of the good," that is, the obligation to express gratitude about a person who bestows beneficence upon another. In this connection I repeat here what I wrote about such a person in the preface of a previous book of mine, *The Land of Israel: Its Theological Dimensions*:

There is another person to whom I owe thanks for the seminal influence he had on me in the area of biblical studies. He is the late Dr. Nahum Sarna, who served for many years as Professor of Biblical Studies at Brandeis University outside of Boston. At the time I was Director of the New England Region of the United Synagogue of America headquartered in Brookline, Mass.

For five consecutive years we sat together as congregants in the pews of Congregation Kehillath Israel in Brookline. This was every Shabbat and holiday service, the consistency about which we both complained yet from which we rarely absented ourselves. Nahum was a warm and friendly and embracing persona and most especially a profoundly informed and creative biblical scholar. I had arranged a wide-ranging seminar program for rabbis and educators in Boston featuring Dr. Sarna and his path-breaking approach to Bible study which successfully reconciled biblical tradition with the new literary, historical and archaeological findings that have emerged from the studies of scholars of the ancient Near Eastern milieu. This helped cement a bond between us.

At each of the Shabbat and holiday services before, during and after the Torah reading (yes, we were a bit out of line on this score), Nahum would share with me his interpretations, replete with documented data, insights, bon mots that illumined for me fascinating traditional and modern approaches to the world of the Bible. The utter consistency and substantive content of these encounters constituted an education (tuition-free) in scripture of the first order.

Before leaving Boston for Pittsburgh to take up my post as a pulpit rabbi, Nahum gifted me with a fourteenth-century illuminated manuscript reproduced from the original. It was a prayer from an Ashkenazic Yom Kippur prayerbook. Framed by an *Aron Kodesh* (Holy Ark), towers, birds and figures in various praying postures was the text:

*Barukh Ata Adonoy Elohaynu Melekh Ha-olom Hapotayakh Lanu Sha-ar.*
*Blessed are You O God, King of the universe, who opens for us the gates.*

Nahum reminded me that this, of course, meant the gates to heaven asking for forgiveness; but also, he said, it meant the "gates to learning" as I proceed to my new task.

Nahum also took me with him to the Andover Theological Seminary library in Newton to study the collection of biblical books and made sure that I had the latest comprehensive publications containing the standard resources for intensive biblical study.

I've long since been persuaded that the five-year encounter with Nahum Sarna laid the groundwork for the kind of work a book of this nature required. Yet more: When I applied for admission to the doctoral program in biblical studies at the University of Pittsburgh/Pittsburgh Theological Seminary, Nahum wrote a recommendation for me which helped in no small measure. Nahum has since passed away. The memory of him is, indeed, a blessing.

And then there is my scholarly wife, Leah. As usual, she kept me focused on the ideological authenticity of this topic, on the accurate use of the content of scripture, and on the correct usage of Hebrew. It is difficult to thank Leah enough for all this and much more. God was good when He brought us together.

Terri Nigro. This highly skilled literary technician has been at my side for a number of years now in my writing pursuits. She has carefully typed the manuscript of this book from my "old-fashioned" handwriting. (I've long since been self-trained to think with pen rather than with typewriter/computer.) For this, and for many other helpful ways, many thanks are due to Terri.

And then the manuscript reached the hands of the competent professionals at Rowman & Littlefield and its Hamilton Books imprint. Robert Swanson prepared the index and Brianna Westervelt guided the production process. Julie Kirsch, who manages an array of the company's publications, took special interest in this book. Her pronounced skill and focus on the work's numerous details—major and minor—was accompanied with benign demeanor and constant encouragement. This all helped considerably for this work to now emerge into the light of day.

*Introduction*

# On Monotheism

*The Patriarchs planted the seed.*
*Moses nurtured it.*
*The Prophets made it bloom.*
*The Rabbis harvested its fruits.*

The concept of development is indispensable for understanding the origin and growth of the Jewish religion.

### THE OBJECTIVE OF THIS WORK

This undertaking is designed to trace the idea of Monotheism as it has evolved over the centuries: the belief in the existence of the One God who fashioned the world, and remains involved in it and with humanity and its values. The tracing begins with the era of the Patriarchs, continues through the Mosaic and prophetic periods, into the classical rabbinic/early Christian era, and then to the realm of the mystics up to the early modern age. It concludes with elucidation of the monotheistic idea in modern terms.

What has made an effort such as this possible is the biblical scholarship of the last century, which has enabled the arrangement of the documents of scripture in their approximate chronological order. Thus an important result of seeing the biblical writings in sequence is the ability to study the development of biblical ideas. Added to this is the assured knowledge we have of the timeframe of the classical rabbinic/early Christian era and beyond, which followed the close of the biblical period. Hence, the "history" of ideas (the idea of Monotheism in this work), has become a feasible undertaking.

Ziony Zevit has described the various methodologies with which to gain insightful access to human affairs—among them the process of writing history in general and the history of Israelite religion in particular. General history from a bird's-eye view sees events as connected and these connected events "comprise a trajectory and are goal oriented, driven by some inner force or logic either exterior to people or embodied in them." As to the history of

Israelite religion, much the same is involved. It seeks to locate connections of events in which significant lessons can be learned from the past and applied to the present. To this end biblical historians arranged their source materials chronologically. Thus, as Israelite history viewed the past, it determined that the various interactions between individuals and communities resulted in *patterns of behavior and ideology that persisted in one form or another from era to era*. And this historical methodology, writes Zevit, "explained most major events within the pattern in terms of *divine causality*."[1]

## On the Developmental Process

And so, the approach of this work is an historical one in that it traces the idea of God as it developed in the ongoing life of the people in specific time periods; it reflects the newly perceived perspectives about the deity due to changing times, locales, and climates of opinion. When, for example, Nahum Sarna shows how Moses introduced the name YHWH in his time, he pointed to an awareness of the deity that did not exist in the period of his patriarchal ancestors.[2] When Yosef Yerushalmi notes the transformation of the Israelite festivals from agricultural to historical commemorations, this demonstrates the newly discovered role God played in the life of His people.[3] When Robert Gordis traces the new insights of the Prophets—"the rod of God's anger" as the purging of the power of evil, the doctrines of the "Saving Remnant," the "Suffering Servant," and "The Day of The Lord," each developed out of the conditions on the ground at particular times in Israelite history—this points to expanded awareness of God's character.[4] And when Isadore Epstein asserts that the Prophets emphasized as never before the concept of God's universality, this perceives an expanded consciousness of God's character.[5] Walter Eichrodt encapsulates the essence of the developmental, evolving nature of the God idea in scripture:

> The development of Old Testament religion shows that the essential factor in the emergence of a vital and moral Monotheism was not philosophical speculation, but the experience of God's close and living reality. If monotheistic belief had secured a foothold in Israel prematurely, it would have made no progress, but would have become a pale abstraction devoid of inner force. This has been the fate of all monotheistic conceptions arrived at by speculative methods, from the Aton of Amenophis IV and the Brahman of Indian religion to the Proton Kinoun (unmoved mover) of the Greeks. It was only because their God YHWH was at hand to dominate the whole of life and to give practical evidence of His reality that Israel's picture of God was able to grow, and that *her concepts could be expanded without endangering the inward vitality of her religion.*[6]

What needs to be stressed about the nature of this developmental process is that the new formulations about the nature of God's character *were projected as discoveries rather than as newly minted ideas*. The process of spiritual development in the Bible seems to me to involve *not human invention but Divine self-disclosure*. This is what the general historians hinted at when they pointed to events as "driven by some inner force or logic either exterior to people or embodied in them," and what Zevit termed "divine causality" as explaining Israelite events. What man did was to *uncover* God's true nature; he unraveled that which was always there. Man did this via experiencing the *Sturm und Drang* of human life in historical time. As events confronted him and circumstances changed, he saw the *always One God's hand at work*— this without fully realizing it, for, in the flux of time and pulsating change, God's work was still for man somewhat hazy and His presence equivocal. Yet the people of the Bible communicated with God, heard His voice in the happenings of the day. Gradually, they came to discern His true nature in the vicissitudes of the lives of nations and individuals. Indeed, the Bible's visionary figures were afforded insights into the meaning of historical events through what was for them encounters with a Higher Power. And they viewed this Higher Power as the *source* of the world's reaching for moral order, and as the very *animating force* of the historical process itself, which ultimately revealed God's true singular character.[7] Salo Baron has articulated well the essence of this perspective:

> God's realization in this universe as reflected in our mind comes through the endless flow of time. In this long historical process God may assume different shapes in the minds of men. He may divest Himself of one historical form and take on another to suit the new conceptions of the age. So profoundly imageless is God in Judaism, however, that *these transformations have no effect whatever upon His eternally uniform substance*. . . . Thus God, eternal and therefore indifferent to time, brooded over history and waited, as it were, for a clearer articulation when circumstances should favor or demand it.[8]

Yet another basic characteristic of this developmental process is to be found in a parallel notion to the *abiding presence of the One God* as the animating force in the historical process: *the abiding root principles of the faith* established in the Mosaic age. Thus, even as the authentic character of the One God was slowly uncovered in the flux of time, so were the specific properties of the One God idea unfolded over time.

Indeed, such has been the pattern throughout Jewish religious history. The social and economic, political and religious conditions change in the course of life's flow *but not the core principles established in the Mosaic period launched at Mt. Sinai*. For it was at that unique creative period that the fundamental principles of the faith were established. What subsequent generations have done was to adopt and proceed to adapt these basic principles and to do so in the spirit and conditions of their own time and clime in order to make them relevant to their generation(s) and operative in their people's lives. Indeed, these subsequent adaptations were always seen as *implicit* in the teaching of the Mosaic-Sinai period.

Abraham Geiger has described this perspective in this way:

> The history of Judaism is wonderfully unique in that it spans a period extending from remote antiquity down to the immediate present. It is, therefore, not mere curiosity which acts as a spur to its study, not merely the desire to eavesdrop on the mystery of the origins of Judaism, but at least equally *the desire to detect the extent to which all of its later development was essentially already inherent in the growth and flowering process of the original seeds*. These beginnings are elusive . . . but without the revelation which only study of them affords, one can never succeed in gaining the proper insight into Judaism's subsequent history which lies more fully recorded before him.[9]

And later Rabbi Jonathan Sacks reinforced this perspective in striking modern terms. In his Koren Rosh Hashana Makhzor he writes,

> In the earliest stages of an embryo, when a fetus is still no more than a small bundle of cells, already it contains the genome, the long string of DNA from which the child and eventually the adult will emerge. *The genetic structure that will shape the person it becomes is there from the beginning*. So it is with Judaism. The Jerusalem Talmud (Peah 2:4) states this: *Mikra, Mishna, Talmud and Aggadah, afilu mah shetalmid vatic atid l'horot lifnay rabo kvar ne-emar l'moshe* b'sinai, "Bible, Talmud, Mishna and Aggadah, even what a senior disciple is destined to teach in the presence of his master, were already stated to Moses at Sinai."[10]

The evolution of the specific properties of the One God idea was prefigured, or, put another way, implied. To see how these properties developed is one of the basic tasks of this book.

## ABOUT THE WORK

This work is the fruit of many years of teaching "The Evolution of Biblical Ideas" in the rabbinical school at the University of Judaism in Los Angeles, and for Catholic priests-to-be at St. John's Seminary in Camarillo, California. I have found that the approach employed in the course of study—tracing the development of a single basic idea in scripture from its origin in the hoary past down to its normative form at the turn of the millennium—to be of great value. The ideas in scripture are, of course, many: God, man, right and wrong, suffering, prayer, immortality, and they intermingle, making for ideational complexity difficult for some students of scripture to grasp. Disentangling as far as possible the ideas one from another, and examining them separately in their chronological development, makes for demonstrable clarity, enabling students to gain coherent and usable understanding of the Bible for personal enrichment and religious knowledge as well as for practical purposes. Thus the focus here is solely on the Bible's central idea—Monotheism—from which a set of basic tenets flow: *The Deity is a supreme God; He is a God of people, not place; He is Creator of heaven and earth; He protects and cares for people; He requires justice and righteousness.* Each of these tenets is traced as it evolved through the centuries as depicted in scripture and the rabbinic literature.

Our book reflects my long-time work as a professional university educator for the public at large. In this role I have sought to translate often complex and abstract historical and religious texts and ideas encountered via scholarly endeavor into accessible reading and study for the general reader; this reader is one who seeks entry into the world of Jews and Judaism, in the case of this book, the world of the Bible. I do hope that this work will have succeeded in some measure in this regard. I hope, as well, that scholars of the subject will benefit from perusal of the material.

This field, of course, has been traversed by many an expert, as the text will show. Thus, the reader will note that I have freely used the established data and works of the recognized authorities in the various subjects involved. However, I did find a need for a more detailed clarification of the ideational development within each of the tenets (enumerated above) that flow from the Oneness of God that is at the core of the monotheistic idea. I have also sought to organize the materials at hand so that the reader can readily follow the similar thought lines that thread their ways from the period of the Patriarchs down to the classical rabbinic-early Christian era. The last two chapters flow directly from the basic theme of the previous ones—one that later in time seems to alter somewhat the "normative" monotheistic idea, and a concluding one that seeks to articulate why this entire subject is of such great consequence.

## ABOUT THE TETRAGRAMMATON—YHWH—
## THE FOUR HEBREW LETTERS THAT FORM
## THE BIBLICAL PROPER NAME FOR GOD

YHWH is the standard name for the God of Monotheism. It is used only at the beginning of this book in order to make clear its meaning for Monotheism. Because of the religious sensitivity about employing the name inappropriately, we have used in its stead *The Lord* everywhere else. It needs to be kept in mind, however, that the standard name—*not* its substitute—harbors the authentic connotations of the monotheistic doctrine in Hebrew scripture and in subsequent Jewish literature and tradition.

## ABOUT CHRONOLOGY

The eras during which the idea of Monotheism developed is discussed are the following:

Chapter 1: The Patriarchal Era: 1800–1300 BCE
Chapter 2: The Mosaic Era: 1300–800 BCE
Chapter 3: The Prophetic Era: 800–300 BCE
Chapters 4 and 5: The Classical Rabbinic/Early Christian Era: 300 BCE–200 CE

The above are approximate dates projected by recognized authorities on the subject, specifically William Foxwell Albright in his *From the Stone Age to Christianity*, Chronological Table, p. 404, and John Bright in his *A History of Israel*, Chronological Charts, p. 465.

Chapter 6: The era of the major Jewish mystics (from the Zohar, 1300 CE to Shneur Zalman of Ladi, 1800 CE), the early modern period.
Chapter 7: The modern period.

## ABOUT THE SETTLEMENT IN CANAAN: IN
## TWO DIFFERENT ERAS

Bible readers often conflate the two periods in history when the Hebrews/Israelites settled in Canaan. The Hebrews in the patriarchal era settled in Canaan from their nomadic/semi-nomadic milieu from approximately 1800–1700 BCE. On the other hand, the Israelites during the Mosaic period under

Joshua settled in Canaan from approximately 1200–1100 BCE. Thus approximately six hundred years separated the two periods of settlement.

*Chapter 1*

# The Patriarchs and Monotheism

## *Where It All Began: The Patriarchs as Nomads and Migrating Shepherds*

> The seeds were planted by Abraham, Isaac and Jacob, who came before Moses; and we can now follow the path that led from their notion of God to the God of Israel. —Albrecht Alt, *The God of the Fathers*

### DID MONOTHEISM ORIGINATE WITH THE PATRIARCHS?

We begin examination of the evolution of the idea of Monotheism—the belief in the One God—in the era of the Patriarchs: Abraham, Isaac and Jacob and their descendants.[1]

From the perspective of the faith of Israel, the idea of Monotheism is traditionally thought to have originated with Abraham who launched the patriarchal era. From the perspective of history, such is not the case. In fact, as we shall see, the monotheistic idea in its near-normative form originated with Moses who inaugurated the Mosaic era. And the idea was further developed later in the era of the Prophets into its fully normative form. Historically, however, it does appear accurate to assert that *the seeds of the idea were planted in the era of the Patriarchs.* It is this contention that is examined in this chapter.

Before proceeding, we need to explain the usage of the term *YHWH*,[2] the standard name for the God of Monotheism, which term was introduced in Mosaic times. The apparent problem: the name *YHWH is* found in the patriarchal narratives such as, for example, in the encounter with Abraham in Haran.[3] How then can we account for the usage of "YHWH" in these narratives if, as we claim, that name and its new connotations were introduced in the Mosaic era?

The response: the biblical record shows that, while the name was used in connection with the Patriarchs, in other places of scripture (Exodus 6:2–3) it is explicitly stated, "God spoke to Moses and said to him, 'I am *YHWH*. I appeared to Abraham, Isaac and Jacob as El Shaddai, but *I did not make Myself known to them by my name YHWH.*'"[4] Clearly, the Patriarchs did not know the name *YHWH* as God in their lifetime. Moreover, other areas of the Genesis narrative studiously avoid the use of that name prior to the era of Moses; these passages speak of the deity as *Elohim*.[5] All accounts agree that the Patriarchs worshipped the deity by various other names, such as *Shaddai, Pahad, Abir*, as we shall soon see.

How, then, do we account for use of the name *YHWH* in the encounter with Abraham at Haran and elsewhere in the patriarchal narratives? The answer is that *these narratives were recorded later from the point of view of subsequent monotheist theology*, that is, approximately between 900–800 BCE, many centuries after the patriarchal period, 1800–1300 BCE.[6]

John Bright has articulated this characteristic biblical phenomenon this way:

> Now, theologically speaking, there is really no contradiction in this. All the patriarchal narratives were written from the point of view of Yahwistic theology by men who were worshipers of YHWH; whether they used the name or not, they had no doubt that the God of the Patriarchs was actually YHWH, God of Israel, who the Patriarchs, whether consciously or unconsciously, worshiped. Nevertheless, we cannot impose the faith of later Israel on the Patriarchs. Theologically legitimate though it may be to do so, it is not historically accurate to say that the God of the Patriarchs was YHWH. Yahwism began with Moses, as the Bible explicitly states ("I did not make Myself known to them [the Patriarchs] by my name YHWH," Exodus 6:3) and as all the evidence agrees. Whatever the origins of the worship of YHWH, we have no knowledge of it as the God of the patriarchs in pre-Mosaic times. We cannot, therefore, read normative Yahwism, or even primitive Yahwism, back upon the Patriarchs.[7]

James Kugel adds to Bright on this matter. Modern biblical scholars tell us that a God known by the letters Y-H-W-H is out of place in these patriarchal stories in that there is no indication anywhere that such a deity was worshipped during Abraham's time. Moreover, "a modern scholar's account of the emergence of Israel's religion would be far more complex and evolutionary than anything attached to the person of Abraham as depicted in Genesis." Abraham as an exponent of only one true God in the world is an idea that appears to have been wholly created by the ancient interpreters.

> When it comes to cases, not a single word in the book of Genesis actually says that Abraham believed in the existence of only one God. . . . He is presented as

worshipping his own God but not as an exponent of monotheism. . . . On this matter of Abraham as monotheist, there is general agreement among modern scholars.[8]

## THE SEEDS PLANTED

As indicated, though the Patriarchs cannot be seen as the originators of the idea of Monotheism, the biblical record shows that the seeds for later Monotheism were planted in the patriarchal era—that a set of rudimentary notions in that earlier period pointed to the idea. And as the history of Israel proceeded in time, these nascent notions evolved into the near-normative Monotheism of Moses and subsequently into the fully normative Monotheism projected by the Prophets of Israel.

And so, in accordance with our discussion in the introduction to this book—the developmental process in the realm of ideas, Geiger on the system inherent in the growth and flowering of original seeds, and Sacks about the DNA process—we begin with tracing the idea of Monotheism with the religion of the patriarchal era.

## THE GOD OF THE FATHERS: A DEITY OF PEOPLE, NOT PLACE

Albrecht Alt, in his seminal essay *The God of the Fathers*,[9] established the basic thought line concerning the nascent notion of Israel's God. According to Alt, some of the essential elements of the idea grew out of the life of the people still organized on the basis of families and clans.

In Genesis each Patriarch chooses to worship *his* God to whom the Patriarch thereafter entrusted himself. What we see here is a close personal tie between the clan father and his God—

- In connection with Abraham

    When Abram was ninety-nine years old, the Lord appeared to Abram and said to him, "*I am El Shaddai.* Walk in my ways and be blameless. [I will establish my covenant between Me and you, and I will make you exceedingly numerous.[10]]

This deity was again so designated when God, speaking to Moses, recalled His having appeared to Abraham and his successors as *Shaddai*.[11] (*Shaddai* was originally the name of the god who resided on the cosmic mountain that was the center of the earth and thus connoted the essence of might.[12]) *Shaddai* was also the god of Abraham's descendant, Joseph, who was blessed by this god, who extricated Joseph from many a tribulation.[13]

- In connection with Isaac

> Had not the God of my father, the God of Abraham and the *Pahad* (fear) of Isaac been with me, you would have sent me (Jacob) away empty-handed. But God took notice of my plight and the toil of my hands, and He gave judgment that night.[14]

Now, *Pahad* (literally "fear") means "kinsman," i.e., "Kinsman of Isaac." In patriarchal religion the personal deity of the head of the clan was the protector of the group.[15] Thus here Isaac's clan god was his (Isaac's) kinsman to whom Jacob attributed his relief from Laban.

- In connection with Jacob

> Archers bitterly assailed him (Jacob), they shot at him and harried him. Yet his bow stayed taut, and his arms were made firm by the hand of the *Abir* (Mighty One) of Jacob.[16]

Now, "the *Abir* (Mighty One) is the "redeemer" of the clan in patriarchal religion.[17] Thus, this is the clan god who helped Jacob parry his harassers.

As we see from the above, in patriarchal religion these gods were the patron deities of a clan. Abraham served *Shaddai*, Jacob swore by the *Pahad* of Isaac, and Jacob made a vow sealing an agreement with his uncle Laban in the name of the *Abir* of his clan.

Parallels to this clan god phenomenon during the patriarchal era are found in Aramean and Arab societies, and from Cappadocian texts in Asia Minor and other documents of the age and later.[18] This demonstrates that establishing a personal and contractual relationship between a clan and its god was a widespread and ancient phenomenon amongst the Semitic nomads, which included the Patriarchs of Israel.

This patriarchal religion prepared the ground for elements of later Monotheism in a crucial respect. Frank Moore Cross points to the essential traits of this religion. It differs radically from the cults of the Canaanite *elim*, the *numina* of particular holy places. Cross explains that the God of the Fathers is not attached to a shrine, but is designated by the name of the Patriarch with whom he has a special relation, or rather, in Alt's view, by the name of the founder of his cult. He is not a local deity, but the patron of the clan, the social group. He may be described as an "historical" god, that is, one who enters into a kinship or covenantal relationship with a clan, and who guides the social group in its peregrinations, its wars, in short throughout historical vicissitudes to its destiny. The special traits of the patriarchal gods, in fact, anticipate a number of points characteristic of the religion of YHWH, the Lord of covenant and community.

In these ways, Cross discerns continuity between the old (i.e., patriarchal) religious forms and the new (later Yahwistic)—an historically credible background for emergent Yahwism, in this instance the deity being a god of people and not place.[19]

Salo Baron, in encapsulating the essence of Albrecht Alt's authoritative view on this subject, as amplified by Frank Cross, puts it this way:

> In contrast to the Canaanite creeds, this was a religion with a preponderant emphasis on the relation between God and man, especially on that of God and human society *without close attachment to any particular place*. That is why it was so well adapted to all the changes in the destiny of its adherents.[20]

The relationship between a man and his group with the deity was not determined by a specific locality in which people naturally served the god of their territory, but was an alliance voluntarily assumed by the migrating tribes. Hence, this was a different sort of religion from that of the religion of nature that the Patriarchs found amongst the Canaanites amidst whom they subsequently settled. *It was a tie to people rather than to places*; it was rooted in a divinity's protective relationship with persons always on the move—the clan father and the members of his tribe. This relationship did not depend on encounter with the deity in concrete ways such as at specific locations nor via a physical image of the deity in the form of an idol. In this early Hebrew conception the divine could be encountered wherever the people were on their ways and without the limitations that images/idols implied. Herein was a seed planted for later Monotheism.

## THE DEITY PROTECTS AND CARES FOR PEOPLE

There are additional notions that characterize the religion of the God of the Fathers.[21] The Hebrews, prior to their settlement in Canaan, lived in the desert as nomads or semi-nomads. It was thus natural that such a life entailed a distinct pattern of society, and established a code of behavior all its own. These living patterns were initially rooted in the conditions of life of the environment; they subsequently became virtues in and of themselves and were attributed to the will of the groups' gods. Core ideas in early patriarchal religion resulted from this circumstance.

In the desert, the unit of society, the tribe (a collection of clans themselves comprising a set of individual families) must be compact enough to be mobile yet strong enough to ensure its own safety and that of its individual members. In the desert environment, an individual who is separated from his own group must be able to count without question on a welcome from the groups through which he passes or which he joins. *Anyone may need help and therefore everyone must give it. This is the basis for the law of hospitality and asylum.*[22]

Indeed, hospitality is a necessity in the desert the nomad traverses, and this necessity became a virtue as such and a highly esteemed one—a virtue seen as a requirement of the gods. The guest is sacred. It is an honor to provide for him. In this ancient Near Eastern setting the stranger can avail himself of this hospitality for three days, for example, and even after leaving he has the right of protection for a given period of time and within a prescribed geographical area. A set of other details about this phenomenon is on record.[23]

Biblical parallels during subsequent times in Canaan reflect this. Abraham gave a lavish reception to three visitors in Mamre.[24] Laban is eager to welcome Abraham's servant, Eliezer, at Aram.[25] Examples of the extreme commitment to the virtue of hospitality are the stories of the people who stayed in Lot's house in Sodom[26] and of the crime at Gibeah.[27] Both Lot and the old man of Gibeah are ready to sacrifice the honor of their daughters in order to protect their guests, and the reason is stated in both cases: it is simply because these guests have come under their roof.[28]

Nomadic life also gives rise to the law of asylum. In this type of society it is impossible and inconceivable that an individual could live isolated, unattached to any clan or tribe. Thus, if a man must leave his tribe because he involuntarily committed murder or some other offense, or leaves of his own free will for whatever reason, he has to seek protection of another tribe. There he becomes what modern Arabs call a *dahil*, "he who has come in," and what their forefathers called *jar*. The tribe undertakes to protect him, to defend him against his enemies and, if necessary, to avenge his "blood" if his enemy got to him. These early nomadic customs are reflected in the Bible in the person of the *ger* (sojourner), which is the same word as the Arabic *jar*, and in the institution of the cities of refuge, which were ordained by God, i.e., "The Lord spoke to Moses" (Numbers 34:9–12 and Deuteronomy 4:41–43). Thus, another seed was planted for later Monotheism: *God protects and cares for people.*

## THE DEITY REQUIRES JUSTICE AND RIGHTEOUS BEHAVIOR

Yet another seed of Monotheism was planted in the patriarchal era: *The deity requires justice*. In the desert there is no police force or court of justice with authority over the tribes; thus, the group as a whole is held responsible for a crime and liable for its punishment—the law of "blood vengeance," i.e., the law of reciprocity for hurt inflicted on one's own.

Now, a tribe is an autonomous group of clans who believe they are descended from a common ancestor. Hence every individual is related by "blood." It is that key factor that unites all the tribesmen, all of whom thus consider themselves "brothers" in a generic sense. Indeed, this bond creates a sense of solidarity among all the members of the tribe. It is a deep-rooted feeling imbibed by the patriarchal nomads from the general condition of nomadism of their time, and this feeling persisted long after the Patriarchs' settlement in Canaan. This solidarity is seen especially in the group's duty to protect its weak and oppressed members. It is the obligation that lies behind the later biblical institution of the *goel* (to buy back, restore), who was a protector, a defender of the interests of the unfortunate in his group.[29]

More: this sense of solidarity and brotherhood that prevailed amongst the nomads gave rise to a *decided drive for justice. The life of a kinsman must be avenged by the death of the one who shed it*, or, failing him, by the life of one of his family. Here again the early nomadic Patriarchs absorbed a notion from their general environment which, in turn, showed up in its later settled period in Canaan. Thus Joab kills Abner to avenge the death of his brother.[30] Mitigations of this system were later introduced.[31]

In sum, nascent notions about the deity inhered in the religion of the God of the Fathers: *a deity of people, not places, who protects and cares for people*, and *requires justice and righteous behavior*. These notions, when fused, as we shall see, with similar ideational tendencies of the Canaanites amongst whom the nomadic Patriarchs later settled, persisted as seeds from which Monotheism grew. How did this come about?

## THE GOD OF THE FATHERS AND EL: SYNCRETISM AND HEBREW TENACITY

Now, when the Hebrews in the early patriarchal period[32] settled in among the Canaanites who were long rooted in the land, their nomadic ideal of the peripatetic clan god inevitably became significantly (not fully) assimilated with the native peoples' god, El. El is the common Semitic name for deity in ancient Near Eastern cultures. He is the divine patriarch, the father of gods and men, sometimes stern, often compassionate, always wise in judgment. He is the ruler of the family of gods. He is a tent dweller situated on the mount of assembly where cosmic decisions are made. He is creator, the ancient one whose extraordinary procreative powers have populated heaven and earth, which he himself fashioned. He fights with the younger gods, Baal in particular, with whom he shares, at times, subordinate rule. He has several wives. His three important consorts are his two sisters, Asherah and Astarte, and his daughter, Anat. Thus Polytheism (along with a number of characteristics that hint at aspects of the Divinity embraced by the Hebrews) and the worship of El were basic components of Canaanite religion.[33]

The Bible records this Canaanite supreme god, *El*, with whom the Hebrews associated, and *El*'s local manifestations in connection with the Hebrews in various locations. Now, as we have pointed out, the patriarchal religion which the early Hebrews brought with them into Canaan was unconnected to the soil or any fixed point in its environment. However, when in Canaan, such was not the case: Canaanite religion was rooted in the soil and in specific locales, and the Hebrews joined in worshipping their gods in these locales. Thus,

- *El Elyon* ("god most high") was absorbed by the Hebrews in Sodom.[34]

- *El Roi* ("god of seeing/divination") was worshipped by the Hebrews in Kadesh/Bered.[35]

- *El Olam* ("god of the world/eternity") was worshipped by the Hebrews in Beersheba.[36]

- *El Bethel* ("god of house of El") was worshipped by the Hebrews in Bethel.[37]

This demonstrates that patriarchal worship became assimilated to specific native local gods and locales—the deities and sanctuaries of the Canaanites. Indeed, when the nomadic Hebrews moved into Canaan their own clan deities came to be identified with *El*, who was worshipped locally under various names. Thus, for example, God appeared to the Patriarchs as *El Shaddai*.[38]

However, and this is a crucial and consequential point: despite the syncretism depicted, *the notion of the patriarchal "God of the Fathers"—a clan god linked to people primarily rather than to places and unconnected to any polytheistic pantheon—did not die among the Hebrews*. And this tenacity was destined to bear mighty fruit, as we shall see. At this point in time, in practice, the Canaanite notion of a god in a specific place and the patriarchal nomadic notion of god with people on the move stood side by side, as it were, the former the dominant strain, and the latter the minor though persistent strain. Indeed, later Israel never forgot that its God was a God of the wilderness and of nomads.

The very involvement of the Hebrews[39] with the Canaanite *El* harbored rudimentary elements of later Monotheism. These elements made *El* religion somewhat more palatable for the previously nomadic Hebrews. The reason for this was that for these non-Hebrew Semites within whom the Hebrews settled, *budding ideas about the Deity and his characteristics existed and these were tolerable for the Hebrews. What were these ideas?*

As described earlier, the nomadic Patriarchs harbored the notion of a *deity who protected and cared for people. So, too, the Canaanites' El was believed to have concern for humans.* We are told that following Abraham's rescue of his nephew Lot, who had been taken captive along with his people and possessions—an act of positive concern for family—Melkizedek, king of Salem and priest of *El Elyon* ("god most high") greets Abraham with bread and wine and blesses him, saying,

> Blessed be Abram of god most high,
> Creator of heaven and earth.
> And blessed be god most high
> who has delivered your foes into your hand.[40]

Here *El* is praised as a good god who acts with sympathy for human beings in straits. Abraham is lauded for his action that evinced concern for kindred. It is El, acting through Abraham, who rescues captives from merciless marauders. Indeed, this god shows care for people. We see a similar attitude among the Hebrews where, in the Abraham saga, God is portrayed as intolerant of the sinful Sodomites, "who were very wicked sinners against the Lord" (Genesis 13:13). Abraham pleads for compassion for its people even for the sake of only ten righteous Sodomites. God assents. Indeed, patriarchal religion had internalized the seed of morality as it had meshed its own nomadic past with related notions it encountered after it settled down in Canaan.[41]

Yet more: The notion developed by the early nomadic Patriarchs of a *deity who requires justice and righteous behavior on the part of humans also existed in nascent form among the Canaanites*, and this too made practical fusion of the notions possible. As indicated, the clan god of the Patriarchs required just behavior on the part of his followers. In the case of the Canaanites the very name *Melkizedek* implied just character: "My King (El) is just." Similarly, *Adonizedek*, "My Lord (El) is just."[42] Moreover, the extra-biblical literature produced in the northern city-state of Ugarit (second millennium BCE) reveals a conception of *El* as having good character. He is not only "creator of the earth" and "the father of years," and "the father of humankind," but also "a gray beard," a source of "wisdom," of "compassion," of "beneficence."[43]

The hint of humane characteristics of *El* with whom the Hebrews were involved could not help but re-enforce their notion of the deity at this point in their history. The biblical record testifies to patriarchal religion's understanding of a God who is himself moral and thus expects moral behavior on the part of his people. Thus God says to Abraham,

> I have singled him (Abraham) out, that he may instruct his children and his posterity to keep the way of The Lord by doing what is *just and right* in order that The Lord may bring about for Abraham what He has promised him.[44]

*To recapitulate*, patriarchal religion harbored three nascent notions about the deity. One, that he was *a deity of people, not place*—a minor though persistent view in contrast to the dominant Canaanite notion of a god in a specific place. Second, that the *deity protects and cares for people*—a notion shared with the Canaanites. Third, that the *deity requires just and right behavior*, a notion also shared with the Canaanites. These were notions about deity that emerged in patriarchal religion.

## Further Notions in Patriarchal Religion

In addition to the above ideas, other nascent notions about the deity emerged within patriarchal religion in this period. These appear to have been adopted from the Canaanites, for which there seemed to be no precedent in the earlier nomadic period of the Hebrews.

*The deity is a supreme god.* El was supreme among other existing gods. He was the father of the gods; he ordered their world as well as that of humans. Indeed, El is the common Semite name for deity in the cultures of the ancient Near East. He is, for example, the head of the pantheon in Ugarit in northern Canaan. El is the king, the ruler of the gods. In their assembly he holds the highest position.[45]

As pointed out above, patriarchal religion in this period embraced El, which pointed to embrace of its property of supremacy.

*The deity is creator of heaven and earth.* King Melkizedek blessed Abraham in the name of his god: "Blessed be Abram of El Elyon ['god most high'], *creator of heaven and earth*, and blessed be god most high."[46] Further, in the extra-biblical Ugarit literature El is similarly viewed as a creator, being called "builder of things built," described as "creator of the earth," and as the ultimate ruler of the earth who, for example allowed the building of a palace for his contemporary god, Baal—this only with El's permission."[47]

Abraham's acceptance of Melkizedek's blessing, which included El as *creator of heaven and earth*, pointed to patriarchal religion's absorption of the notion of a deity as creator. This is hinted at, as well, when Abraham, in this period, pleads on behalf of the sinful Sodomites, "Shall not *the judge of all the earth* deal justly?"

## Summary and Conclusion

This syncretic form of religion wherein the Hebrews' God of the Fathers and the Canaanite El were in a sense "integrated" (Jacob's altar in Shechem was called *El Elohay Yisrael*)[48] constituted the notion of deity in the patriarchal period. And it possessed a set of properties that contained the seeds of later Monotheism. These "seeds" were the following:

1) The deity is a supreme god.

2) The deity is a god of people, not place.

3) The deity is creator of heaven and earth.

4) The deity protects and cares for people.

5) The deity requires justice and righteousness.

Though we may assume that this "combination god" was the primary object of worship, it would be inaccurate to call this type of religion "Monotheism," i.e., the one and only god because other gods were recognized as existing with power and influence. Moreover, images of gods existed among the Hebrews, witness the household idols that Rachel stole.[49] And yet, this form of religion resembled neither the official Polytheism of Mesopotamia nor the fertility cults of Canaan whose orgies, as practiced by the followers of Baal, for example, have no trace in the Genesis narrative.[50]

We thus conclude: the patriarchal notion of the deity and his properties sowed the seeds of the Monotheism of Moses and of the era he inaugurated. As Albrecht Alt put it, *"Abraham, Isaac and Jacob came before Moses; but we can now follow the path which led from their gods to the God of Israel."*[51]

*Chapter 2*

# Moses and Monotheism

## The Exodus of the Israelites From Egypt

A new definition of the Deity initiated by Moses followed what seemed to him and his people to be a unique, divinely guided experience—the Exodus from Egypt—an event that provoked a widening and deepening and transforming knowledge of God's character and power.

### THE PROBLEM

As we saw in chapter 1, the idea of deity in the patriarchal period was a creative blend between the "God of the Fathers" and of El, who had long been the supreme deity of Canaan into whose midst the Hebrews settled sometime between 1800–1700 BCE. And we concluded that the patriarchal notion of god harbored a set of ideational seeds ready for development on the part of Moses and the era he inaugurated. It is this development we seek to trace in this chapter.

At the root of the theological activity of the Mosaic period was awareness of a profound problem: while the inherited "fused" religion rendered elements that pointed to Monotheism, a highly consequential negative condition within that fusion prevailed. Israel continued to harbor many of *El*'s local practices that were connected to revered sanctuaries, *places* where the deities were encountered, and to the physical objects that represented these deities. These local cults in which Israel participated promoted the idea *not only of a supreme El but of multiple deities* to be worshipped. This is what Polytheism was about. It was clear that the God of the Fathers notion had but faintly taken root in the patriarchal period. Anchored as it was in Israel's nomadic past, which posited a deity of people *and not places, the notion was at odds with a religion of place.* Yes, the original notion was still alive, but was overlaid by the dominant Canaanite religion. Here is where the breakthrough of Mosaic religion enters the picture.[1]

## The Exodus, and a New Name Introduced: YHWH (The Lord)

The time had come when this blend of the patriarchal nomadic view of the deity combined with the Canaanite view needed a new definition. This would not only fashion wholly new perspectives on the notion of deity per se, but also enable the development in new and creative ways of the promising seeds that the patriarchal notion planted. This initiative on Moses' part followed what he and his people considered to be a unique, divinely guided experience: the exodus of the Israelites from Egypt—an event that provoked a widening and deepening and transforming knowledge of God's character and power.[2] Indeed, as Mark Smith has observed, the Exodus experience marked the emergence of Israel as a people, a conscious collective unit which, in turn, coincided with the appearance of the Lord as her central Deity.[3] David Noel Friedman put it this way . . .

> The irresistible power of YHWH, demonstrated through a decisive action against a leading military power, and the way it was exercised by YHWH as sole champion . . . gives definition and structure to the faith of Israel that carries through the remainder of its history as well as its sacred books. Recognition of the Lord's monopoly of power and His exclusive claim on Israel, which He gained through the decisive victory at the Red Sea, constitutes the main content of biblical tradition and the ongoing purpose of its religion. Israel was saved at the sea and was sealed to the Lord as its sole and exclusive Lord from that moment on.[4]

In later times, the Rabbis intuited the state of mind at this momentous juncture. They indicate that when the Israelites crossed the Sea of Reeds in safety they became especially conscious of God in their midst. Even the humblest amongst them were filled with the feeling of the Deity's nearness, so that everyone—young and old, newcomer and native alike—cried out, *Zeh Eli V'anvayu*, "this is my God and I will glorify Him" (Talmud, Sota 30b). This experience enabled the Israelites to see God with a clearer vision and hear His voice with a finer ear.

G. Ernest Wright and James Sanders have further amplified the impact of the Exodus happening—Wright on the God idea and Sanders on the Exodus happening itself.[5] The latter cites some fifty biblical passages in which *the story of the Exodus—the wanderings in the desert—the entrance into Canaan* became a pivotal and constantly repeated narrative in scripture. For Israel, this basic story became a touchstone for authority, a kind of "early canon" for numerous speakers and writers—early and late—in the Bible. Reference to the authority of Israel's defining story was invoked to support a point they wanted to stress.

Thus, for example, the Prophet Amos cited the story (2:10) by comparing the justice of God for the slaves in Egypt with the injustice Israel's heirs were perpetrating on the poor and dispossessed in their own country under Jeroboam II. Among numerous other examples, Sanders points to the passages where the Exodus is cited as authority for the Festival of Sukkot (Leviticus 23:43), for the *kashrut* laws (Leviticus 11:45), for the first commandment (Deuteronomy 4:20), for loving the sojourner (Deuteronomy 10:19), for the Passover (Deuteronomy 16:1), for God's judging the people for desiring a king (I Samuel 8:8), for the uniqueness of Israel (I Chronicles 17:21–22). And I would add to this list the contemporary recital over wine (the *kiddush*) at the Jewish table on Friday evening when the Shabbat is cited "in remembrance of the Exodus from Egypt." Indeed, what had happened "back then"—at the time of the founding story—was indicative of what was happening at the time of the writing, and now.

And so, as a result of the Exodus experience, the Deity became known under a different name than hitherto, with new and widening implications . . .

> Moses said to God: "When I come to the Israelites and say to them, 'The God of your fathers has sent me to you,' and they ask me, 'What is His name?' what shall I say to them?" God said to Moses, *Eheyeh-Asher-Eheyeh*. He (God) continued, "Thus shall you say to the Israelites, '*Eheyeh* sent me to you.'" And God said further to Moses, "Thus shall you speak to the Israelites: *YHWH*, The Lord, the God of your fathers, the God of Abraham, the God of Isaac, and the God of Jacob, has sent me to you: This shall be my name forever. This is my appellation for all eternity.[6]

God is disclosed here via a new name, as a Deity whose nature and power the Patriarchs did not experience. Yet more: with the disclosure of the name *YHWH*, the El Shaddai of the Patriarchs as in Genesis 6:3 became obsolete; it is preserved only in poetic texts.[7] Indeed, the name *YHWH* came into prominence as a characteristic personal name for the God of Israel only in the time of Moses.[8] This disclosure was equivalent to the disclosure of God's true nature, since a name in biblical times was regarded as an effective expression of character and essence. Words had power, conveying the sense of forces and energies. Knowing the name of a god might give the knower an inner connection with the object of his knowledge. And so, the knowledge of the name of the Deity—in this case Israel's God as *YHWH*—meant that Moses and his people were initiated into a new and potent insight into God's true nature, purposes and actions.[9]

## The Meaning(s) of YHWH

What are the implications of this new name introduced into the religion of Israel at this time that led to the transformation of the notion of God? Several have been cited by scholars as they understand Exodus 3:14—*Eheyeh Asher Eheyeh*, from the Hebrew stem "to be."[10]

- *I am the One who is*. This connotes that God exists—*He is* (present tense), which means that God is a Presence in the world. We realize this because we experience Him in our natural surroundings and in our personal lives everywhere and at all times. He is present in the miracles of nature, in the very air humans breathe. Most of all, He is a God who guides the destiny of collective and individual humanity. Indeed, He is The Lord of history. Thus, there is no need for a divine mythological history like those attached to the gods in whom other peoples believe, because The Lord exists eternally, without birth and without death, and is revealed in His actions.

- *I shall be what I shall be* (future tense). Israel's life and faith have a future. Her faith is characterized by confidence in the Divine promises to her ancestors of progeny and land and prosperity—an exuberant belief in good things to come. Thus Moses heard God saying, "I shall be what I shall be" to mean He (God) will be revealed by His *future* Presence. Just as God will have granted freedom to the Israelites in the past via His liberating them from Egyptian bondage, so will He grant them "salvation" (i.e., fulfillment, self-realization) in days to come. The Israelite people, as it goes forward into the future, will be accompanied by God's protection and cause them to gain ever deeper knowledge of His purposes.

- *He (God) causes to be what exists* (causative form, the Hebrew *hiphil*). God is the Creator of the world and all living things. He is, as well, the ultimate fashioner of human events, the Ruler of history.

- *I shall be what I shall be*. I, God, am in the process of becoming known. Human understanding of Me is not yet complete. People will come to know Me through my acts as time progresses. My self-revelation will be ongoing. (See pages 2–4 in the Introduction, "On the Developmental Process.")

Thus via these connotations of the new name for the Deity, fresh meaning was infused into the notion inherited from the patriarchal era. These new insights removed the shortcomings of the received religion while, at the same time, nurtured the ideational seeds planted by the Patriarchs, which development, in turn, reflects the continuities between the God of the Fathers and YHWH, the God of Israel.

What follows is an analysis of the five "seeds" Mosaic religion nurtured into Monotheism, with the Deity as "The Lord" being the driving "Force" (henceforth "The Lord" is used instead of YHWH).

## The Deity Is a Supreme God

As pointed out in chapter 1, when the early Patriarchs settled in among the Canaanites, they adopted an aspect of the religion of the time—the notion that the Canaanite god, El, was the *supreme god* amongst the other existing gods. El was the father of the gods; he ordered their world as well as that of humans. Indeed, El is the common Semitic name for deity in the ancient Near-Eastern cultures; he is, for example, the head of the pantheon in Ugarit in northern Canaan. El is the king, the ruler of the gods. In their assembly he holds the highest position.[11]

This rudimentary notion of divine supremacy was transformed for Israel into the central pillar of Monotheism: *the absolute supremacy of the Deity to the exclusion of other gods.* El, though supreme, existed along with other deities. Thus the first and second of the Ten Commandments Moses brought to the people: "I am The Lord your God who brought you out of the land of Egypt, the house of Bondage. You shall have no other gods besides Me."[12] Israel was not to recognize in any manner or form what other people (the Canaanites and their El and his progeny) accept as deities. Israel's God demands uncompromising and exclusive loyalty.[13] This stress on the Deity's exclusivity was further emphasized by the sole-ness of God, by His Oneness: "Shema Yisrael, Hear O Israel, The Lord is our God, *The Lord is One.*"[14] Indeed, for Israel God is the sole God, He is one and not many.

The notion that The Lord alone is God is what we today might term a "conceptual" one, an "idea" that our intellect needs to absorb. This concept was important but it was not enough. *It was to be acted out in the ongoing life of the people.* It was to be a living experience. This is the import of the emphasis following the declaration of the Shema.

> You shall love The Lord your God with all your heart and with all your soul and with all your might. Take to heart these instructions with which I charge you this day. Impress them upon your children. Recite them when you stay at home and when you are away, when you lie down and when you get up. Bind them as a sign on your hand and let them serve as a symbol on your forehead; inscribe them on the doorposts of your house and on your gates.[15]

And then Moses continues by emphasizing that Israel must

revere only The Lord your God and worship Him alone, and swear only by His name. Do not follow other gods, any gods of the peoples about you—for The Lord your God in your midst is an impassioned God—lest the anger of The Lord your God blaze forth against you and He wipe you off the face of the earth.[16]

A strong admonition indeed.

In a sense, what Mosaic religion accomplished here was to extract the core notion of divine supremacy from the syncretic patriarchal context and proceed to develop it into the basic property of the God of Israel.

## *The Egyptian Sun God—and Monotheism*

A factor that might well have been in place in connection with the Mosaic notion of the One Supreme God was an apparent form of Monotheism that existed before and during the very same era of Moses, i.e., 1400–1300 BCE, and that is the worship and worldwide (at the time) influence of a deity—the sun god of Egypt.

The Egyptian King Akhenaten (ca. 1364–1347 BCE) proclaimed the existence of the solar disk, called Aten, to be the supreme god. Aten was to be worshipped exclusively and representation of him in either human or animal form was not allowed. This notion of the deity had long been germinating in Egyptian society. Indeed, the sun was one of the fundamentals of Egyptian life and was personified as a deity. It was looked upon as the founder of kingship in Egypt from whom the pharaohs claimed biological descent. The prominence of the cult of the sun god, his universal sovereignty, the notion that other gods of the pantheon were but variant forms and manifestations of him, were all well rooted in Egyptian culture. And Akhenaten's great hymn to Aten refers to that deity as "the sole god apart from whom no other exists." It is thus clear that the notion of a universal, cosmic deity was in existence during the very Mosaic period when the Israelite idea of Monotheism was conceptualized[17]

Scholars differ about the possible influence of the Aten solar god on Mosaic Monotheism. Nahum Sarna claims that the specific Aten form of Egyptian religion lasted no more than fifteen years, that it was confined to members of the royal family, that the new aristocracy Akhenaten had created had no impact on the Egyptian people, that Aten had no concern for the common man, and that its ethical content was ambiguous at best. He thus concluded that this sun god religion of Egypt did not advance in the direction of Monotheism.[18]

Donald Redford similarly demurs from seeing influences of this Egyptian form of Monotheism on Mosaic Monotheism. He depicts in detail the existence of what he calls the "One-God" phenomenon, which prevailed a good century before Akhenaten's specific form of the notion in practice, and adumbrations of the sun-worship phenomenon long after. Yet Redford sees too many factors that characterize the differences between Egypt's version of Monotheism and that of the Mosaic era. For example, he contends (erroneously, according to a good deal of scholarly consensus) that Monotheism is a much later development in Israel's history gestating, as it did, in the prophetic movement and culminating with Jeremiah and Second Isaiah in the late seventh and mid-sixth centuries—long after the Mosaic and Akhenaten fourteenth-century period.[19]

Salo Baron differs.[20] He contends that the circumstance of the Exodus and Moses' "theological" work being located in fourteenth century BCE, which the weight of evidence now at hand favors, encourages a more positive view of the sun god religion's influence on Monotheism. This is because Moses grew to maturity not very long after the death of Akhenaten in 1347 BCE. Hence, because the existence of the sun god religion in the very atmosphere in which Moses lived and thought, and the fact that a notion of a universal deity was cherished for centuries in Egypt, it seems not unfair to contend that Moses must have been aware of a single all-powerful god. Indeed, this palpable monotheistic tendency could well have had an influence on the development of Mosaic Monotheism.

Two additional factors tend to confirm Israel's awareness of the Egyptian sun god and its possible influence on its monotheistic notion immediately following the advent of Moses. The Israelites had settled in Canaan, and Canaan was under the control of Egypt during this period of settlement. Donald Redford has himself documented that Egypt in this era dominated not only Canaan but the entire Fertile Crescent region. It thus seems reasonable to claim that Egypt's sun god religion, although officially deposed as it was at the time, must have penetrated the Canaanite villages in which the Israelites were settled. And this circumstance might well have helped reinforce the more advanced Mosaic notion of Monotheism these settlers adopted. Moreover, the very fact that scripture, reflecting Mosaic teaching, specifically prohibited making any image of whatever "is in the heaven above," and even more pointedly, the sun and the moon and the stars," demonstrates this awareness.[21]

## The Deity Is a God of People, Not Place

The notion of a God of people, not place that Israel clung to tenaciously from her nomadic past, in Mosaic times morphed into passionate war against idolatry, which was characterized by imaging the gods. The patriarchal narratives do not evince negative attitudes to such pagan practice. "It is the arrival of Moses on the scene of history that heralds the first appearance of the notion of a war on Polytheism."²² Thus, a key assertion in the Ten Commandments reads:

> You shall not make for yourself a sculptured image, or any likeness of what is in the heavens above, or on the earth below, or in the waters under the earth. You shall not bow down to them or serve them.²³

This was a specific, striking and permanent innovation—a logical implication of the patriarchal concept of a deity being a god of people on the move rather than one in the fixed places of concrete nature. According to Salo Baron, these fixed places that the gods presumably inhabited limited the gods' influence and accessibility. For the same reason, plastic representations of the deity were taboo. "Imagery is concrete; it is localized. It tends to focus worship in a certain place. Imagery makes the local sanctuary supreme, and with it a special attachment to a particular territory."²⁴ Moreover, the Israelites at the time, like their Mesopotamian and Canaanite contemporaries, viewed concrete images such as a wooden pole or tree and a pillar made of stone as embodying the deity. Thus, for example, Benjamin Sommer points out that some Israelites regarded the goddess *Asherah* as the Lord's partner and, in turn, as a cultic object consisting of a live tree, a tree stump or a wooden pole (e.g., Exodus 34:13).²⁵ And Ziony Zevit has shown that the *matzeva* (stone pillar) in Bethel (Genesis 28:10–13) where Jacob anoints the pillar after he sets it up, is respectful acknowledgment of the power manifest within the stone and that God speaks from that place (Genesis 31:13). "Nowhere," writes Zevit, "does the narrative equate the *matzevah* with the deity, but it *does allow that the god could somehow be a presence in, but apart from, the stone*."²⁶ Hence the commandment that prohibits concrete representation of things in the physical world, particularly an image that appears to embody the deity itself. And later, in keeping with this commandment, these wooden and stone images were soundly condemned by mainline scripture. Indeed, the intensity with which these images were destroyed was proportional to the perceived inherent sacred power they were believed to possess (see 2 Kings 10:26–27).

Nahum Sarna and Benjamin Sommer add to the rationale for this prohibition.

> *Sarna:* An image that depicts natural forces and objects is not simply symbolic in function. The image or statue inevitably becomes endowed with divinity. As such, it is automatically invested with influence, and the representation is somehow ultimately identified with the deity itself. *It is looked upon as the place and presence of the deity,* and becomes the focus of veneration and worship.²⁷

*Sommer:* For the Deuteronomists there can be no incarnations of the exclusively transcendent God. Even representations of that God are illicit lest they come to be viewed as embodying the divine. Indeed, for Deuteronomy any representation of God should be regarded as a false god, a god of other nations. The Deuteronomists employ here what the Rabbis would later call a *seeyug* or fence: in order to make clear that no physical object can embody God, they further insist that no object should even portray Him, *lest the portrayal come to be regarded as an incarnation.*[28]

People before and during Moses' time who were accustomed to pagan attachment to places of worship and to statues and statuettes of various gods in those places no doubt found Moses' prohibition difficult to understand and accept. However, the principle established at this juncture with great emphasis was that nothing in nature can be compared to The Lord and that nothing can represent Him. Indeed, asserts scripture, "My face you cannot see, for no mortal man can see me and live."[29] Moses' conviction about the God of Israel was that The Lord was wholly independent of the world He created; He does not inhabit a place or a concrete object; distance between Him and humans was at all times to be maintained.

## The Deity Protects and Cares for People

In our discussion about the "God of the Fathers" in chapter 1, we noted that one of the characteristics of this deity was that he was a god who uses his power to work for his people, who helps them in their trials, who promises them a positive future. Thus the patron god, *Shaddai*, promised Abraham, Isaac and Jacob a land in which they and their progeny will dwell.[30] The clan god of Isaac, *Pahad*, protects Jacob from the machinations of his father-in-law, Laban.[31] And the clan god of Jacob, *Abir*, helps Jacob parry his harassers.[32] This portrays a close personal relationship between the patriarchal clan and its god—a fundamental characteristic of a deity who protects and cares for people.

Here again Mosaic religion proceeds to expand and deepen a notion inherited from the patriarchal period. It did so by introducing The Lord into the Israelite religion. In responding to Moses' query about God's name, which would thus lend authority for his mission before Pharaoh, God responds, *Eheye Asher Eheyeh,*[33] a translation of which is, "I shall be what I shall be." This meant that Israel's life and faith have a future. Indeed, The Lord cares for His people. Her faith is characterized by confidence in the Divine promises to her ancestors of land and progeny and prosperity. What Mosaic religion did in adopting this element of help and promise for people was to substitute The Lord, the single God for the multiple gods of the past—*Shaddai, Pahad, Abir*. This Deity constituted *one unambiguous authority, one voice*, as it were, whose promises of care and protection could therefore be relied upon, a God who could be believed in and worshiped with confidence.

The seed had been planted. Mosaic religion nurtured it by infusing the received notion of the Godhood with a sturdy confidence in the destiny of the people Israel. He heard God saying, as it were, "I shall be what I shall be." That is, God will be revealed by His future presence. Just as He granted a good tomorrow for Israel's patriarchal ancestors, and just as He granted freedom to the Israelites in the past by liberating them from Egyptian bondage, so will He grant them fulfillment in days to come.[34]

## The Deity Is Creator of Heaven and Earth

As we have seen in chapter 1 depicting the religion of the Patriarchs, King Melkizedek blessed Abraham in the name of his god: *"Blessed be Abram of El Elyon ['god most high'], creator of heaven and earth*, and blessed be god most high."[35] Further, in the extra-biblical Ugarit literature El is similarly viewed as a creator, being called "builder of things built," described as "creator of the earth," and as the ultimate ruler of the earth who, for example allowed the building of a palace for his contemporary god, Baal—this only with El's permission."[36]

Here, too, Moses inherited a rudimentary idea of deity—this time as creator—and transformed it into a basic element of Monotheism. He did this via introduction of the name The Lord into the religion of Israel, along with one of its fundamental connotations. Thus God's response to Moses' request for the name of Israel's God was *Eheyeh Asher Eheyeh*, which means, "The Lord causes to be what exists." *The Lord, the One God—and not El, one of many gods—is the Creator of heaven and earth and all within it.* Thus,

> Remember the Sabbath day to keep it holy. Six days you shall labor and do all your work, but the seventh day is a Sabbath to The Lord your God. . . . *For in six days The Lord made heaven and earth*, the sea, and all that is in them, and rested the seventh day; therefore The Lord blessed the Sabbath day and hallowed it.[37]

The notion of The Lord as Creator is attested to not only in the book of Exodus (as above), but also in the Deuteronomistic literature (i.e., from Deuteronomy proper to the books of Kings). This literature, composed much later than this Mosaic period, in the seventh century BCE, was, according to William Foxwell Albright, "A conscious effort to recapture both the letter and spirit of Mosaicism, which, the Deuteronomists believed, had been neglected by the Israelites of the Monarchy."[38] Thus in the book of Deuteronomy proper,

> Ask now of the days that are past, which were before you, since the day that God created man upon the earth, and ask from one end of heaven to the other, whether such a great thing as this as has ever happened or was ever heard of.[39]

And a bit later we are told,

> Behold, to The Lord your God belong heaven and the heaven of heavens, the earth with all that is in it.[40]

And subsequently in the Deuteronomistic books of Samuel and Kings,

> The Lord raises up the poor from the dust; He lifts the needy from the ash heap to make them sit with princes and inherit a seat of honor. For the pillars of the earth are The Lord's and on them He has set the world.[41]

And finally,

> (King) Hezekiah prayed before The Lord and said: O Lord the God of Israel who art enthroned above the cherubim, Thou art the God, Thou alone, of all the kingdoms of the earth; Thou hast made heaven and earth.[42]

## The Deity Is Identified with Justice and Righteousness

As we saw in our chapter on the Patriarchs, patriarchal religion harbored nascent notions of justice and righteousness. These notions matured and were expanded in the Mosaic age.

While the patriarchal El Elyon was, indeed, "the god most high," this deity was not the exclusive god at the time. Many other gods with power and authority existed in the minds of the people, and were recognized as active in their lives, and authoritative in matters of religious law and practice. Hence, El Elyon did have notions of morality, but so did other god-authorities whose notions were more often than not at variance with those of El and of each other. It was a system of morality unsteady, unreliable and inconsistent and, indeed, in need of fundamental change.

And so it was at this juncture in time that Mosaic religion introduced The Lord into Israelite religion. God was not to be seen as many but as singular: *He is one God who demands one set of moral standards*. This notion resides at the very root of Monotheism. It was first explicated in the Mosaic period and thereafter animates all of biblical literature. It asserts that the welfare of society is conditioned on adherence to *a single God's single set of laws*. And this God is deemed to be *absolutely moral* and correspondingly demands moral behavior on the part of all human beings.

What Mosaic religion did was to extrapolate on the moral and ethical notions inherited from the patriarchal period—the virtues of compassion, justice, beneficence. To cite but a few representative examples of the Mosaic ethical system as recorded in the book of Exodus alone, which are seen as rooted in a single authority:

- Six days shall you labor and do all your work, but the seventh day is a Sabbath of The Lord your God: you shall not do any work—you, your son or daughter, your male or female servant, or your cattle, or the stranger who is within your settlements (22:9–10).

- You shall not wrong a stranger or oppress him, for you were strangers in the land of Egypt (22:19).

- You shall not ill treat any widow or orphan. If you do mistreat them, I will heed their outcry (22:21–22).

- If you take your neighbor's garment in pledge, you must return it to him before the sun sets; it is his only clothing, the sole clothing of his skin, in what else shall he sleep? Therefore, if he cries out to Me, I will pay heed, for I am compassionate (22:26).

- You must not carry false rumors; you shall not join hands with the guilty to act as a malicious witness: You shall neither side with the mighty to do wrong—you shall not give perverse testimony in a dispute so as to pervert it in favor of the mighty—nor shall you show deference to a poor man in his dispute (23:1–3).

- When you encounter your enemy's ox or ass wandering, you must take it back to him. When you see the ass of your enemy lying under its burden and would refrain from raising it, you must nevertheless raise it with him. You shall not subvert the rights of your needy in their disputes (23:4–6).

- Keep far from a false charge; do not bring death on those who are innocent and in the right, for I will not acquit the wrongdoer. Do not take bribes, for bribes blind the clear-sighted and upset the pleas of those who are in the right (23:7–8).

- Six years you shall sow your land and gather in its yield; but in the seventh you shall let it rest and lie fallow. Let the needy among your people eat of it, and what they leave let the wild beasts eat. You shall do the same with your vineyards and your olive groves (23:10–11).

A basic tenet of Monotheism is affirmed in expansive fashion.

## Was Mosaic Religion Pure Monotheism?

As Baruch Halpern has observed, "Early Israelite religion is not self-consciously monotheistic. It defines itself in terms of loyalty to the Lord, in terms of the Lord's incomparability, *but not in terms of His transcending uniqueness*. It has not as yet the fully developed notion that being monotheistic (to use the term as it is applied to modern monotheisms) is central to its identity."[43] Thus, if "pure" Monotheism means that but one God exists everywhere in the world and for all people everywhere, which is to say that apart from The Lord no gods whatsoever even existed, it is questionable if Mosaic Monotheism may be considered pure Monotheism. Indeed, the reality of other gods besides The Lord was still a condition to be reckoned with. The very fact that a particular name—"The Lord"—was newly chosen in the Mosaic age for Israel's own God shows that religionists at the time felt the need of special nomenclature to distinguish this God of theirs from the other gods whose existence was thus surely assumed.[44]

Scripture depicts The Lord as having a "heavenly host," an assembly of angels, to wit: "And The Lord God said, now that the man has become *like one of us* knowing good and bad . . . ,"[45] and, says God, when men sought to build a tower with its top to the sky: "*Let us* go down and confound their speech there."[46] Indeed, Benjamin Sommer has documented via several biblical passages that angels were perceived by some at the time as having elements of divine character. Thus, for example, among many others, in Exodus we read: "I will now send an angel in front of you. . . . Take care with him and obey him. . . . For *My name is within* him."[47] By stating that His name is in the angel, God indicates that the angel carries something of God's own essence or self; it is not an entirely separate entity, but it clearly is not fully identical with God either.[48] The notion of a heavenly host was shared by Israel with her pagan neighbors and there was always the temptation to worship these figures. Thus, Deuteronomy asserts, "And when you look up to the sky and behold the sun and the moon and the stars, the whole heavenly host, you must not be lured into bowing down to them or serving them."[49]

A set of Psalms similarly appears to view celestial powers as existing, though, of course, as lesser beings: *God is exalted over all celestial beings* (Psalm 93:3); they *reverently fulfill the will of their Creator* (Psalm 103:20). *The heavenly host give praise to God, whose greatness the celestial beings proclaim* (Psalm 148:2). As Halpern pointedly quotes a hypothetical student asking an (over)-confident monotheist: "Do angels not live forever, enjoy supernatural powers, exist in a dimension different from that inhabited by mortals?"[50]

Yet more: The assumption of the existence of gods other than The Lord along with their power to affect forces and events is clearly indicated in numerous passages reflecting the religion of the Mosaic period, to wit:

- The iconic Shema is addressed solely to the people Israel: "*Hear O Israel, The Lord is our God, The Lord is One.*" The Lord is Israel's God. It does not proclaim that The Lord is God of people other than Israelites. The gods of non-Israel are left in place; nothing about their non-existence is asserted. Further, in the passage following the first paragraph of the Shema, Moses asserts in The Lord's name, "Do not follow other gods, any gods of the people about you." Indeed, these gods are not to be followed, but they are there, they exist for other people.[51]

- The equally iconic second of the Ten Commandments states, "You shall have no other gods besides Me." This means "in addition to Me." Indeed, other gods exist in addition to The Lord but these, the commandment asserts, Israel must not "have," must not recognize or worship."[52]

- Moses' father-in-law, Jethro, enthuses, "Now I know that he Lord is greater than all gods by the result of their very schemes against the people of Israel." The gods of Egypt failed but were active in opposition to Israel.[53]

- Moses declares, "When you look up to the sky and behold the sun and the moon and the stars, the whole heavenly host, you must not be lured into bowing down to them or serving them. *These The Lord your God allotted to other peoples everywhere under heaven.*" Here the gods of other people are not only assumed to exist, but that The Lord Himself gave them to others.[54]

- The Israelites sing at the sea they traversed in safety: "Who is like You among the gods, O Lord." The Lord is God among the other existing gods.[55]

- The Judge Jephtha is speaking to the Amorites, who were seeking to seize land Israel held east of the Jordan: "Do you not hold what Chemosh your god gives you to possess? So, we will hold on to everything that The Lord our God, has given us to possess." Israel was well aware of the existence and power of a rival god.[56]

- David is remonstrating against King Saul for having driven him out of his homeland, saying, "Go serve other gods." So other gods were thought to be functioning.[57]

Indeed, examination of Israelite life in Canaan as depicted in the books of Joshua, Judges and Samuel, *ca. 1200–800 BCE, i.e., the extended period during which Mosaic religion functioned*, reveals assumption of the existence of foreign gods.

This condition has been corroborated by numerous extra-biblical archaeological findings throughout this period as limned in detail by scholars such as Baruch Halpern, William Dever, and Kyle McCarter. These include a variety of figurines discovered in Israelite locales that were understood to represent the gods who served the Lord, cultic pillars, various lists of pagan names of Israelites, and inscriptions such as the Mesha Stele, which depicts the national god Chemosh in both defeat and victory with the inscription mentioning the Lord as Israel's god.[58]

And so, Israel's notion of God as formulated in the Mosaic era cannot be considered pure Monotheism. On the other hand, if we avoid the term "Monotheism" as such, it would be difficult to find a more satisfactory one to define the God of Moses. "Polytheism" certainly was not the religion of Moses. "Henotheism," the belief in one God without actually asserting that The Lord is the only God, and "Monolatry," the worship of God and no other, both, though usually and legitimately employed, do not seem to capture the essential nature of the situation—this because though the existence of other gods was not expressly denied, neither was their status tolerantly granted. Moreover, the two terms do not effectively presage what is to come with regard to the development of Monotheism. Thus some scholars seek compromise terms such as "incipient Monotheism" or "implicit Monotheism."[59]

It is these latter two terms, "incipient" and "implicit" Monotheism, which the writer of these lines prefers. This is because they illustrate the basic thesis of this book. Its operating principle is that one era contains the seeds of an idea that a following era adopts and adapts to a higher level of awareness. Thus, Mosaic religion nourished the seeds of the God idea it inherited from the patriarchal era and brought it to a much-advanced level of consciousness, details of which are chronicled in this chapter. More: in so doing, Mosaic religion laid its considerably advanced notion of the God idea at the feet of the Prophets who followed it and who, in turn, transcribed it into pure authentic Monotheism, as we shall soon see. Thus, Mosaic religion was "incipient Monotheism" in that it brought the notion of God to the brink of its fullest meaning and "implicit Monotheism" in that it contained already elevated elements that made possible the prophetic expansion of the God idea to include the Deity as a God of all the world and of all mankind. What was it about Moses' work that made this happen?

Walter Eichrodt[60] focuses on the Mosaic era notion of the singularity of the Deity and what made it so compelling in this period. Though, as we have indicated, the existence of deities for peoples other than their own was recognized, Israel's religious ideologues affirmed with unequivocal passion the existence of the One God as Israel's sole Deity. Eichrodt points out that in the early religion of the Patriarchs there is emphasis on the exclusiveness of the relationship to their god, El, and thus an ascription of uniqueness to the tribal deity. So it was in the Mosaic age, that the conviction of the God's absolute Oneness for Israel emerged in a truly dominant manner. What made it so influential was the nature of the idea which was adhered to by the "official" leadership. Such was the case in the face of ceaseless challenge on the part of the people at large, many of whom (including in various periods some of the leaders themselves) deviated in practice from the establishment's norms. And so it was that Mosaic religion's advanced God idea, adhered to with such ideological tenacity as it was, rendered it "implicit" and "incipient" Monotheism.

It is now that the Prophets enter the historical and theological picture and move the Mosaic notion of the Godhead and its characteristics to the next level of consciousness.

*Chapter 3*

# The Prophets and Monotheism

## *The God of Israel Is the God of All Mankind*

Amos and Hosea, First Isaiah, Jeremiah and Ezekiel made major contributions to the developing idea of Monotheism. However, it was Second Isaiah who gave Monotheism, always implicit in Israel's faith, its clearest and most consistent expression.

### THE PROPHETS CONTINUE MONOTHEISM'S DEVELOPMENT

As we have been pointing out, each era in the history of Israelite religion based its teachings on notions inherited from its past. Such is the case with the Prophets, those extraordinary men who regarded themselves as links in the chain of religious teachers who preceded them. Each sought to deepen and expand the ideas about the One God, while retaining the essential thrust of the ideas received. Thus their formulations grew out of earlier formulations which appeared as "implicit" in what they came to teach. And so, the received Mosaic notion of Monotheism was adopted by the Prophets, who proceeded to adapt it in the context of their own time and clime and religious sensibilities.[1]

#### The Deity Is a Supreme God

The Prophets expanded the Mosaic notion of Deity in two basic ways: A) from tacit acceptance of the existence of other gods to insistence that no gods other than The Lord even exist, and B) from God being the God of Israel alone to His being the God of all people—Israelite and non-Israelite alike.

## The Non-Existence of Other Gods

Mosaic religion assumed the existence of gods other than The Lord, who was for Israel supreme. However, in the pre-exilic prophetic period, historical events and the Bible itself pointed to The Lord's continuing emerging character. These elements appear to add to the mosaic notion of "implicit" or "incipient" Monotheism we have designated at the conclusion of our previous chapter.

The situation on the ground: The centralization of national worship during the period of the monarchy *encouraged the notion of a single deity* and devalued local manifestations of the Godhood. As P. K. McCarter has commented on the Davidic kings, "Their policies, by unifying the worship of YHWH, had the effect of unifying the way in which He was conceived by His worshippers."[2] Which is to say that this focused ever strongly in practice on the idea of God's singularity. A practical factor especially developed during the period of the monarchy, which helped establish the worship of the One God, which, in turn, pointed to His total singularity, was the role of writing in Israelite society (i.e., chiseled inscriptions on stone monuments and clay tablets, writing with stylus on potsherds, papyrus and parchment, etc.). Even as the development of printing in the Middle Ages made possible widespread dissemination of religious doctrine, so too was the consequence of writing in this ancient time. It gave the doctrines and practices of the heretofore oral law more general application and enhanced its authoritative status in society. In Israel at this point in time, the notion of the sole worship of the One and Only God (of Israel) was emerging with special emphasis.[3]

The Hebrew Bible's theological perspective as Yehezkel Kaufmann interprets it is illuminating in this regard. What Kaufmann does is to show the vast superiority of The Lord over the gods of Canaan and Mesopotamia, and this provided further evidence of the continued advance of the idea of Monotheism toward its fullest meaning articulated in the period of the exile. In effect, Kaufmann strengthens the picture of "incipient" Monotheism in the pre-exilic prophetic period. What follows is Benjamin Sommer's summary of Kaufmann's analysis.[4]

Kaufmann depicts the consistent differences between the Bible's descriptions of "The Lord" and the Canaanites' and Mesopotamians' descriptions of their gods. In each of these cases the biblical God is seen, in one way or another, as vastly superior in terms of godhood.

- Thus, the divine retinue we know from the Hebrew Bible differs from that of the pagans because the latter's lower beings do not realistically challenge The Lord in the Bible; and when they do, the revolt is put down without any difficulty.

- The Lord is the High God from the very beginning in scripture as compared to the pagan gods who took on their roles at one point.

- The pagan gods were created or born from something prior to them, whereas about the Lord we know nothing of His origin.

- Whereas in polytheistic theologies the gods are subject to matter and to forces stronger than themselves, The Lord is never frustrated by the forces of nature, by matter or by other gods.

- Finally, though the Hebrew Bible *does mention the existence of other gods*, those gods do not appear as important characters in their own right, but rather are portrayed only as part of an anonymous mass; The Lord, on the other hand, is of ultimate importance and of distinct character.

Kaufmann's analysis *does not reveal a deity as precluding the very existence of other gods*, but it does portray the pagan gods as characters of profound hollowness as compared to The Lord. Indeed, the pre-exilic Prophets portray them as such. (First) Isaiah, in the mid-eighth century BCE, proclaimed that the pagan gods were *elilim*, "nothings."[5] Jeremiah understood the Lord as a generative, life-giving force, "the source of living waters." All other deities, the host of heaven included, he considers *borot nishbarim asher lo yukhilu ha-mayim*, "broken cisterns which cannot even hold water."[6] They are bad imitations of empty receptacles. To turn from the Lord to any other god is to forsake reality for deception.[7] *Shikutzim*, "abominations," and *gilulim*, "gods of dung," are favorite appellations with Ezekiel.[8]

The Deuteronomist, reflecting the prophetic scorn and mockery of pagan images, saw them as *ma-asay yadayim*, "the work of human hands."[9] However, he went further with a general assertion about the matter: the images of the pagan gods were not only mere human creations, but that the God of Israel, by contrast, was "the real thing," as it were, "It has been clearly demonstrated to you that *the Lord alone is God*,"[10] and again, "Know, therefore, this day and keep in mind that *the Lord alone is God* in the heaven above and on the earth below; *there is no other*."[11] Though the context of these assertions is a speech in Moses' name admonishing Israel about her God,[12] these statements, combined with those of (First) Isaiah, Jeremiah and Ezekiel, bring the notion of the singularity of Deity in the late pre-exile period yet closer to the brink of its fullness. This morphed into the work of Second Isaiah, who projected the removal, at long last, of any ambiguity about the Oneness of God by establishing the principle that *no other gods, besides the Lord, in any sense even exist*. George Adam Smith put it this way: "Second

Isaiah treated the gods of the nations as things in whose existence no reasonable person could possibly believe.[13] Indeed, it was this Prophet who spelled out the notion of Deity clearly implicit in the assertions of his mosaic and prophetic predecessors. As John Bright wrote, "It was Second Isaiah who gave Monotheism, always implicit in Israel's faith, its clearest and most consistent expression.[14]

In addition to the factors above, there were historical conditions that the exile from the homeland brought about that contributed to an articulation of this full Monotheism on the part of Second Isaiah. Mark Smith, in his depiction of Monotheism as it evolved through the centuries, explains. "Israel stands at the bottom of political power, and it exalts its Deity *inversely* as ruler of the whole universe."[15] Disaster had befallen Israel. The Babylonians had destroyed the Jerusalem Temple. The nation was dismembered. The people fled to foreign lands, exile. Israel's customs and traditions were waylaid. The pagan gods of Babylon were now in full power. This was a national and psychological trauma of the first order.

The catastrophe inevitably stimulated serious renewed thinking about God's role in Israel's affairs and those of the larger world. What was God's true nature? Was He really in control of events as claimed? Could Israel's history and present suffering be explained? What does the rise of Cyrus imply about God's role in the life of nations besides Israel? Indeed, Israel's exile and the rest was a searing experience, and response to these questions was demanded.

The response to the catastrophe? That God had failed and abandoned His people was unthinkable. No, Israel's faith in The Lord was tenacious and could or would never be abandoned. To the contrary, she concluded that *this terrible experience had been the Lord's will. Indeed, the Lord was even stronger than had been previously evident.* "After all," Robert Wright observes, "the Babylonians had conquered the mighty Assyrians. If wielding Assyria as 'the rod of My anger'[16] was testament to The Lord's strength and control of world affairs, what did it mean when The Lord showed His strength and control of the Babylonians in wreaking havoc on Israel?" According to the book of Habakkuk, *The Lord Himself directed the Babylonian onslaught.*

> Look at the nations, and see! Be astonished! Be astounded! For a work is being done in your days that you would not believe if you were told. For I am rousing the Chaldeans [Babylonians], that fierce and impetuous nation, who march through the breadth of the earth to seize dwellings not their own. . . . At kings they scoff, and of rulers they make sport.[17]

This is what Mark Smith meant when he observed that from the depths of Israel's condition she *inversely* exalts The Lord as ruler of the entire world. Deep irony is involved here, but the notion it harbors is compelling: a God who governs the action of the greatest empire of its time is a God who governs history itself, and thus is the one and only God of the world. This not only explained the reason for Israel's collapse—punishment for backsliding—but also constituted a definitive self-disclosure on The Lord's part.

Herein are the routes to an explicit and uncompromising Monotheism as articulated by Second Isaiah, and done so as never before.

> I am the Lord and there is none else;
> Beside Me, there is no god.
> I engird you, though you have not known Me,
> So that they may know, from east to west,
> That there is none but Me.
> I am the Lord and there is none else,
> I form light and create darkness,
> I make weal and create woe—
> I the Lord do all these things.[18]

The pagan nations are challenged to prove the validity of their claims and of their gods.

> Submit your case, says The Lord;
> Offer your pleas, says the king of Jacob.
> Let them approach and tell us what will happen.
> Tell us what has occurred,
> And we will take note of it;
> Or announce to us what will occur,
> That we may know the outcome.
> Foretell what is yet to happen,
> That we may know that you are gods!
> Do anything, good or bad,
> That we may be awed and see.
> *Why, you are less than nothing,*
> *Your effect is less than nullity;*
> *One who chooses you is an abomination.*[19]

The prophet, speaking in God's name, makes it crystal clear that God is unique in that there is no such thing as other gods.

> Thus said The Lord, the King of Israel,
> Their Redeemer, The Lord of Hosts:

> *I am the first and I am the last,*
> *And there is no god, but me.*
> Who like me can announce,
> Can foretell it—and match me thereby?
> Even as I told the future to an ancient people
> So let him foretell coming events to them.
> Do not be frightened, do not be shaken!
> Have I not from of old predicted to you?
> I foretold, and you are my witnesses.
> *Is there any god, then, but me?*
> "There is no other rock; I know none!"[20]

And then the prophet again emphasizes God's Oneness; His uniqueness, His eternity. The implication of his words here is plain: only this can be said about The Lord:

> Listen to me, O Jacob,
> Israel, whom I have called:
> *I am he—I am the first,*
> *And I am the last as well.*
> *My* own *hand founded the earth,*
> *My* right *hand spread out the skies.*
> I call unto them, let them stand up.
> Assemble, all of you, and listen!
> Who among you foretold these things:
> "He whom The Lord loves
> Shall work His will against Babylon,
> And, with His might, against Chaldea"?
> I, I predicted, and I called him;
> I have brought him and he shall succeed in his mission.
> Draw *near to me and hear this:*
> *From the beginning, I did not speak in secret;*
> *From the time anything existed, I was there.*[21]

In sum, God is the sovereign Lord of all that transpires in the world. All things take place within His power and purpose for The Lord alone is God. Indeed, as H. W. Robinson has said about the phenomenal theological achievement here articulated: "Isaiah drops the keystone of the Monotheistic arch into its place."[22]

## The Universality of God

Mosaic religion viewed God as The Lord of the people Israel alone. However, as was the case with the notion of the Oneness of God depicted previously, another seed for the future period was planted in pre-exilic times. The patron of the monarchy, *The Lord, supported Israel in international conflicts. Divine power became transnational in scope, thereby pointing in the direction of an early form of universalist faith.* So, for example, the Elijah-Elisha cycles communicate the scope of The Lord's power over other deities *even outside* Israel. The story of Naaman in 2 Kings 5 sets the stage for an assertion that the actions of The Lord extend beyond Israel's national borders; Naaman declares in recognition of this fact, "There is no God in all the earth but in Israel" (2 Kings 5:15). As Mark Smith put it, "This notion of the Lord's power over the nations *continued* among the prophets of the eighth century and reached full flower with the emergence of (unambiguous) Israelite Monotheism in the exile."[23]

And so, the Prophets, based on the Mosaic notion of The Lord's overarching sovereignty, expanded that notion to include, without equivocation or qualification, God's rule over all peoples and nations—Israelites and non-Israelites alike. Listen to the pre-exilic Prophets and then to Second Isaiah:

*Amos:* "Are you not as the children of the Ethiopians to Me, O people of Israel? says The Lord. Did I not bring Israel up from the land of Egypt, and the *Philistines from Caphtor and the Syrians from Kir*?"[24] Yes, God cares not only for Israel but for non-Israel as well, for He is also their God.

*Micah:* "And it shall come to pass in the latter days that the mountain of the house of The Lord shall be established as the highest of the mountains . . . and all nations shall flow to it."[25] Yes, the God of Israel shall now be worshiped by non-Israel, for they will recognize The Lord as theirs as well.

*Isaiah* declares that the day will come when the people of Egypt will "swear allegiance to The Lord of hosts," that they will know The Lord and worship Him and that when they call upon Him. "He will hear their supplications and heal them."[26] Yes, The Lord cares for all people.

*Zephaniah:* "Yea, at that time I will change the speech of the peoples to a pure speech, that all of them may call on the name of The Lord and serve him with one accord. From beyond the rivers of Ethiopia my suppliants, the daughters of my dispersed ones, shall bring my offering."[27] Yes, those of Israel who have long since "assimilated" and live far and wide will one day recognize The Lord as their God.

And then there are the extraordinary Prophets who lived and taught in the period after 586 BCE, who articulated the universality of The Lord.

*Jeremiah:* It is with this Prophet that the notion of God's accessibility being independent of a specific place comes into full and unclouded view. When the exiled Jews in Babylonia, in dismay, asked Jeremiah, "Where now is your God who allowed such a catastrophe?" the Prophet wrote them a letter while yet in Jerusalem: "When you call me, and come and pray to me, I will give heed to you. You will search for me and find me, if only you seek me wholeheartedly."[28] God is available *everywhere*, declares the prophet. He can be sought and found in personal prayer *anywhere* and *anytime*—not just in Jerusalem and not just via the ritual of the Temple. He is thus the God of each country where the people happen to live.

Indeed, Jeremiah's advice was revolutionary in that it viewed God's presence beyond the confines of Israel's own land: He was a God of people and not place. More: Jeremiah, along with his predecessors, Isaiah and Micah, envisioned that "the nations from the ends of the earth" will come to recognize The Lord.[29] So, too, Zechariah, who proclaimed, "And many nations shall join themselves to The Lord, in that day, and they shall be my people."[30]

*Second Isaiah:* This great herald of universalism speaks of God assembling the nations of the world and telling them to see God's hand in the present overturn of Babylon on the part of Persia.[31] God expected the great Cyrus, "His anointed one," to recognize His role in Cyrus' triumph over Babylon and therefore acknowledge The Lord as the true God.[32] In this assembly of the heathen nations the Prophet declares that their people pray "to a god who cannot save," that only The Lord is a "righteous God and Savior" and that there is none beside Him. "Therefore, turn to me and be saved, all the ends of the earth . . . from my mouth has gone forth righteousness, a word that shall not return." (i.e., a permanent moral obligation). The prophet hears The Lord, the One and only God, proclaiming for all the world to hear: "I will give you as a light to the nations, that my salvation may reach to the end of the earth."[33]

And so, with the Prophets of Israel, the universalism of Monotheism comes to full fruition. The notion was articulated by them with the utmost emphasis and clarity. Israel's concept of God and the elements it harbored were given universal dimensions.

## WHAT DIFFERENCE DOES IT MAKE IF IT WAS MOSES OR ISAIAH WHO ESTABLISHED DEFINITIVE MONOTHEISM?

The notion that it was the prophet Isaiah in the exilic period who established the definitive monotheistic idea, to wit: the Deity's universality and the total non-existence of other gods is, indeed, a radical departure from the longstanding tradition. In this construct the Mosaic idea was not yet full Monotheism as Isaiah understood it. Rather, as we have noted, "it was Second Isaiah who gave Monotheism, always implicit in Israel's Mosaic faith, its clearest and most consistent expression" (John Bright). And, even more emphatically, was H. W. Robinson's assertion that "Isaiah drops the keystone of the monotheistic arch into its place."

The evolving awareness of scriptural ideas is thus apparent. The biblical writers wrote from the perspectives of their own time and clime, though, as we have pointed out, in the spirit of their predecessors. This phenomenon is not only the work of Benedict Spinoza in the seventeenth century, who is viewed as the "father" of the so-called higher criticism of the Bible, and, of course, of modern scholarship, which has documented the multiple strata in scripture developed over time. It was in nascent form long before in the Middle Ages by the renowned Bible commentator Abraham Ibn Ezra (1092–1167), whose work graces the traditional editions of the Pentateuch (and other biblical books). Ibn Ezra himself pointed to the book of Isaiah's chapters from 40 on as having been written in the period of the exile that followed destruction of the Temple and nation in 586 BCE. He also (cautiously) explains Psalms 69 (verse 10), 85, 120, 137 as pertaining to the Babylonian exile.[34] Indeed, Ibn Ezra, in these and other varied ways, accepted this "radical" notion of biblical writers' penning their work from the perspective of their own historical condition.

Nahum Sarna has noted Ibn Ezra's comments on a set of biblical passages that appear to be anachronisms in the Torah and so later interpolations. In his commentary on Deuteronomy 1:2, Ibn Ezra cryptically writes this,

> If you understand the deep meaning of the twelve [final verses of the book of Deuteronomy 34:1–12], and the passage, "That day Moses wrote down the poem: 'The Canaanites were then in the land' (Genesis 12:6), and the passage, 'In the mountains of the Lord it will be seen' (Genesis 22:14), and the passage, 'his bedstead is an iron bedstead,' *you will recognize the truth.*

Concerning this comment Sarna writes,

> "The twelve" refers to the closing 12 verses of Deuteronomy; unlike the body of the book, which is couched in autobiographical style, these twelve verses speak of Moses in the third person, indicating that they were not written by him. In fact, on Deuteronomy 34:1 our commentator explicitly says, "In my opinion, Joshua wrote from this verse on, for once Moses ascended the summit of Pisgah (where he died), he wrote no more; or he wrote prophetically (about himself)."

Sarna's analysis continues. Ibn Ezra lists the other passages he took to be later interpolations: Deuteronomy 31:22, which also refers to Moses in the third person. Genesis 22:14, which records that in consequence of Abraham's naming the site of the binding of Isaac, *Adonai-yireh*, there arose a saying: "On the mountain of the Lord there is vision." Says Sarna, "Such an appellation would be applicable only subsequent to Solomon's temple building." As to the reference to the iron casket of the king of Bashan in Deuteronomy 3:11 mentioning that the relic survived at Rabbah of the Amonites, Sarna indicates that the Israelites would not have placed it there after defeating the monarch. "The archaeological note suggests that this passage was written from the perspective of a later age, and is an interpolation."[35]

Of additional significance in this regard is Ibn Ezra's comment on the narrative in Genesis 12 concerning the patriarch Abraham's travels from Haran to Canaan. He focuses on the statement in verse 6, *v'hakna-ani uz b'aretz*, "The Canaanites were *then* in the land." Clearly this statement reflects a later biblical writer in whose era the Canaanites were not in the land, having been decimated by Joshua. This biblical writer is looking back, as it were, into the earlier Mosaic period—centuries before his century—when, indeed, the Canaanites were in the land. Hence, as E. A. Speiser has averred, Ibn Ezra is guardedly telling us here that Moses could not have authored the *then* statement and notes Ibn Ezra's concluding remark: *yesh lo sod v'hamaskil yidom*, "There is a mystery here, and the wise had best keep silent" (Anchor Bible: Genesis, p. 87).

There is a work called the *Tzafnas Paneyakh*, which examines in detail the commentary of Ibn Ezra. It was written in the 1300s by a Spanish Jew by the name of Yosef ben Eliezer who was recognized as a major expert on the writings of Ibn Ezra. Ben Eliezer analyses the sentence, "And the Canaanites were then in the land," and amplifies Ibn Ezra's understanding of the matter, writing this:

> *lo yitakhen she-amar Moshe "uz"* . . .
> It is not possible that Moses uttered "then" because our *reason* tells us that the word "then" was written when the Canaanites were not in the land . . . accordingly, it appears that Moses did not write this word but rather it was Joshua or one of the other prophets who wrote it.

Ben Eliezer then asks tellingly:

> *Ma li shekatvoo moshe o shekatvoo navi akher? Ho-eel divray kulam emet v'haym b'nivoo-ah.*
> What difference does it make if Moshe wrote these words or some other prophet did, since the words of all of them are true and originate in prophecy?[36]

The reasoned approach of Ibn Ezra and Yosef ben Eliezer, and this book's thesis about the evolutionary unfolding of the monotheistic idea, cannot be cavalierly dismissed in the name of traditional faith, hallowed and longstanding as it is. Indeed, faith is not allowed to be jettisoned by non-awareness to the findings of the critical mind guided as it is by "reason," as Yosef ben Eliezer put it in his analysis of Ibn Ezra. Critical thinking is one of God's marvelous endowments on His human children, as Ibn Ezra himself emphasized in the introduction to of his commentary to the book of Genesis. A guiding principle he employs in interpreting scripture was that the human intellect is *a malakh Hashem*, "an angel sent by God," and he further emphasized that he who believes in something that contradicts the *sekhel* (that is, common sense, logic, reason) abuses the finest gift God has given him.[37]

Yet more: Ibn Ezra echoed his famous Muslim predecessor, theologian and jurist Abu Hamid al-Ghazali (1058–1111), who emphasized that *lo barah Hashem b'riah yotair nikhbedet min hasekhel*, "God has created nothing more honored/distinguished than reason" (translated from the Arabic into Hebrew by Rabbi Avraham ben Hasdai [ca. 1230], an enthusiastic scholarly partisan of Moses Maimonides, who was a champion of rational thought in the pursuit of religious studies). So, too, Thomas Aquinas (1224–1274), the preeminent spokesman of the Catholic tradition, who saw reason in harmony with faith. The critical mind, Acquinas emphasized, was a divine gift highly to be cherished (Aquinas notion, for example, if a Prime Mover/Causeless Cause demonstrated his reasoned thinking about the existence of God).[38]

In sum, man's search for God was (and continues to be) uncovered in progressive stages; it is an evolving process. It strengthens rather than weakens faith, for it reveals the presence of the Divine in Israel and the world not solely in one period of history (e.g., the Mosaic) and on the part of one seer (e.g., Moses), but in multiple periods (e.g., the prophetic) and by other seers (e.g., Isaiah). Such has been the case throughout the annals of history. It just took humanity time—historic time—to realize that extraordinary phenomenon of faith.

## God Is a God of People, Not Place

As pointed out in the two previous chapters, the patriarchal notion of the deity as a God of people on the move rather than one localized in a fixed place was zealously clung to even amidst the prevailing religious climate of Canaan El worship. Fixed places inhabited by the gods limited the deity's accessibility, and plastic images similarly tended to localize the deity and to create attachment to one place or another. Further, images and statues inevitably became themselves endowed with divinity. Hence the Mosaic prohibition of any concrete representation of a deity—a condition contrary to the One God.

The Prophets, in turn, inherited this imperative and articulated it with even greater passion than in the past. A key amplification: they removed, at long last, any and all ambiguity about the Oneness of God by establishing the principle that no other gods in any sense exist. Hence, it was emphasized more than ever that no images or idols are to be fashioned, no cult around them practiced, for these were seen to challenge the absolute Oneness of The Lord. Thus the Prophets continued, in their ways, the Mosaic war on Polytheism.

Baruch Halpern has amplified the rationale for this stance on the part of the prophets: their jettisoning of the process of attributing concrete reality to the Deity. The makings of this stance are found in the extant writings of the early prophets (Amos, Hosea, First Isaiah, and Micah) and more fully articulated by Jeremiah and the Deuteronomistic school in the last quarter of the seventh century—the period at the brink of the exile to Babylonia.[39] (As we proceed with this analysis, it must be stressed that the prophetic stance here depicted is the fruit of the ideologues of the time. The stance was not necessarily that of the Israelite people in practice.)

An icon is not a god, and those who worship an icon are accused of worshipping the icon rather than the god. Ritual, a symbol of submission, is not submission itself, so that those who participate in ritual are accused of mistaking the symbol for the act itself. The temple is not God's literal dwelling, and those who rely on God's presence on Zion—God's presumed place—stand accused of trusting in the temple rather than in God. This dissonance between metaphor and reality, between language and what language refers to, was the premise of the critique the prophets leveled with ever clearer emphasis. The Lord could not be limited in any way. He was free of concrete attributes and representatives. *He was not especially present in any one location.* Any symbol of the Lord was a fraud, any concretization of Him a deception.

A logical consequence of this stance was that the angels, the localization of the "living God," were cast as "divisions" of that which was "indivisible" (i.e., God). *Here the prophets viewed God as One, Alone, the All.* His total presence suffused the totality of His creation. He was the One and Only source of the cosmos. As this stance proceeded to take hold in the minds of the prophets, and as they strove to grasp God's reality as directly as Israel had at Sinai (Deuteronomy 4:9f), they succeeded, indeed, to cast serious doubt about the worthwhileness of the prevailing ritual regalia, cult and temple. To all this Halpern added parenthetically,

> That this theological position had already been consolidated in Josiah's reign explains more than anything else the survival of Judah and Israel as peoples after the trauma of the temple's destruction and the Babylonian exile. Simply,

in the Deuteronomistic school, the temple had been emptied of concrete content by means of the prophetic critique.

Perusal of the writings of the classical prophets testifies to their fervent opposition to pagan religious practice, and the rationale for this opposition.

*Amos* is chastising his people about their busy religious practices, including worship of two known Assyrian deities, Sakkuth and Kaiwan. Amos asserts the Divine word:

> Did you bring me sacrifices and offerings the forty years in the wilderness, O house of Israel? You shall take up Sakkuth, your king, and Kaiwan, your star-god, which you made for yourselves; therefore I will take you into exile beyond Damascus, says The Lord, whose name is God of hosts.[40]

*Hosea*, in numerous ways and in different contexts in the life of his people, condemns their idolatrous practices—with pillar and ephod and seraphim, and sacrifices with cult prostitutes—this all while drunk with wine.[41] And then this,

> Like grapes in the wilderness I found Israel,
> Like the first fruits on the fig tree in its first season, I
>   saw your failures.
> But they came to Ba-al-peor and consecrated
> Themselves to Baal, and became detestable
> Like the things they loved.[42]

Such furious condemnation characterizes the thinking and preaching of Hosea throughout his career.[43]

*Isaiah expresses* utter contempt for man-made objects of worship.[44] Indeed, Israel must rid herself from these corrupting images, and she will do so.

> Your ears shall hear a word (from your Teacher) behind you saying, this is the way, walk in it; when you turn to the right or when you turn to the left, then you will defile your silver-covered graven images and your gold-plated molten images. You will scatter them as unclean things; you will say to them, "Begone!"

Isaiah has much more to say about this in many an instance.[45]

*Micah* hurls threats against Samaria and Jerusalem because of their religious corruption that includes their nefarious idol worship.[46] God will follow through with His threats because of Israel's obduracy.

> I will cut off sorceries from your hand and you shall have no more soothsayers; and I will cut off your images and your pillars from among you, and you shall bow down no more to the work of your hands; and I will root out your Asherim from among you, and destroy your cities.[47]

*Jeremiah*, out of deep personal anguish being unable to resist God's insistent call that he speak to his people's abominable religious behavior, has his say throughout a tumultuous career: Israel is an idolatrous folk, "They have burned incense to other gods and worshiped the works of their own hands."[48] "How can you say, I am not defiled, I have not gone after the Baals?" Not only are these gods useless, but they are everywhere: "for as many of your cities are your gods, O Judah."[49] Worst of all, was the most terrible of all Israel's aberrations—the sacrifice of children on a burning pagan platform in the infamous Valley of Hinnom in Jerusalem.[50] Jeremiah persisted in his negation of idolatry in various other ways and settings.[51]

With *Ezekiel*, throughout his early life and career there flows a constant stream of denunciation of Israel's fashioning idols of wood and stone, of silver and gold, of sanctimonious obeisance to them, of constant worship of these contrary to the covenant of The Lord with Israel. God, says the prophet, will "destroy your high places, your altars shall become desolate, your incense altars shall be broken, I will cast down your slain men before your idols."[52] More: "Their beautiful ornaments they used for vain glory and they made their abominable images and their detestable things of it; therefore I will make it an unclean thing to them."[53] And on and on about images which provoke "jealousy" in man, about "elders—fire house of Israel," "burning clouds of incense" to a god (Osiris), of "women weeping for Tammuz," of "twenty-five men . . . worshiping the sun."[54]

What is especially disturbing to Ezekiel is Israel's *internalizing* the ideology and practice of idolatry:

> Then came the elders of Israel to me (Ezekiel), and sat before me. And the word of The Lord came to me. Son of man, *these men have taken their idols into their hearts*, and set the stumbling block of their iniquity before their faces; should I let myself be inquired of by them? . . . I, The Lord, will answer them myself; I will set my face against these men, I will make them a sign and a byword and cut them off from the midst of my people, and you shall know that *I* am The Lord.[55]

And *Second Isaiah*: The Lord will turn away from those "who trust in graven images, who say to molten images: You are our gods."[56] The craftsmen, the ironsmith, the carpenter fashion an image, bake bread, kindle a fire and fall down before it. They "fall down before a block of wood." Those who do these things "shall be put to shame."[57] They carry about wooden idols and keep on praying to a god that cannot save.[58] It is the sharp contrast Isaiah makes between the futility of the pagan gods and The Lord, which brings into stark relief the absolute Oneness and supremacy of The Lord, whose promises to Israel therefore carry so much weight.

> Bel bows down, Nebo stoops, their idols are on beasts and cattle; these things you carry are loaded as burdens on weary beasts. They stoop, they bow down together, they cannot save the burden.[59]

In sum, the pagan gods, rooted as they were in place, in fixed locations for worship, in representation of the deity in concrete form are the factors which provoked continuation of the Mosaic war on Polytheism in the prophetic age.

Jeffrey Tigay has a different take on this subject. Based on a comprehensive and nuanced analysis of evidence gathered from discovery of pagan and Israelite personal names and engraved inscriptions from the eighth century BCE, Tigay concludes that the Israelites of this era—the period of the major Prophets—were *not* for the most part polytheistic. "After the united monarchy, perhaps even earlier, the evidence currently available makes it difficult to suppose that many Israelites worshipped gods other than YHWH." As to the voluminous and vociferous condemnations of Israelite idol worship on the part of the Prophets during this period, Tigay attributes these to exaggeration prompted by the need to explain national calamity as the result of the sin of idolatry. "The sweeping biblical indictments, in sum, are based more on theological axioms than on historical data," Tigay concludes. (See "Conclusions" in his *You Shall Have No Other Gods*, pp. 37–41.)

The content of this book's chapter on the Prophets and Monotheism clearly diverges from Tigay's argument. I would counter as follows:

The biblical testimony about Israelite pagan worship detailed in this chapter cannot be dismissed on theological grounds as exaggeration or hyperbole. The Israelites of this era lived in a vast and intense polytheistic setting; they were relatively small in number; the upper classes were often highly assimilated; the middle and lower classes were in regular, even daily contact with their pagan neighbors. It is thus difficult to evade the social, economic and political factors which are more likely than not to have heavily influenced religious behavior that is intimately bound to such factors. It is this condition that the Prophets of Israel reflect in their observations about much polytheistic behavior on the part of the Israelites of their time. Moreover, the plethora of extra-biblical data that Tigay cites—pagan figurines, seals, personal names, inscriptions of various kinds et al.—do not, of course, persuade Tigay about their influence on the Israelites of their time as polytheists. However, their very existence testifies to their persistent hovering over and probable insinuating into the religious life of the Israelites.

## The Miracle of Jewish Survival

Another highly consequential product of Israelite religion's notion of The Lord as a God of people and not place needs our attention here. The question: how was it possible for a people cast out of her land, without temple and cult and stated priests, without king and nationhood, to survive? These conditions, after all, are the usual, indispensable elements of the life of a people if it is to endure. In fact, for centuries Israel was deeply attached to her own land in which she encountered her God, in which she nourished her inner life, in which she had the opportunity to implement her faith in everyday life—in its social and economic, political and military facets. Without all this, how was it conceivable that such a people could persist as a distinct entity? Indeed, in Israelite early annals, God *was* a God of place!

### Survival Despite Absence of the Land: Religion

A basis for the answer to this insistent question is provided by Israel's relationship to the land embedded in the tradition the Prophets inherited. As we have explained on several occasions in this work, prior to Israel's settlement in Canaan, the prevailing notion was that Divinity was necessarily *detached from soil*. As Salo Baron has put it,

> Since it would have been impossible to abstract God so abruptly from all locality, He remained the God of the desert long after Israel's settlement in Canaan. From the days of Debra to those of the writing Prophets, God appears in poetic vision as having His seat at Mount Sinai, or Mount Seir, in the desert of Paran, or in other places—*all outside Palestine*. Not even the combined efforts of the kings and priests in Jerusalem to associate the divine presence with the Temple on Zion could succeed. *Israel's God thus became definitely dissociated from exclusive residence on Israel's soil.*[60]

The prophets Jeremiah and Ezekiel thus had the ground upon which to provide the answer to the question about Israel's survival minus her land. *Israel, indeed could have a relationship to her God without the land she had inhabited, without temple and cult, without traditional nationhood.* Both assured her of this. The people could meet God and survive in the land of their exile if they sought Him there with their whole heart.

The Lord, Jeremiah explains, will visit the people in Babylon and fulfill His promises. He has plans for Israel's welfare to give them a future and hope.

Then they will call upon me and come and pray to me, and *I will hear you. You will seek me and find me*; when you seek me with all your heart *I will be found by you*, says The Lord, and I will restore your fortunes and gather you from all the nations and all the places where I have driven you and bring you back to the land from which I sent you into exile.[61]

And God speaks through Ezekiel and says,

Though I removed them far off among the nations, and though I scattered them among the countries, *yet I have been a sanctuary to them in the countries where they have gone.* Therefore . . . I will give you (back) the land of Israel.[62]

Thus in the days of great suffering the idea of a people beyond state and territory was firmly established. It was their tenacious clinging to the One and Only God who could be accessed even in exile that made their survival as a people possible. Yes, they continued to yearn for return to their ancestral land, and this was ever a source of hope for the morrow. Yet the people were without state or territory in the days of Moses. What ultimately mattered was to obey the commands of The Lord *in all places*. Salo Baron has articulated the essential core thought of this "amazing" development in the life of the people Israel.

New leaders arose. A transcendent and holy God, they taught, has selected the people of Israel as His holy nation, for reasons known only to Him. Through a life of holiness and, if necessary, of suffering, this people will continue to make known the name of God until the end of days, when all nations will recognize their error and worship the One God. In the meantime, Israel must keep aloof from these other nations, in order not to be contaminated by their errors and their unholy life. Such an aim can only be achieved by a full, specific, and peculiar law in all its ramifications. *The life thus demanded is necessarily artificial and contrary to nature in many ways [i.e., a people without its own land and all that goes with it]. Thus the Jew has to live, if necessary, in defiance of nature.*[63]

The answer to our question about Israel's survival without her land was thus planted. Here was a people in exile, scattered to the ends of the earth—a condition that under normal circumstances would inevitably lead to their being swallowed up by their surroundings. Why did this not happen? A set of major Jewish historians, each in his own way, echoed Baron, in answer to our question about the exile.

Nahman Krochmal:

God bestowed his grace upon the people of Israel—a grace for which we can find the reason neither in ourselves nor in any of the preceding generations.

... This grace presented us with a God idea that is supreme over all rational thought. We have always maintained this conception.... This idea became engraved upon the tablet of our hearts and never departed from our history. Through it we have become teachers of the nations, and through it *we continue to exist to this day, and with it we shall be forever redeemed.*[64]

Heinrich Graetz:

What prevented this ever-wandering people from degenerating into brutish vagrants or a vagabond horde of gypsies? The answer: during its desolate history of 1800 years in the diaspora, the Jewish people carried with it the Ark of the Covenant, which placed an ideal striving in its heart and transfigured the badge of shame on its garment with an apostolic radiance designed to educate the nations to the knowledge of God and morality.... Such a people for whom the present meant nothing and the future everything *which seemed to exist by virtue of its hope, is for that very reason as eternal as hope itself.*[65]

Simon Dubnow:

Bereft of country and dispersed as it is, the Jewish people lives, and will go on living, because a creative principle permeates it, one that is the root of its being and an indigenous product of its history. This principle consists in a sum of definite religious and moral ideals whose exponent at all times was the Jewish people.... It consists in the consciousness that true Judaism, which has accomplished great things for humanity in the past, has not yet played out its part, and therefore may not perish. In short, *the Jewish people lives because it contains a living soul which refuses to separate from its skin and cannot be forced out of it by its misfortunes.*[66]

Yehezkel Kaufmann:

What is the reason for the fact that the people of Israel persisted in being a people despite its being scattered among the nations?... When we examine the people's consciousness in the diaspora, we see that all of the values to which it clung were *religious* values—the language, the memories, the past with all its heroes, its destiny, race, customs—all were not secular matters but were sublimated and became religious values.... This all was the word and will of God with Israel as their bearer.... As such, these were permanent values harbored by a permanent people.[67]

### *Survival Despite Absence of the Land: Peoplehood*

All the above does not exhaust this subject nor fully answer the question posed: why the Jewish people's persistence in the diaspora?

The intimate relationship between the Jewish people and its religion is a basic phenomenon of Israel's history. G. Ernest Wright has pointed to this: "The Israelites point of view toward the apprehension of the Divine is to be seen, *not primarily in abstract discussion of the merits of the one over against the many, but in the fact that the God of the Bible is first of all the God of Israel.*"[68]

Walter Eichrodt alluded to this as well when he pointed out that the idea of Monotheism *took hold in the world because it was embedded in the life of the people Israel who lived the idea and thus anchored it in the world.* It was not arrived at by philosophical speculation and thus an abstraction hovering about in thin air.[69] This too was emphasized by the historians quoted above. Heinrich Graetz wrote for all of them when he asserted that *the God idea was indeed the core reason for Jewish survival in the diaspora; however, this was because it became lodged in a people who husbanded it.* Nationhood, now gone, was replaced by *peoplehood*, which became a working "substitute," as it were, a surrogate, however poor, for Israel's territory; and this accounts for the Jewish people's implacable tenacity in the diaspora: a living people harboring and proclaiming the living God.

A pronounced characteristic of Judaism, Graetz pointed out, was its drive to find concrete application for the most abstract and idealistic doctrine. The unique God-idea was not left in the ethereal region of vacuous abstraction, but sought concrete embodiment in human life. Thus the Jewish people became the *vital bearer* of God's central position and role in the affairs of the world and humanity, this in the form of their ongoing life and practices as a community. The revealed God idea did not and does not exist for its own sake, so that it might be known merely theoretically, but has a practical aim, that of promoting a temporal good life. "That it may be well with you on the land which the Lord your God gives you" is a phrase that recurs in the most diverse ordinances, for example, when Exodus 20:12 speaks of honoring father and mother, and Deuteronomy 22:6–7 forbids taking a mother bird together with her fledgling. Salo Baron amplifies this notion.

> *The seamless connection between Jewish peoplehood and its faith was felt at the very threshold of the history of both.* It is no accident that among the oldest literary documents of the people are not only war songs, legends and tales such as are found in other civilizations, but primarily laws and religious and moral teachings. One of the oldest parts of the Bible is the so-called Book of the Covenant (Exodus 20-22-23:33) containing essentially civil and criminal laws. The Decalogue itself deals with creed only in the first two (or three) commandments, devoting all the rest to laws concerning the conduct of daily life.[70]

*Thus the God idea was also a social and political idea.* This accounts for the constant formation of Jewish communities throughout the diaspora period. These communities, often despite great distances, sought and found connections with the collectivities of fellow Jews, thus forming a distinct peoplehood. Driven to this condition by religious conviction, this circumstance took on the appearance of a life of its own, as it were, especially in the modern period. The communities were reinforced by physical living enclaves, by historic memory, by an encompassing system of law, by a vast literature, by its own language, by an array of custom, by tenacious hope for resuming life in the land of her ancestors. Yet more, and especially significant, by geographical centers of authority such as in Babylonia, Spain, France and Germany, whose leaders were looked upon as arbiters of law and life for Jews in the far-flung regions of the diaspora.[71]

Yehezkel Kaufmann cautions not to overstate the independent character of this Jewish peoplehood. He stresses the faith as the determining factor in the connection . . .

> The laws and way of life did not create the attachment of the people to the religious idea; they were its natural result, they were not means invented to preserve the people from extinction, but the result of a *primary cause*, the internal force which was the power of faith: the power of the fundamental idea of the existence of Israel, the bearer of the religion of God.[72]

Leo Baeck stressed this same point. He noted the sundering of Jewish peoplehood from the religion of Israel in the modern age. This was due, he pointed out, to the enlightenment and emancipation whereby the traditional religion of the Jews that he had so completely experienced in the past became blunted with the Jewish exodus from the old culture. The "history" of the people, its identity as a community, its purely political and social agenda, became dominant, with the religious element either absent entirely or a relatively minor component of this new condition. Baeck contended that this condition refused to concern itself with the ultimate meaning of the history of Judaism, that which gave Jewish life "its dynamic element and motive power." Baeck, in rather lofty language, articulated his reminder to the Jews in his time about that which characterizes authentic Judaism, its true strength, and the capacity of the Jewish people to persist in the past, the present and into the future, and that is,

> The incursion of the Infinite, Eternal, the One and unconditional into the finite, temporal, manifold and limited—and the spiritual and moral tension of the human fiber which is the result. Whatever ideas and hopes Judaism has created within its own sphere and beyond it emanate from here.[73]

[To paraphrase: God has entered the world of the here and now, and mankind's spiritual and moral response to that phenomenon is the result. Whatever ideas and hopes Jews fashion emanate from that encounter.]

And then Baeck asserts, "The community and the transcendent were bound together. The narrow Jewish street knew that it is encompassed by the world of Divine spheres . . . the renewal of this bond is Jewry's ordained task."

These factors, taken together, motored as they were by basic religious idea, as Kaufmann and Baeck and the historians emphasized, crystallized and strengthened diaspora Jewry's sense of peoplehood within the very nations in which Jews lived—this all a people without the possession of soil and homeland, without geographical boundaries and state organisms. This is what Salo Baron meant when he said that diaspora life was "living contrary to nature," that is, living without a land of its own and all that goes with it. But it was a life lived as a people—a peculiar people indeed—which endured in the midst of, and, it must be said, in spite of the centrifugal vicissitudes of a stormy diaspora.

In sum, the Jewish people's tenacious, landless persistence is rooted in a double aspect that constitutes an essence of Judaism: knowledge of the One God and the sense of peoplehood that nurtures and propagates it. These two streams are inextricable; they interpenetrate and converge, making Judaism what it is and what it has always been in its long period of exile.

## God Protects and Cares for People

As we concluded in our previous chapter, Moses infused his received notion of the Godhead who uses His power to help people with a new name for the Deity: The Lord. This is a Deity who is ever at the side of His people with promise for a better future, along with protection, support and compassionate concern.

The Prophets seized on this notion and amplified it with extended and special emphasis on God's love for His people as the *source* for His protection and care for them. This emphasis is embedded in the term *berit*, "covenant," a pact, a mutual agreement between the Lord and Israel.[74] Thus, at Mt. Sinai God established such a covenant with His people (Exodus 19:4) in which, if the people did their part by adhering to the stipulations indicated, God will make them "a treasured possession," a "kingdom of priests" and a "holy nation." This covenant was also established with King David, proclaimed the Prophet Nathan in God's name, in this case with no conditions attached for David to attain renown and his throne an everlasting one.

Indeed, these covenants contained for Israel heavy emphasis on God's love—His loyalty and support, security and prosperity, promise and forgiveness. The Prophet Ezekiel encapsulates the prophetic understanding of this matter when he hears God's voice proclaiming, "I will remember the covenant which I made with you as an everlasting covenant" (Ezekiel 16:60). This despite Israel's shortcomings (verse 63).

And so, what the Prophets focused on was the motivating factor, as it were, that accounted for God's protection and care for His people. Indeed, *it is God's love* that is at the root of the relationship between Him and Israel. The authors of the Bible do not concern themselves primarily with abstract ideas about God's nature. Rather, they portray Him via people's experiences with Him: what specific deeds He performs on their behalf—how He deals with them kindly, giving them security and prosperity, and the rest. Yet more, how even within the drumbeat of condemnation of Israel's sinfulness, God emerges predominantly as a God who, despite all His people's shortcomings, loves them and thus protects and cares for them. Indeed, it is a love that is implacable.

This covenantal love, Jon Levenson stresses, is not a sentimental, emotional expression of affection, what modern western culture views as a "romantic" feeling. Rather, in the biblical context, it is a concept of love that is action-oriented and practical. It is an expression of love derived from deeds of service where affectionate language is not necessarily present.

> What if we were to speak of the love of parents and their children? In that case, it seems to me, we are more likely to speak of actions than affects. A mother and a father work extra hours to put their children through school, to pay for music lessons, or for orthodontia; parents of a rebellious and unruly adolescent quietly endure the provocations, responding as seems appropriate to the situation at hand but never simply walking away from their own child. For their part, children take on extra responsibilities around the house or a part-time job to help a disabled parent; adult children assume special burdens to assure that their aging parents are receiving good care and dwelling in appropriate quarters. In all these cases, is it not reasonable to infer a relationship of love from the practices themselves, even in the near or total absence of verbal expressions of affection or of kisses and hugs?[75]

This analogy to the relationship between The Lord and the people is far from farfetched. Scripture, in fact, is replete with images of relationships within families that reveal this kind of love. Witness the following.

## The Notion of God's Love for His People: Articulated via the Prism of "Family"

In ancient societies when a man wanted to adopt a child, the ceremony was simple: "I will be to him a father, and he will become my son."

The marriage ceremony was similar: "She is my wife, and I am her husband." In front of witnesses they stated the relationship they had with each other, and these words made it official.

When God wanted to state His relationship with the Israel of biblical times, He used similar words: "I am Israel's Father and Ephraim is my firstborn son." He is stating the terms of the relationship: like that of a parent and child. Scripture also used marriage as a description of a relationship: "Your Maker (i.e., God) is your husband . . . as if you were a wife."[76] And as Hosea 2:19 put it: "I will betroth you to me forever." Thus, when God declares that He is Israel's "Father" or "Husband," He is stressing a special relationship; saying in effect: "I am bonded to you; you are like family to me." Indeed, this is expressed very often by the Prophets.

### First and Second Isaiah Tell the Story

"I reared children and brought them up," God says through Isaiah. "But they have rebelled against me. . . . They have forsaken The Lord; they have spurned the Holy One of Israel and turned their backs on Him" (*Isaiah 1:2, 4*).

It looked like the relationship had come to an end. "You have abandoned your people," Isaiah says in 2:6. But it was not permanent. "My people who live in Zion, do not be afraid. . . . Very soon my anger against you will end" (*10:24–25*). "I will not forget you" (*44:21*). "The Lord comforts his people and will have compassion on his afflicted ones" (*49:13*).

The Prophets spoke of a huge regathering: "I will say to the north, 'Give them up!' and to the south, 'Do not hold them back.' Bring my sons from afar and my daughters from the ends of the earth" (*43:6*).

"My people will live in peaceful dwelling places, in secure homes, in undisturbed places of rest" (*32:18*). "The Sovereign Lord will wipe away the tears from all faces. . . . In that day they will say, 'Surely this is our God; we trusted in him, and He saved us'" (*25:8–9*). And God says to them, "You are my people" (*51:16*). "Surely they are my people, children who will be true to me" (*63:8*).[77]

### Jeremiah Tells the Story

Jeremiah combines the family metaphors: "How gladly would I treat you like my children and give you a pleasant land. . . . I thought you would call me 'Father' and not turn away. . . . But like a woman unfaithful to her husband, so you, Israel, have been unfaithful to me" (*3:19–20*). "They broke my covenant, though I was a husband to them" (*31:32*).

Jeremiah initially prophesies that the relationship is over: "These people do not belong to The Lord. The people of Israel and the people of Judah have been utterly unfaithful to me" (*5:10–11*). "I gave faithless Israel her certificate of divorce and sent her away because of all her adulteries" (*3:8*). But this is not a permanent rejection. "Is not Ephraim my dear son, the child in whom I delight? . . . My heart yearns for him; I have great compassion for him" (*31:20*). "How long will you wander, unfaithful daughter Israel?" (*31:22*).

God promises a renewal of their relationship, which is the equivalent to making a new covenant with them: "They will be my people, and I will be their God" (*24:7; 30:22, 31:33, 32:38*). "I will be the God of all the families of Israel, and they will be my people" (*31:1*). "I will make a new covenant with the people of Israel and with the people of Judah" (*31:31*). "I will make an everlasting covenant with them: I will never stop doing good to them" (*32:40*).

## *Ezekiel Tells a Similar Story*

Ezekiel also describes God's relationship with Israel as a marriage: "When I looked at you and saw that you were old enough for love, I spread the corner of my garment over you and covered your naked body. I gave you my solemn oath and entered into a covenant with you, declares the Sovereign Lord, and you became mine" (*16:8*).

As indicated above, the relationship is described as a covenant: "I will remember the covenant I made with you in the *days of your youth,* and I will establish an everlasting covenant with you" (*16:60*).

## *More Prophets Tell the Story*

Hosea and Micah, Zechariah and Malachi also spoke in terms of family to depict the relationship between God and the people of Israel.[78]

*Indeed, because God loves His people, He protects them, He cares for them.*

## **God Is Creator of Heaven and Earth**

As indicated in chapter 2, Moses inherited a rudimentary notion of the deity from the patriarchal age and transformed it into a basic element of Monotheism: The Lord is Creator of heaven and earth and all within it. The Prophets, in turn, inherited this Mosaic notion and proceeded to put even greater emphasis on God as the Creator and Sustainer of humanity and of heaven and earth.[79]

Witness the consensus view on the matter embedded in the prophetic writings:

*Amos* proclaims:

> For lo, *He who forms the mountains and creates the wind,* and declares to man what is His thought, who makes the morning darkness, and treads on the heights of the earth—The Lord, the God of hosts, is His name.[80]

Amos then proceeds to see the creative work of God in yet wider expanses.

> *He who made the Pleiades and Orion*, and turns deep darkness into the morning, and darkens the day into night, who calls for the waters of the sea and pours them out upon the surface of the earth, The Lord is His name.[81]

*Isaiah* is eager to emphasize *God's creative role in all facets of human life as well as those of the world "above."*

> Woe to these who hide deep from The Lord their counsel, whose deeds are in the dark, and who say, "Who sees us, who knows us?" You turn things upside down! Shall the potter be regarded as the clay; that the thing made should say of its maker, "He did not make me"; or the thing formed say of him who formed it, "He did not form me"?[82]

Isaiah proceeds to relate the content of King Hezekiah's prayer after the Israelite monarch received a letter from the King of Assyria concerning his planned attack on Jerusalem. Hezekiah went up to the Temple and spread the letter before God and prayed.

> O Lord of hosts, God of Israel, who art enthroned above the cherubim, Thou art the God, Thou alone, of all the kingdoms of the earth; *thou has made heaven and earth.*[83]

*Jeremiah thunders* against the "uncircumcised in heart," those in Egypt and Judah, in Edom, Ammon, and Moab.

> Thus shall you say to them: Their gods *who did not make the heavens and the earth* shall perish from the earth and from under the heavens. *It is He (The Lord) who made the earth* by His power, and established the world by His wisdom, and by His understanding stretched out the heavens.[84]

And then Jeremiah stresses that God has not only fashioned the earth and all on it, but He also has full control of its history. He tells Zedekiah, king of Judah, to tell the leaders of the nations who were challenging him,

Give from this charge to these masters: Thus says The Lord of Hosts, the God of Israel: *It is I who by my great power and my outstretched arm have made the earth, with the men and animals that are on the earth,* and I give it to whomever it seems right to me.[85]

*Second Isaiah,* the great prophet of the exile, juxtaposes with telling consequences The Lord, the Creator and Sustainer of the universe and of all that lives, with the pagan idols of his time.

Thus says God, *The Lord, who created the heavens and stretched them out, who spread forth the earth and what comes from it,* who gives breath to the people upon it and spirit to those who walk in it. . . . I am The Lord, my glory I give to no one, nor my praise to graven images.[86]

And significantly, God's creation of the earth was to fashion order out of chaos, this so that human beings would be able to live in a world with sturdy confidence.

Thus says The Lord, Israel's Maker: will you question me about my children, or command me concerning the work of my hands? I made the earth and created man upon it; it was my hands that stretched out the heavens, and I commanded all their host. . . . For thus says The Lord who created the heavens—He is God— who formed the earth and made it; *He did not create it a chaos, He formed it to be inhabited*!

*Zechariah:* "The word of The Lord concerning Israel. Thus says *The Lord who stretched out the heavens and founded the earth* and formed the spirit of man within him: Lo and behold, I am about to make Jerusalem a cup of reeling."[87]

*Genesis'* account of God as Creator can be invoked here because it reflects the prophetic era's perspective on the notion.[88]

## God Demands Justice and Righteousness

In our previous chapter, *Moses and Monotheism,* we concluded that the idea of One God who Moses affirmed implies that there can be but one set of moral standards. And because God is deemed to be absolutely moral, man is mandated to replicate such principle. Hence, the virtues of justice and beneficence of the patriarchal era, the dicta in the Ten Commandments about murder, adultery, stealing, etc.,[89] and the laws of the *Book of the Covenant* about compassion for widow, orphan and stranger, honest weights and measures, etc.[90]—these from the Mosaic era.

The Prophets inherited these principles and proceeded to expand and deepen them in major and highly consequential fashion—in two basic ways: the imperative of social justice and the primacy of morality. They applied these principles and proceeded to expand and deepen them in major and highly consequential fashion.

*Social Justice*

Special focus was placed on the social ills of their time. With great vehemence they castigated the oppression of the poor, the exploitation of laborers, the expropriation of small landholders, and the political, administrative and judicial system which sanctioned these crimes. And they made a special point of linking these moral ills with the religion itself. "In fact," writes Salo Baron, "these preachers regarded themselves as primarily religious rather than social reformers. If asked, they probably would have objected violently to the distinction; their view was precisely that *social life is part of religious life*, that social crimes become religious sins."[91] Lamentable social conditions are abominations to God. Social justice is at the root of the religion of Israel.

Amos: *Thus said The Lord:* for three transgressions of Israel, for four I will not revoke the punishment, for they have sold for silver those whose cause was just, and the needy for a pair of sandals.[92]

Isaiah: *Hear the word of The Lord*. Learn to do good. Devote yourselves to justice, correct oppression, uphold the rights of the orphan, defend the cause of the widow.[93]

Zechariah: *Thus says The Lord of hosts*: Render true judgments, show kindness and mercy to one another, do not oppress the widow, the fatherless, the sojourner, the poor, and let none of you devise evil against one another in your heart.[94]

Jeremiah: *Thus says The Lord*: Do justice and righteousness, and deliver from the hand of the oppressor him who has been robbed. And do no wrong or violence to the resident alien, the fatherless and the widow, nor shed innocent blood in this place.[95]

Ezekiel: *Now O harlot, hear the word of The Lord*. Behold this was the guilt of your sister Sodom: she and her daughters had pride, excess of food and prosperous care, but did not aid the poor and needy. They were haughty ... so I removed them when I saw it.[96]

## Moral and Ethical Behavior Must Accompany Busy Religious Ritual

The Prophets placed heavy emphasis on the primacy of morality, that the essence of God's demand of man is not solely cultic, but moral. This view regards human goodness as the realization of the will of God on earth. It does not deny the importance of religious ritual per se, but does negate its value when unaccompanied by moral and ethical behavior. This perspective provided further ground for rebuke of the people. *Morality (as a basic principle) and ethics (as the application of that principle in specific circumstances)* were regarded as decisive for the very destiny of Israel.

"The older view," Yehezkel Kaufmann asserts, "was that the fate of the people was determined by their religious practice; idolatry entailed national punishment. But the Prophets conceived the idea that moral corruption too was a national historical factor. Moreover, they have a new evaluation of social morality: not merely bloodshed and sexual crimes, but injustice, taking bribes, and oppressing the poor and defenseless, harbor consequences for the fate of the nation."[97] Of significance, as well, was inclusion of "righteousness" as a guiding principle in the affairs of state, of the military, of politics, of international relations. Here is the way the Prophets heard God's "voice," as it were, articulating morality as a cornerstone of religion–both for Israel and ultimately for all the world.

*Amos*: "I loathe, I spurn your festivals, I am not appeased by your solemn assemblies. If your offer me burnt offerings . . . I will not accept them. . . . Spare me the sound of your hymns, and let me not hear the music of your lutes. But let justice well up like water, righteousness like an unfailing stream."[98]

*Micah*: "With what shall I approach The Lord, do homage to God on high? Shall I approach Him with burnt offerings, with calves a year old? . . . He has told you, O man, what is good, and what The Lord requires of you: only to do justice, and love goodness, and to walk humbly with your God."[99]

*Isaiah*: "What need have I of all your sacrifices . . . your new moons and fixed seasons fill me with loathing . . . and when you lift up your hands, I will turn my eyes away from you . . . your hands are stained with crime . . . devote yourselves to justice, aid the wronged, uphold the rights of the orphan, defend the cause of the widow."[100]

*Jeremiah*: "To what purpose is to me the frankincense that comes from Sheba, and the sweet cane from a far country? Your burnt offerings are not acceptable to me."[101] There is nothing to suggest that Jeremiah opposed sacrifices as such. What he and the others denounced was external conformity to the demands of the Temple services without observance of the moral law. With despairing sarcasm, Jeremiah exclaims: "Will you steal and murder and commit adultery and swear falsely and (then) come and stand before me in this house . . . and say: we are delivered that you may do all these abominations? Is this house . . . become a den of robbers in your eyes?"[102]

*Zechariah*: The people of Bethel came to entreat the favor of The Lord; they were in straits and needed help. One of the priests asked, "Should I mourn and fast as I have done for so many years? Zechariah responded that these rituals were really for their own sake and not for God's sake, and the Prophet hears God saying: render judgment, show kindness and mercy each to his brother; do not oppress the widow, the fatherless, the sojourner or the poor, and let none of you devise evil against his brother in his heart.[103]

*Second Isaiah* does want to smash the altars of idolatry and does condemn the people's insincere and hypocritical rote ritual, *but he also testifies that God longs for properly-motivated ritual observance*: "I will bring them to my holy mountain and make them joyful in my house of prayer. *These burnt offerings and their sacrifices will be acceptable upon my altar*, for my house shall be called a house of prayer for all peoples."[104]

Parenthetically, we must note here a crucial point. Isaiah's clear affirmation of ritual observance in this passage calls out the stereotypical and persistent contention on the part of those who assert the negativity of religious ritual, as such—this on the part of the Prophets. The heart of religion, it is claimed, is moral and ethical behavior with religious ritual both a burden and impediment to such good behavior. Would Isaiah's affirmation of sacrifice and sanctuary have been so emphasized by him if he agreed with such a one-sided attitude?

A vital fallout from this stress on the principles of morality and ethical behavior is what we have previously noted about the work of the Prophets. Embedded in these virtues was the compelling element of universality. They have a "generic" character, as it were. They were not "local" obligations confined to just some people and not others. They were applicable not only in some locations but in all locations everywhere. They were to be observed not only by some nations such as that of Israel, but by all nations in God's universe (Amos, chapter 1).

*In sum*, the Prophets proclaimed with great power and eloquence that the One and only God harbored an uncompromising ethic—the demand that justice and righteousness are to govern human affairs. Herein is what has been famously called "Ethical Monotheism."

Isadore Epstein has articulated the essence of this tenet of Monotheism:

> Judaism emphasized two revolutionary concepts of God that transformed the idea of the conditions of divine favor and, with it, the whole conception of historical events. The first is the moral character of the Deity and the second God's universality. . . . As a moral God, He demands righteous action . . . and all events in history must, therefore, be interpreted in terms of this divine call to morality. His universality carries with it the idea that there is only one moral law for all men, and that His divine call to righteousness goes forth not only to Israel but to all the nations on the earth.[105]

## CONCLUSION

And so, the Mosaic notion of Monotheism and the tenets that flowed from its core—the Oneness of the Deity—were affirmed by the Prophets. They proceeded to expand both in detail and scope what they deemed as implicit in what they inherited—this all in tandem with the basic thrust and animating spirit of the faith of their predecessors. This leads us to the rabbinic period in which the sages served as heirs to the Prophets who preceded them.

*Chapter 4*

# The Rabbis and Monotheism

*Observance of Mitzvot*
*Intensive Learning*
*Emphasis on Prayer*
*Focus on Good Deeds*

It was through these mechanisms that the fruits of the God idea inherited from the Patriarchs, Moses and the Prophets were harvested.

### THE RABBIS: HEIRS TO THE PROPHETS

We now arrive at the classical rabbinic period which followed the conclusion of the prophetic era. Jews were still in Palestine and others in Egypt and Babylonia. It was the perspective of the Rabbis in Palestine in this period which predominated in the realms of religious thought and practice.

Yosef Yerushalmi has articulated the basic stance of the Rabbis regarding the past bequeathed to them.

> Prophecy had ceased, but the Rabbis regarded themselves as heirs to the Prophets, and this was proper, for they had thoroughly assimilated the prophetic world view and made it their own. . . . For the Rabbis the Bible was not only a repository of past history, but a revealed pattern of the whole of history, and they had learned their scriptures well. *They knew that history had a purpose—the establishment of the Kingdom of God on earth and that the Jewish people has a central role to play in the process*. . . .Above all, they had learned from the Bible that the true pulse of history often beats beneath its manifest surfaces, an invisible history that was more real than what the world could recognize.[1]

It is with this perspective that the Rabbis dealt with the notion of Monotheism inherited from their prophetic forebears. They proceeded to cultivate the notion in accordance with their own time and clime, striving to interpret it in living terms for their own and future generations. What follows is an analysis of their take on the five elements of the monotheistic idea that came to them.

## The Deity is a Supreme God

As we concluded in our previous chapter about the prophetic stance on the Deity, God was absolutely One, no other gods existed, and this Supreme God was universal in that He could be accessed anywhere and everywhere by all people, Israelite and non-Israelite alike. Such is the essence of Monotheism in the prophetic mind.

The Rabbis inherited this basic understanding. For them Monotheism, as for Moses and the Prophets, was the cornerstone of Judaism. They emphasized this in a number of ways.

### *Opposition to Zoroastrian Dualism*[2]

The main intellectual challenge to Monotheism in this rabbinic period—the first four centuries of the Common Era—was the Persian doctrine that there were two gods: Ormuzd, the god of goodness and light, and Ahriman, the god of evil and darkness. It was a doctrine motivated by the desire to disassociate the deity from the manifest evil in the world. How can the god of goodness and compassion be the cause of evil and cruelty? Surely there must be—there is—another divine power responsible for the latter.

Here was a doctrine that was embraced by many Jews at the time because of its apparent compelling character. Hence, the leaders of Palestinian Jewry were deeply concerned about this; they saw it as a defection from the strict monotheistic principle of the absolute singularity of the Godhood; they feared its morphing into a different kind of belief that there were *shtay reshuyot*, "two authorities." This doctrine not only posited the notion that since God is good, He cannot be the cause of any kind of evil, but also that he was so transcendent, so remote in his exalted heavenly abode, that it was necessary to interpose between this God and the world an inferior power—a divine power nonetheless—closer to the human world of the here and now. Moreover, as George Foote Moore has asserted, "It is evident also that Gentile Christianity at the time, with its Supreme God, the Father, and its Son as savior, was founded on a doctrine of 'two powers'" (*Judaism*, Vol. 1, p. 354).

This all, taken together, provoked resistance. Since for the stated Rabbis Monotheism meant the absolute singularity of the Godhood as a doctrine that could brook no compromise, they condemned this dualistic heresy, and did so with all the means at their disposal. Thus they adopted the assertion in the book of Isaiah (45:7): "I *form light and create darkness*, I make peace and create evil. I, the Lord, do all these things," and incorporated it as an opening statement in the morning service after the *Borkhu*, "Bless the Lord," which is the formal summons to the congregation to engage in the act of collective prayer.

> Blessed are You, Lord our God,
> King of the Universe,
> *who forms light and creates darkness*
> makes peace and creates all.

This is clearly a protest against the prevailing dualism with its vision of perpetual cosmic struggle. Judaism in the rabbinic mind affirmed its received notion insisting that all reality derives from a single source.

More was involved in this adoption. Note the change the Rabbis made in the phrase, from "I make peace and *create evil*," to "makes peace and *creates all*." They could not attribute to God the creation of evil in the world, so they had the audacity to alter a biblical verse! It appears that they simply sought in this context to avoid the troubling issue. Later Maimonides made a valiant attempt to explain away the notion that God could be the author of evil. God only fashions the good, Maimonides claimed; evil is but the absence of good, the fruit of the good which, when it recedes, reveals evil. Much like when the sun sets, darkness appears. Thus God created the sun, an act of goodness, but not the darkness, which a good God could not possibly have created. Thus Maimonides made what we might call a "labored" effort to attack a vexing problem (Rambam's analysis of Isaiah 45:7 in his *Guide for the Perplexed*, chapter 10, pp. 265–267).

This struggle against dualism is articulated in rabbinic literature in numerous other ways. The rabbinic term for dualism is *shtay reshuyot*, "two powers" or "two authorities," i.e., two gods in control of the world. The Midrash,[3] the Sifre to Deuteronomy 32:39, quotes the verse: "See now, that *Ani* (I), even *Ani* (I) am He, and there is no god with me. If anyone says," comments the Midrash, "that there are two powers in heaven (based on the double use of the term *Ani*) the retort is to be given to him: *There is no god with me*." Similarly, the Mishna[4] rules that if a man says in his prayers, "We acknowledge Thee, we acknowledge Thee" (i.e., he repeats the formula *modim anakhnu lakh*) "he is to be silenced."

And then there is the Midrash[5] on the Shema, "Hear, O Israel, the Lord our God, the Lord is One." It comments, "The Holy One, blessed be He, said to Israel: 'My children, everything that I created in the universe is in pairs—e.g., heaven and earth, the sun and the moon, Adam and Eve, this world and the world to come; *but I am One and alone in the universe*." That two powers gave the law and two powers created the world was argued by some from *Elohim* in Exodus 20:1, and from "let *us* make man in *our* image, in *our* likeness" (Genesis 1:26). These verses were taken as numerical plurals to which answer was given that in both cases the verbs of which *Elohim* is the subject is in singular number (Genesis Rabbah 8:8–9). The Talmud[6] expressed this attitude with "tongue in cheek," as it were. It tells the story of a Zoroastrian Magus who declared to a Rabbi that the upper part of the body (containing the brain and the heart) belongs to Ormuzd and the lower part to Ahriman. The Rabbi replied that if this were the case, why did Ahriman permit Ormuzd to send water through his territory, i.e., if the dualism alleged to be present in the universe is reflected in man's body, how are the digestive processes possible?[7]

Indeed, this dualism notion challenged the idea of God's total oneness and was jettisoned by the Rabbis in multiple ways.

George Foote Moore has summarized the condition of this dualism matter in the rabbinic period this way:

> The difficulty of reconciling the evils of the world with the goodness of God was so strongly felt in the early centuries of our era in the East and the West, and a dualistic solution of one kind or another was so widely accepted in philosophy and religion, that it is idle to attempt to identify the Jewish circles which accepted this solution. It must suffice that we know there were such circles; that they tried to fortify their position with texts of Scripture; and that the Rabbis refuted them with their own weapons. (See, for example, the story of the *min* [apostate] in Talmud Hullin 87a). It is certain also that, whatever leanings there may have been in this direction, Judaism, with its inveterate Monotheism, was not rent by dualistic heresies as Christianity was for centuries.[8]

### Contemporary Version of Zoroastrianism Dualism

The perplexing problem of reconciling the God of goodness with the evil in the world has never been fully put to rest, neither by the classical Rabbis nor the idealogues since. Indeed, the dualism of the godhood has reappeared yet again in the modern era.

In Northridge, California in January 1994, a major sector of Los Angeles was stricken by a devastating earthquake. Everywhere people were perplexed by an occurrence over which they had no control, shaken by the terrible damage and loss, and moved to question a basic tenet of their faith. Many sought guidance from Jewish tradition. Rabbi Harold Schulweis, an eminent spiritual leader in Los Angeles, swiftly penned a column entitled "Where was God in the Earthquake?" published by the *Los Angeles Jewish Journal*, in which he sought to make sense of the happening from a theological perspective. The essence of Rabbi Schulweis's message was this:

God *(Elohim)* is the author of nature, the God of gravitation, of physical laws. But God's role ends there; He is not involved as nature relates to humanity. However, when it comes to humanity's reaction to the nature's devastating havoc wreaked on its world, God is *Adonai* who is not responsible for this havoc, but rather functions positively in the lives of people, prompting them to creatively cope with and compassionately deal with the effects of nature's fury.

What is problematic about this formulation? It is certainly helpful to people confused and anguished; it is timely and "relevant" to the immediate situation; it is conveniently soothing. But it is also inconsistent and confusing theology.

To ask the question, "Where was God in the Earthquake?" is equivalent to asking, "Where is God in the physical universe?" In the Jewish theological scheme of things, God is everywhere—not just in the inspiring, beneficent and beautiful in nature—in spring blossoms, aromatic plants and delicious fruit—but also in the not so beneficent: in natural physical havoc as well. Indeed, our prayer book enjoins us not only to acknowledge God for our food and clothing, for heaven's rain and rainbow, but also for thunder and earthquake as well: "Blessed are you Lord our God, Master of the Universe, whose strength and might fill the world." The rabbinic tradition goes further and enjoins to discern God not only in that which human beings deem to be the good things in life, but in the not so good as well. Rabbi Meir (*Berachot 48b*) tells us: "Just as one praises God for the good, so is one to praise Him for the bad." Similarly, when a person passes away, one is enjoined to ascribe to God wisdom in judgment: "Praised be the True Judge."

It is apparent theological legerdemain to ascribe to God only the good and the positive in the world, and simultaneously remove Him from the scene when something negative occurs. This thought pattern has one unabashedly thanking and praising God when one benefits from the beauty and bounty of nature. It then has one conveniently disassociating God from nature's havoc—thus visiting upon one tortuous inconsistency.

- One lauds God for the rain that waters the earth, which makes it possible to cultivate our crops thus enabling us to eat—and live. But when it rains too abundantly and the flood comes, we absent God from the picture.

- One praises God for the moving air in the natural atmosphere, which gives us the very breath of life. But when the wind blows too strongly bringing on a hurricane, we hastily deal God out of the equation.

- One stands in awe of God and thanks Him as we watch the miracle of a normal and healthy baby emerge from a mother's womb. But when tragically a baby emerges malformed, a new insight springs to mind: in this God was not involved!

If the proponents of this stance would be just as unwilling to attribute to God nature's positive beneficence toward humanity as they are unwilling to attribute to God nature's negative manifestations toward humanity, then there would be no theological quarrel with them. If they are not, maintaining the belief that God is only present in the good things in our world and not in the bad, then this position is not only inconsistent but flawed insofar as normative Jewish theology is concerned. Why? Because it *suggests the old dualism of the deity notion, wherein separate powers in the world appear to be functioning, and doing so independently: one the source of the good (God) and another the source of the bad (not-God).* Thus, an aspect of the world of nature such as an earthquake appears to function via a power other than God, and this is a notion unacceptable to the religious mindset of the monotheist.

In Jewish theology, *kvodo malay ha-olam*, "God's presence permeates the whole world," the natural and the human, not just part of it and not just some of the time, but all of it and at all times. The non-normative theology long since jettisoned by the classical Rabbis and reformulated in modern times was and is embraced by many earnest religionists in the wake of such things as an earthquake. Such a view provides balm, calm and some measure of meaning for people hurting and for perplexed minds and troubled spirits engendered by natural phenomena that periodically wreaks havoc.

While this approach is quite understandable and seems to bring meaning to real problems, in the long run it evades the complexities, the mystery, the bittersweet, the existential reality of the often tragic pain of the world—the real world.

## *The One God Everywhere in the World*

The Rabbis affirmed the one God in yet another way. As we have seen, the Prophets discerned the presence of God anywhere and everywhere in the world when the faithful call upon Him. The sages were on the same track in this regard.

Thus they cited King Solomon's dedicatory prayer upon construction of the temple to the effect that, while God is in the heavens, He is available to humans who call upon Him from wherever they are.[9] In reality God is everywhere present as the author of the Book of Barukh in the Apocrypha sets forth: "How great, O Israel, is God's dwelling place, how vast the extent of His domain. Great it is and boundless, lofty and immeasurable."[10] Because He is in one place, He is no less elsewhere, Rabbi Levi contends: "The tabernacle was like a cave that adjoined the sea. The sea came rushing in and flooded the cave; the cave was filled, but the sea was not in the least diminished. So the tabernacle was filled with the radiance of the Divine Presence, but the world lost nothing of that Presence.[11]

Another Midrash compares the presence of God in the world to the soul of man. As the soul fills the body, so God fills the world; as the soul sustains the body, God sustains the world; as the soul outlasts the body, God outlasts the world; *as the soul is the only one in the body, God is the only God in the world*; like God, the soul sees but is not seen; it is pure; it never sleeps, etc.[12]

Yet another Midrash comments on Exodus 3:3 where God appears to Moses in a craggy thorn bush rather than a carob or sycamore tree that people value.

A heathen once asked Rabbi Joshua ben Korkha: Why did God choose a thornbush from which to speak to Moses? He replied: Were it a carob or a sycamore tree, you would have asked the same question; but to dismiss you without any reply is not right, so I will tell you why: to teach you that no place is devoid of God's presence, not even a thornbush.[13]

## The Ongoing Experience of the One God

As indicated, the Rabbis affirmed the supremacy of God in strong word. However, they accomplished this task perhaps more significantly via strong deed. And this was *via the experience of the people with the Deity in their everyday lives. And it is here that the primary rabbinic contribution to the monotheistic idea can be located.*

The Proverb (3:6) points us to a basic imperative, *bekhol derakhekha da-ahu*, "Know God *in all your ways.*" One must express awareness of The Lord via the specifics of each person's ways of life. Indeed, no area of life is excluded from reaching for this goal. Moreover, "all your ways" refers to the full resources a person possesses.

The Rabbis took this dictum to heart. And so, the chief characteristic of Jewish life in the extended rabbinic era was development of a religious way which emphasized four basic elements: consistent observance of *mitzvot*; intensive *learning*; strong focus on *prayer*; and *gemilut hasadim*, the practice of good deeds. It was through these mechanisms that the God idea inherited from Moses and the Prophets was anchored in the life of the Jews. This was so despite their precarious existence in a Palestine dominated by Greek and Roman overlords and in exile in Babylonia, Egypt and elsewhere under the thumb of people other than their own where either polytheism or ambiguity about the oneness of the Deity reigned, thus threatening Judaism's monotheistic faith. Indeed, these mechanisms kept alive the reality, role and presence of the One God in the people's midst. Experience with Him is expressed in the following lines in a Jewish evening prayer, which reflects the rabbinic mind.

With everlasting love have You loved the house of Israel, Your people. You have taught us Your Torah, its *commandments, statues, and ordinances* (i.e., *mitzvot*). Therefore, Lord, our God, for all time when we lie down and when we rise up, we will speak of what You have ordained, rejoicing with fervor in *learning* the words of Your Torah and commandments. For they are our life and length of our days and on them we will meditate day and night (*prayer*). May You never take Your love away from us. Blessed are You Lord who loves His people Israel.[14]

And then there is the rabbinic saying in Pirke Avot. Simeon the Righteous taught, "The world depends (literally stands) on three things: on Torah, on Avodah and on *gemilat hasadim*," the practice of good deeds toward fellow human beings.

These are ways that express love for God and are gifts that serve as vital carriers of His presence in the ongoing life of a people. After all, human beings live in the everyday and when mechanisms are in place in the everyday which serve as constant reminders of a people's relationship with their God, one can understand how compelling is this affirmation.

## Mitzvot

When a Jew recites the above prayer about the "commandments, statutes and ordinances" (i.e., *mitzvot*), which he has been taught by his God and that are embedded in his tradition, and then proceeds to incorporate them into his life, he brings awareness of their Author into his everyday. His daily eating regimen, affixing a mezuzah on his doorpost, his donning tallit and tefillin, refraining from work on the Sabbath, the circumcision ceremony, his consuming Passover matzah, sitting in a Sukkah, his acts of charity for the needy and visiting the sick, these all help in "bringing God down from heaven," as it were. With each mitzvah, when its purpose is internalized in the observer's heart and mind, the Jew meets the living God in the living of his life in the here and now.[15]

Examples of this phenomenon:

- *Food*

Michael Fishbane has eloquently observed:

Among the things of the day is food. One does not simply proceed with satisfying the pangs of hunger. An initial preparation of the heart is necessary, undertaken by pausing and directing one's mind to the proper benediction before engaging in the actual act of ingestion. The preparation may include a ritual washing of the hands, if the meal includes bread; but in any case, the act of eating is preceded by a recitation of gratitude to God for the specific gift at hand: "who brings forth food from the earth"; "who creates the fruit of the earth"; "who creates the fruit of the tree"; or more generally, "for all exists through his word." The self is embodied in naturalness, in hunger and physical need; but covenant theology raises the worshiper's consciousness to the spiritual domain, and it is in this realm that one lives out one's natural urges.[16]

- *Shabbat and work*

A basic aspect of Shabbat observance is, of course, refraining from work, this in replication of God ceasing from His work in fashioning the world. Both scripture and rabbinic teaching expanded on this initial rest requirement. Exodus 20:9 declares as the fifth commandment, "Six days shall you labor and do all your work." Note the emphasis: man is *commanded to work* in order to provide for himself, his family and community. Indeed, *even as God labored in the process of creating the world, so is man to work in the process of fashioning his own world.*

Human beings are not to spend all their days "resting" as on Shabbat, do no work, use all of life's time in contemplation or even study. In the talmudic passage the Babylonian Rav urged his disciple, Rav Kahana, "Rather do difficult work for a fee than be supported by charity. Do not say, 'I am a priest or I am a scholar,' as if to say that such work is beneath your dignity."[17] Moreover, according to the Rabbis, a person's work is seen in positive terms because it is an opportunity to secure the future for his fellow humans. Well known is the talmudic tale[18] of one who saw an old man planting trees. "Why do you plant these trees since you will never enjoy the fruit?" he asked. The old man answered, "I found trees planted by my ancestors from whom I enjoyed the fruit. Surely, it is my duty to plant trees that those who come after me might enjoy their fruit." And so, scripture and the Rabbis teach that one must not only work in the world, but also do so diligently and conscientiously if he is to exercise his duty to himself, his family, his society—and ultimately to his God.

- *The ritual of circumcision*

Yet another Jewish way of bringing awareness of God's presence into the life of the world of the here and now is the ritual of circumcision. This way was re-emphasized by the Rabbis in their own time. The ceremony marks the initiation of the newborn into the community. At the same time, it is a mark of the covenant in the Jewish faith—the sign of Abraham's pact with God that established for the Hebrews then and for Jews in the morrow an enduring relationship. Scripture says this: "You shall circumcise the flesh of your foreskin, and that shall be a sign of the covenant between Me and you."[19] The rite, then, is an imprinting experience, stamping the young with peoplehood and with an indelible bond with God.

- *The Seudah Shleesheet (third Shabbat meal)*

Having depicted above the various ways designed to bring God into the everyday, it needs stressing that these rituals and ceremonies do not always accomplish their goals without struggle. Witness the *Seudah Shleesheet*, the "third meal" observance on Shabbat afternoon before Havdalah time, which points to the workweek shortly to come. The mystics invoked the *Ze-ayr Anpin*, the "Miniature Presence," in this setting. It was their way of referring to the Deity who was being invited to the meal. The designation "Miniature Presence" indicates that though God's Presence is everywhere, it is not readily discernible on earth where events can be understood as a result of natural causes rather than as emanating from God. The lack of clarity in our perception of the *Shekhina* is as if we observed an event through a blurred, cloudy lens. The result is that we have diminished appreciation of God's pervasive benevolence. This *aspeklaria she-ayna m'irah, a lens that is unclear* through which man attempts to grasp God's influence, is thus a reference to God as *The Miniature Presence*.

The third "Meal of Faith" on Saturday afternoon, then, is a time of particular spiritual intensity born of a sense of unease about a God who seems to be elusive at this time of transition from holy day to weekday. It has a special atmosphere as now the Shabbat is about to come to conclusion and new challenges loom. On Friday evening we experienced God as the source of special "fragrance" in our lives. On Saturday noon, we experienced Him as a source of "light" for life's betterment, and now on Saturday afternoon we experience Him as through a hazy glass, as somewhat elusive despite our faith in Him. This produces in us a pensive mood. The melodies are more meditative, and the words of Torah at the table more inward. There is awareness that this period is the end of something and the workdays ahead tension-full, unknown and perhaps hazardous. This is a time of spiritual longing as we reluctantly prepare to leave the world-that-ought-to-be to the testing reality of the world-that-is.

To calm and reassure us in the face of this state of mind, Psalm 23 is always chanted at the *Seudah Shleesheet*. The Psalmist speaks of "the valley of the shadow," but then he declares, "I will fear no evil for You are with me." Chanted here toward the end of the Shabbat, these words have particular force. Indeed, even though God appears to us as a "Miniature Presence" at *Seudah Shleesheet* time—distant, elusive—we nevertheless are told to take courage born of faith that we are not to be fearful of the morrow for "You are with me." God will help us fashion this morrow.

- *The Havdalah observance and creation*

There is yet another religious observance that embraces God in human life. It is the Havdalah ceremony, the essence of which adumbrates an aspect of God's creation of the world.

Originally the earth was *tohu v'vohu,* "unformed and void" with darkness over the face of the deep (watery mass) and the wind of God sweeping over the waters.[20] This is a picture of what has been termed "chaos," that is, the confused, unorganized, unstructured state of primordial matter; it had no distinct form; it was an undifferentiated, unseparated mass, an inchoate mixture. In this condition, scripture records God saying, "Let there be light," *vayavdayl, Elohim,* "and God *separated*" the light from the darkness and He called the light day and the darkness He called night. And there was evening and there was morning the first day" (verses 3–5).

From this initial creative act, God proceeds to *separate* water from water, thus fashioning the sky, the earth from the seas, *distinct* earth species, *different* animal species, *different* heavenly lights—sun and moon, and finally *different* human beings—man and woman. What God did was to create what has been termed a "cosmos" out of the existing "chaos." He fashioned an orderly world, a structured enterprise—this all based on the fundamental act of invading, as it were, the original chaotic mass and separating it into distinct elements. Thus the process of creation is one of making distinctions, "separations," *havdalot,* imposing order when there had been randomness.

Now, scripture (and subsequent Jewish tradition) expanded on this emphasis on distinctions, to include, among other matters, permitted and forbidden foods, no cross-breeding of animal species, no mixing of diverse seeds, the distinction between sacred and profane behavior, and the separation between sacred and secular time, i.e., the Sabbath from the weekday.

To use the above paradigm projected by Mircea Eliade in his famous *Sacred and the* Profane[21] as it pertains to this context: what the Havdalah ritual does is to carry its observer back to that original creative act of God, to the time of the world's very beginning, when God completed the work (He "rested" on the seventh day). *This religious man does via the ritual of the Havdalah in order to recapture the immense purity, freshness and strength of that creative act of making distinctions, so that he can renew his own strength and creativity.* He generates anew his own human capacity by replicating God's original creativity. This all so that he can face the inevitably challenging forces he must encounter in the week ahead.

- *Learning*

When a Jew rejoices "with fervor in *learning* the words of Your Torah and commandments" he senses the Deity's presence in his midst. When two or three students scan the scriptures and engage in their exegetical methods as they study together, they pioneer a spirituality in which Torah study replaces the temple as the chief means of encountering the Divine Presence. Moreover, a Jew senses God's reality when he reads and studies scripture in public on Saturdays, Mondays and Thursdays. In Jewish life, study becomes a form of piety and mode of worship as one exposes himself to the testimonies of the written and oral tradition about God's word and deed. Via such activity we are even told that God supports the event of learning and guides it to fruition. It is a kind of sacred speech, for God, the source of life, participates in such holy moments.[22]

Significant, as well, is the assertion in the Jewish liturgy that the very capacity for study and learning is credit to God. Thus, in the daily Amida: "You [God] grace us with *knowledge, understanding* and *wisdom* which *come from You*." These are God's "tools," as it were, which He provides men and women, which they employ in examining and affirming His presence in the world.

Yet more: faith in the ever-presence of God is, more often than not, enhanced by modern critical study of the basic biblical and rabbinic texts and of the historical saga of the Jewish people. When, for example, a contemporary bible researcher detects multiple strata in the texts of the Pentateuch that reveal the hands of different writers and different eras in biblical life, we cannot conclude that the Pentateuchal texts are the product of a single hand and their provenance in but one period of time and clime. However, for the faithful modernist, what these researches do show is that *the Divine speaks to humanity in all eras of Jewish life and to the many faithful in their own period and place who are attuned to God's will*. Indeed, genuine faith and basic traditional affirmations about the Divine role in human life are thereby enhanced.

This is what is meant by the notion that the God of Israel is the God of history. The faithful modernist sees God as having manifested His presence and revealed His will not only in early biblical times, but in the prophetic era as well—in His communication with the great prophets, Isaiah, Jeremiah and Ezekiel, Amos, Hosea, and Micah. Yet more: His presence and will were manifest when, earlier, God guided His people during the Exodus from Egypt—and into the Promised Land, when He went into exile with Israel in Babylonia, when He led His people back to the land in the Persian era, when He girded the strength of the Maccabees during the revolt against the Syrian Greeks, when He was with His people during the traumatic period of Roman oppression . . . and on and on through the vicissitudes of the Jewish experience down through the centuries—including our own. Throughout this all, God's presence is seen to be in the midst of the people teaching, sustaining and inspiring them as they delve into the Talmud and Midrash and Responsa, as well as in the historical documents.

- *Prayer*

When a Jew regularly utters the "with everlasting love" *prayer* at the Shabbat morning service, he seeks to sense the ever-present and constant activity of God.

> Truly He alone performs mighty acts, creates new things, conducts battles, sows justice, produces triumphs, creates healing, is revered in renown, is Lord of wonders, Who, in His goodness renews creation every day constantly, as it is said (Psalm 136:7): "To Him who makes the great lights, truly His mercy endures forever."

Reflected in this passage is not only a sense of the Deity's presence in daily life, but in a broader sense as well. Life itself is a miraculous gift "renewed every day constantly." Many of the functions and facets of the human body are seen by the Rabbis as reflective of God's abundant grace. Thus when leaving a bathroom, hearing a sound, opening one's eyes, sitting up and standing up straight, dressing, walking, putting on shoes, one is obliged to bless the Source ultimately responsible for these everyday indispensable activities. These physical functions reflect the mystery and wisdom of The Lord's creation. They also unite Jews to a larger natural drama that expresses the might and love of a God who created the world. All participants in this drama—humans, sun and stars alike—extoll the good God.[23]

Jewish prayer articulates yet more about a God who stimulates in the worshipper high aspiration in the business of everyday living. Witness the *Birkat Hakhodesh*, the Blessing of the New Moon prayer recited each month in the synagogue:

> May it be Your will, Lord our God and God of our fathers, to renew for *us* this coming month for good and blessing. Grant *us long life*, a life of peace, a life of goodness, a life of *sustenance*, a life of *physical health*, a life marked by *reverence for heaven* and *dread of sin*, a life *without shame or disgrace*, a life of *wealth* and honor, a life in which *we* have *love for the Torah*, a life in which *our* hearts' desires are fulfilled for good.
> 
> May He who performed miracles for *our ancestors* and redeemed them from slavery to freedom, redeem *us* soon and gather *our* dispersed people from the

four corners of the earth, so that *all Israel may be united in friendship*, and let *us* say: Amen.

We pray for collective well-being.

Note the repeated use of the word *us*, *we*, and *our* in this prayer. It is yearning in plural terms. Our hope for true well-being is grounded in the well-being of the community of which we are a part. Further, when we pray for freedom, for ingathering exiles, it too is *us* we have in mind; it is *all Israel* (that) may be *united* in friendship.

We pray for physical and material well-being.

Note the terms *long life, physical health, sustenance, wealth*. Judaism has always stressed the importance and decided legitimacy of the material things of life. Thus, the Rabbis tell us that when we arrive at the heavens above, we will be asked if we enjoyed all the legitimate material aspects of life the world fashioned by God offered human beings.

Moreover, taking good care of one's own physical body was a dictum of the sage Hillel because it was seen as an act of reverence for its creator.[24] The mystics added another reason for this: the human physical structure is precious because it harbors God's likeness; even more: a "spark" of Divinity lodges within a human being. Then, too, longevity, physical health, fiscal resources not only make possible a good life, but also provide one with the capacity to do good for others.

We pray for spiritual well-being.

Note the term *reverence for heaven*. This speaks to our aspiration to be aware of the awesome Power in the universe—a Force that is non-human that pervades our world and our own lives. It is to recognize that God is the Source of our lives, that He gives us the resources—the seed and rain, for example—that makes life possible, things that man, though he must himself cultivate, did not himself fashion. *Reverence for heaven* also means that when we behold our wondrous universe, its astonishing order and system and reliability, we see the hand of God—its Fashioner, its Mind, and thus are provoked to profound reverence.

We pray for psychological well-being.

Note the yearning for *a life of peace*, a life *without shame or disgrace*, and *dread of sin*. Often people are seized with internal anxiety causing sleepless nights. The prayer for peace here seeks to ease this condition.

The Hebrew word *shalom*, peace, means more than amicable relationships with others—personal and communal. Genesis 43 tells about Jacob's sons who had traveled from Canaan to Egypt for provisions. On the way back home they discovered that the money they thought they had paid for the provisions was found in the sacks of their donkeys. The brothers were full of anxiety. Maybe one of them *did* take their money back! Perhaps this incident would come to haunt them because of the nefarious deed they inflicted on their brother Joseph in selling him as chattel to the Ishmaelites en route to Egypt! They were conflicted because they felt guilty; yet they needed the provisions to survive and provide for their families. What was to happen to them when they had to return to Egypt for additional provisions?

When they returned, Pharaoh's steward responded to their worries this way:

*Shalom lahkem—Peace be to you* [that is, rest assured], do not be afraid; your God and the God of your fathers must have put treasure [that is, your money] in your sacks for you; I had received your money" (*Genesis 43:23*).[25]

In order to reassure them, the steward asserted that God, through some unknown figure, put that money in their sacks; the steward had already received the money they had legitimately paid for their provisions. And so, when he responded to the brothers with *shalom lakhem*, "peace be to you," he was telling them not to worry, not to be anxious; they were innocent about the money—in a word, that they have peace of mind and heart.

## Good Deeds

When a Jew performs acts of kindness, he builds up the divine image in the world, the living divine image within both himself and his neighbor. In Genesis 1:27 we hear, "And God created man in His image, in the image of God He created him: male and female He created them." The Jew enhances the Divine Image via acts of *gemilat hasadim*, deeds of kindness (*hesed*) typified by clothing the poor, by providing a dowry for indigent women, by burying the dead, by visiting the sick, by treating people with understanding, by giving another confidence when he's down, by easing another's loneliness—good deeds and so many others like them that meet the pressing needs of one's fellow man. I have written elsewhere in this book (chapter 6) about the underlying reason a person is to practice *gemilat hasadim*.

*Reverence for God is shown via reverence for man.* The fear one must feel of offending or hurting another must be as of ultimate importance as one's fear of God for Divinity inheres in that other. An act of violence against an innocent other is a desecration of the Divinity within the violated. To be arrogant toward another person is to be blasphemous toward God: "He who oppresses the poor blasphemes his Maker. He who is gracious to the needy honors Him."[26] The Midrash stresses: "You must not say, since I have been put to shame, let my neighbor be put to shame, for in the likeness of God He (God) made that neighbor.[27] The Rabbis teach that he who sheds the blood of another human being is considered as though he diminished the Divinity.[28]

The fourteen blessings recited in the morning by the faithful embody and illustrate this perspective. The Talmud (*Menakhot 43b*) requires the Jew to recite 100 blessings each day expressing thanks to God for His abundant beneficence. (Listening to others chant the blessings and responding *Amen* counts as a blessing by the listener). With these we thank God for so very much—clarity of mind, freedom, Jewish pride, appreciation of nature, and much more. One of these blessings focuses especially on God's evoking in men and women sensitivity to and concern for the physical and psychic needs of others.

> *Barukh Ata Adonoy Elohaynu Melekh Ha-olom malbish arumim*
> Blessed are You, Lord our God, King of the Universe, who clothes the naked.

. . . to which I have added this amplification:

> Lord, You provide me with so much—clothes to keep me warm, the special raiment for Shabbat and Holy Day, suit and dress for my children, shoes which enable me and my family to go about our daily rounds safely and comfortably. I feel good about these blessings—but I also feel discomfort when I think about others who don't have what I have. I know that You expect help of others from me; so I will try to help. No, I will help.[29]

To summarize,

Fishbane sums up the essential nature and purpose of this pattern of religious action. What it does in effect is to forge connections with the life patterns of the ancestors, and deepens a person's humanity, thus enabling the observer to "walk before God with integrity." But more: he who embraces a pattern of religious deed lives within the naturalness of his natural life, as a creature of the earth who works and eats and labors and thus seeks *to turn those occasions into markers of praise and thankfulness before God, the Life of all life.* The routine happenings of life thus become ways to fashion ongoing awareness of the presence of God.[30]

And so, the idea of the supreme God that the Rabbis inherited from Moses and the Prophets was reaffirmed by both word and deed.

## From Rote Practice to Spiritual Intention

We have depicted the various ways one can keep alive the reality, role and presence of God in one's midst: observance of *mitzvot*, intensive *learning*, strong focus on *prayer*, and the practice of *good deeds*. Experience has long demonstrated that these practices often morph into rote activity. They become external acts, automatic in practice, done without inner drive and enthusiasm, without focus on their true objectives. A problem.

Jon Levenson assists us here.[31] He cites the passage in Deuteronomy 6:5, which immediately follows the Shema (v. 4), the classic affirmation of the Oneness of God. "And you shall love The Lord your God with all your *heart*, and with all your *soul*, and with all your *might*."

*Your heart:* The midrash[32] notes the spelling of the Hebrew word for heart—*levavekha* with two *vets*, whereas *one vet* as *libekha* would have sufficed (v a b are graphically the same)—to make a point. And that is to indicate that love of God is to be expressed with *both* of one's inclinations—the good and the bad. But how can one's inclination to evil be directed to the love of God? Is that not a contradiction in terms? A midrash suggests an answer:

> Nahman [said] in the name of Rabbi Samuel: "[God saw all that He had made], and found it very good" (Gen. 1:31). "Found it good"—this is the Good Inclination. "Found it very good"—this is the Evil Inclination.
> But is the Evil Inclination "very good"?
> Actually, were it not for the Evil Inclination, a man would never build a house, marry a woman, or beget children (*Genesis Rabbah 9:7*).

When the midrash interprets the Evil Inclination as "very good," it is making the point that the inclination that might have gone to evil purposes—to sexual perversion rather than to sex in marriage, or begetting children to perpetuate the faith—to indicate that love of God is to be expressed with *both* one's good and evil inclinations. How so the latter? Because it too can and must be channeled in the service of God and as a way to express love for Him.

*Your soul*: The Hebrew word for soul is *nefesh*. The translation "soul" is problematic for it contradicts the traditional understanding of human identity. Soul, an ancient Greek word prevelant among western philosophers, refers to a detached immortal component of the human self. In the biblical sense, to the contrary, soul and body are one indivisible unit that thus constitutes the entire human being. "Within the original context of Deuteronomy 6:5, then," says Levenson, "*nefesh* refers to the life force, and the commandment to 'love the Lord your God . . . with all your soul' means one should love Him with *all of one's vitality, vigor, energy, selfhood, inner forcefulness and the like*. It does not mean that one should love Him with some immortal, spiritual dimension of the self that is divorced from one's bodily and social identity."

*Your might:* The Hebrew word *m'odekha*, means "very" or "much." Rabbi Hezekiah ben Manoah, a thirteenth-century French commentator known as "Hizquni," stresses the connection with the adverb "very" (*uv'khol*) and thus reads it as "very, very much" (*uv'khol m'odekah*), meaning *set your heart and your soul to love Him*.[33] "So understood," writes Levenson, "*me'od* (might) is not a third noun at all but serves rather to intensify the command 'to love the Lord your God with all your heart and with all your soul.' *The love of God is not to be lukewarm, lethargic or perfunctory. It must mobilize all the capacities of the self and do so to the highest possible degree*."

The point of Levenson's commentary is clear enough. In order to avoid the often mindless, even soul-less character of religious observance, one needs to make a conscious effort to mobilize the manifold capacities of one's inner and outer life—all of one's heart and soul, of one's physical body and social identity—in the process of religious practice. This is, of course, no easy task; however the practice pattern of the religious life, indispensable as it is, needs these equally vital inner and outer forces if it is to effectively fulfill its objectives, again: to fashion ongoing awareness of God's presence in everyday life.

*Why Such Extreme Emphasis On Ritual Detail?*

Experience has long since demonstrated, as well, that fervent adherence by some to a particular pattern of ritual observance often leads to intolerance of others whose ritual patterns differ from their own.

Why is this demonstrably so? Religion deals with man's deepest concerns, with *his attempt at relating himself to the most ultimate reality he can find*, i.e., God, the Transcendent, the Divine, the Ultimate Power of the universe. Thus, *everything attached to that relationship partakes of great seriousness. This is religion's vital nerve; whatever touches it touches religion at the core of its being*; it is instantly alert to any threat in this area. This is what religion signifies by marking off certain things with the mark of "holiness" or "sacredness." It is saying of such things, "These have to do with the most vital concerns known to man; beware how you handle them!"

Here is where the passion for details enters the picture. Since religion's rituals and techniques (its institutions and theological principles) are *methodologies to achieve bonding* with God, they are matters of supreme importance; one cannot afford to jeopardize this supremely important goal, asserts the faithful enthusiast, by neglecting, changing or belittling any part of the process no matter how minute.

Thus, for example, the inappropriate inclusion or the omission of certain prescribed prayers or words in the *Amida* prayer invalidate the entire *Amida*, which the worshipper is then required to repeat in its entirety. In an African ritual dance one wrong word or gesture may invalidate the whole. One who utters a single phrase disparaging Muhammad could be subject to the death penalty. Christians battled intensely over the inclusion or exclusion of the letter "*i*" in a Greek word in a religious statement, and Catholics once fought bitterly over the legitimacy of the language of the Mass: should it remain in Latin or changed to the vernacular? The issue hinged on the validity of the entire prayer process, which could be vitiated by use of the incorrect language. *I've often thought of this phenomenon in this way: picture a ladder reaching from the ground upward toward heaven; if one single rung of the ladder is missing, the whole climb upward to God would be thwarted!*

Granted that religion legitimately attaches great importance to its ritual patterns; granted that this is because these patterns are related to the quest for attachment to the Ultimate; yet there can be ways to ease the zealotry with which this quest is pursued. Religionists might ponder the fact that ritual acts are human-made symbols, are *changing* methodologies elaborately developed and employed in reaching out to God. They are the products of different times and climes and are, therefore, *transient ways of articulating permanent convictions and experiences*. These ways rise and fall in time and are eventually replaced by ritual patterns reflective of new forms of religious observance prompted by different locales and time periods. To cite but one example, among many others, the sacrificial system of pre-exilic days was supplanted by prayer and the study of religious texts. It was the *obligation to worship God which was and is the permanent principle of faith*. Sacrifice and prayer were the changing ways of implementing this principle. To resume the ladder metaphor: missing rungs in a ladder can be, and more often than not are, replaced by new ones in renewing and resuming the climb upward.

It goes without saying that long-established ritual patterns embedded in the life of a religious community are not to be cavalierly changed or abandoned. These are crucial in forging and maintaining bonds between members of community and fellow religionists. In the end, however, living religion calls for the renewal of traditional ritual patterns always done in the recognizable spirit and intent of the tradition, yet also reflecting the mindset and "heartset" of the earnest contemporary religionist. Such an approach might well enable the religionist to approximate the ultimate objective of the religious enterprise: to help make the principles of the faith operative in the life of human beings here on earth.

## The Deity Is a God of People, Not Place: Negation of Polytheism Continued

We concluded in our last chapter that the war on Polytheism initiated in the Mosaic era and continued by the Prophets was based on the conviction that the Deity was attached to people rather than to fixed places inhabited by the gods. The latter notion was deemed as limiting the Deity's accessibility and that plastic images similarly tended to localize the deity and create attachment to one place or another. Further, images and statues inevitably became endowed with divinity—a condition contrary to the absolute Oneness of God. Hence the profound hostility to idols and the worship of them.

The Rabbis carried forth this war on Polytheism in their own way. In the early rabbinic era the Jewish people had largely put idolatry behind them and thus they did not feel compelled to consistently polemicize against the practice. Unlike the Hellenistic Jews, "the problem of idolatry and its *raison d'être*," according to Saul Lieberman, "no longer had practical significance for the Rabbis. However, they were concerned with the heathen rites insofar as they affected the social and commercial contact of the Jew with the gentile."[34] Thus, because the Rabbis were subject to idolatrous Rome in the land of Israel, and were enmeshed with the populace all about them, rules and regulations had to be developed in order to resist the blandishments of pagan practice in everyday life. And so, over time an entire Talmudic tractate, *Avodah Zarah* ("foreign worship"), on the subject came into being.

Numerous precautions were instituted against any acts by Jews that might seem to recognize places or objects gentiles regarded as divine in character or which implied Jewish involvement with them. Jews did not even tolerate Roman ensigns symbolizing the authority of their overlords which were brought into Jerusalem because pagan images were on them. At the risk of their lives they objected to these ensigns in their midst and so Pilate had to withdraw them.[35]

The Mishna records detailed regulations in this vein. For three days before idolatrous festivals, it is prohibited to have business dealings with the idolators—no loans to them and no borrowing from them; when idolatrous services are held in town, Jewish dealers are not permitted to "adorn" their shops for business purposes or leave gratuities for idolatrous priests; where it is Jewish practice to sell small animals to idolators this is permitted, but not large cattle!; Jews are not permitted to assist idolators to build forums, arenas, theatres, niches in walls for idols, although public bathhouses were permitted; fashioning ornaments such as chains, ear-rings, nose-rings for an idol were proscribed. These rules typify the rabbinic stance on "appearances" vis-à-vis the gentile idolatry of their time.[36]

In addition, there were warnings about vices which were felt to be rooted in idolatry. Indeed, there was palpable fear at the time that immoral behavior was linked to such practice. Note this recorded outburst from around 100 BCE: "All is in chaos—bloody murder, theft and fraud . . . moral corruption, sexual perversion, breakdown of marriage, adultery. . . . For *the worship of idols*, whose names it is wrong even to mention, *is the beginning cause and end of every evil*." Such were the words of the author of The Wisdom of Solomon book in the Apocrypha.[37]

## Why Does God Allow Idolatry to Exist?

There were times when polemics were called for, particularly when the Rabbis were challenged.

> The Jewish elders in Rome were asked: If your God has no desire for idolatry, why does He not abolish it? They replied: if it were something which the people did not need that was worshipped, God would abolish it. But people worship the sun, moon and stars and planets. Should He destroy these on account of fools? *Olam ke-minhago noheg, the world pursues its normal course*; and as for the fools who act wrongly, they will have to render an account. Another illustration: suppose a man stole a measure of wheat and went and sowed it in the ground. *It is right* that it should not grow. But *the world pursues its normal course*; and as for the fools who act wrongly, they will have to render an account. Another illustration: suppose a man has intercourse with his neighbor's wife. *It is right* that she should not conceive. *But the world pursues its normal course*; and as for the fools who act wrongly, they will have to render an account.[38]

In analyzing this passage, David Hartman notes that the pious Jew is correct in feeling that the stolen wheat ought not to grow, nor should the adulterous wife conceive. The thieves and adulterers will eventually have to render account for their deeds, but the Jew must accept the existence of a natural order and can do so without disavowing his personal expectations of God. Indeed, o*lam ke-minhago noheg, the world pursues its normal course— the natural order has its own built-in rules* making it immutable. In the short term fools frustrate God's purpose by exploiting the natural order He created. They do so by fashioning their idols representing elements in this natural order—the sun, the moon, the stars, the planets. For this they will eventually pay a price. Herein is the reply to the question posed to the Jewish elders, and herein is a lesson learned. The Jew faces the fact that the natural order God created "pursues its normal course" and that is God's plan as the "Designer" of the world. This condition, the Jew understands, plays a role in idolatry. *He is able to accept this fact knowing that God cannot abolish the elements of nature which idols represent.* At the same time he is able to retain his faith in God's power and eventual judgment of heathen wrongdoing.[39]

## God Protects and Cares for People

The Prophets put special emphasis on God's care and concern for all people— Israelite in particular and non-Israelite in general, as we have seen in our previous chapter. As mentioned earlier, George Foote Moore has observed that such enduring concern had "its origin in the personal love of God for man."[40] Indeed, it was because all people were so loved that God protects and cares for them. The Rabbis embraced this notion and proceeded to explicate it in the context of their own period and environment.

Rabbi Akiba deduced God's love for all mankind as well as for Israel in this Midrash.

> Akiba used to say, *beloved is man*, for he was created in the image of God; but it was by a special love that it was made known to him that he (man) was created in the image of God, as it is said, *betzelem Elohim asa et ha-adam*, "in the image of God He (God) made man."[41] *Beloved are Israel* for to them was given the desirable instrument, the Torah; but it was by a special love that it was made known to them that that desirable instrument was theirs through which the world was created, as it is said, "For I give you good doctrine, forsake not my Torah" (Proverbs 4:2).[42]

This is a compelling statement about the rabbinic conception of God's relationship both to human beings in general and to the people of Israel in particular: Beloved of *man* means God loves *all* human beings regardless of creed. Beloved of Israel means that God loves Israel by giving her the *Torah*, the basic instrument of her religion. And it was the same Rabbi Akiba who deduced from the affirmation of God's "image" man's obligation toward all fellow men, "You shall love your neighbor as yourself" (Leviticus 19:18). Why? Because you need to replicate in your life God's character.[43]

The love of God for Israel is expressed in moving fashion in two prayers in the Sabbath liturgy instituted by the Rabbis that conclude with benedictions before the Shema: *the Ahavah Rabbah*, "with great love You have loved us" and the *Ahavat Olam*, "with everlasting love have You loved Your people the house of Israel."[44] In both prayers the Torah is viewed as the channel through which God's love flows. And in this prayer, "You have loved us and are satisfied with us and have sanctified us through Your mitzvot. Thus you have linked us with Your great and holy name."[45]

The love of God for all people was the view of the Rabbis. So Eliezer ben Jacob: "Who The Lord loves He corrects, even as a father his son in whom he takes pleasure (Prov. 3:12). What makes a son pleasing to his father? It is chastisements, thus Rabbi Meir: "You shall know in your heart that as a man chastises his son, so The Lord your God chastises you" (Deut. 8:5). Yosi ben Judah: "Precious to God are chastisements, for the glory of God lights on those on whom chastisements come, as it is said: The Lord your God chastises you."[46]

Herein is the source of God's protection and care for people—His profound love for them.

## God is Creator of Heaven and Earth

As we have seen, the Mosaic conception of God as Creator of heaven and earth was deepened by the Prophets: He was also the *Designer* and *Sustainer* of the world and all within it. God's world was fashioned in accordance with a carefully designed plan. Moreover, great stress is placed on a God who sustains not only the cosmic world but the world of humanity as well. Indeed, the Prophets helped establish this conception of the Godhood as a fundamental doctrine of religion, a key element of Jewish Monotheism. The Rabbis who followed the Prophets did so, not only in time, but in spirit as well.

That God alone created the world is emphasized in the Midrash. Rabbi Luliani is stressing that the angels the Bible refers to have nothing to do with the creation.

> All agree that no angel was created on the first day, lest you should say that Michael stretched the world in the south and Gabriel in the north, while the Holy One, blessed be He, measured it in the middle; but *I am The Lord that makes all things, who alone stretched forth the heavens, who spread abroad the earth by Myself* (Isaiah 42:24).[47]

That God also created the pre-existent materials from which He fashioned the world (as the Bible in Genesis, chapter 1 has it) is affirmed in the Midrash.

> A certain philosopher (skeptic) asked Rabban Gamliel: your God was indeed a great artist, but surely He found good materials which assisted Him. What are they? Gamliel asked. *Tohu va-vohu, darkness, water, wind* and *the deep*, the philosopher replied. Woe to that man, Gamliel explained, the term "creation" is used by scripture in connection with all of these materials. *Tohu va-vohu: I make peace and create evil; darkness: I form the light and create darkness* (Is. 45:7); *water: praise ye waters that are above the heavens* (Ps. 148:4)—why? *For He*

*commanded and they were created* (Ps. 148:5); *wind: For, lo, He that forms the mountains and creates the wind* (Amos 4:13); *the deep: when there were no depths, I was brought forth* (Proverbs 8:24).[48]

A Midrash that reenforces the above affirmation:

"And there was evening and there was morning" etc. (Genesis one). Rabbi Judah said: Let there be evening is not written here, but and there *was* evening. Hence we know that a time-order existed before this. (i.e., evening *was*, evening existed previous to creation as here described). Rabbi Abbahu said: this proves that the Holy One, blessed be He, went on creating worlds and destroying them until He created this one and declared, this one pleases Me. Rabbi Phineas said, this is Rabbi Abbahu's reason: *And God saw everything that He made and hinay, behold, it was very good* (Gen 1:31): this world pleases Me, those worlds did not please Me. [The deduction is from the Hebrew word *hinay* "now," which implies that only that which exists *now*—in the present—was very good in God's eyes].[49]

Clearly, the Rabbis used creative methods of biblical interpretation to make firm ideological affirmations.

## The "Master Plan" of Creation . . . and Why God Created the World

God is not only the sole Creator of the world, but alone upholds it and maintains its existence. This universal teaching of the Bible is also the doctrine of the Rabbis: "God created and He provides."[50] The maintenance of the world is a kind of continuous creation, as the *Yotzer Or* prayer in the Shabbat liturgy has it: "God in His goodness makes new every day continually the work of creation."

The history of the world, as the prophets maintained, is that of God's "master plan" in which everything moves toward the fulfillment of His purpose, the end that is in His mind. And what constitutes this master plan? It includes a golden age not only for His people Israel but for all mankind, when peace and prosperity will be universal and the physical and human world will be made a suitable dwelling place for wholly changed inhabitants.[51]

The Rabbis did not stop at such lofty rhetoric, but proceeded to be specific about this "master plan." They knew that the human mind by nature was curious, searching, in need of concrete *reasons* for the phenomenon that is the world. That is why they asked for some detail about the issue: why, they wanted to know, did God create the world? They then proceeded to speculate.

- *The world was created for man—not man for the world*

But man who has been formed by Your hands is called Your image because he is made like You, and *for whose sake You have formed all things*, have You also made him like the farmer's seed? No, O, Lord, who is over us! Spare Your people and give mercy to Your inheritance, for You have mercy on Your own creation.[52]

Implied in this statement is that God, out of His abundant love for His human creations, fashioned the world so that man might benefit from what the magnificent world has to offer.

- *The world was made for the sake of the righteous*

The righteous ones, the Patriarchs, *those whom you said the world has come into being on their account*, yes, also that which is coming on their account. For this world is for them a struggle and an effort with much trouble. And to whom will accordingly come a crown with great glory.[53]

The implication: God fashioned the world to serve as the "arena," as it were, in which man was to strive to be righteous. It was to teach that good people emerge from struggling successfully with the difficulties and troubles that the world presents.

- *The world was created for the sake of Israel*

All this I have spoken before You, O Lord, because *You have said that it was for us Israel that you created this world*. And now behold the nations domineer over us and devour us. Your people who You have called Your first-born, only begotten, zealous for You and most dear, have been given into their hands. *If the world has indeed been created for us,* why do we not possess our world as an inheritance? How long will this be so?[54]

The insistent question posed here as to why Israel suffers so in exile, in places not hers, has been answered by the Prophet Isaiah—the substance of which has been embedded in the life of the Jewish people down through the ages. Israel's exilic condition has a purpose. She is to be "a light unto the nations."[55] She is to help make the world a better place in which to live. Such indeed was God's purpose for her—an end that could be realized by an Israel living amidst the nations. God created the world so that Israel could fulfill this purpose. Alas, Israel pays a heavy price for such a task. This is her destiny.

- *The world was created for the sake of the Torah*

"All these things were made by My hand, and thus it all came into being, declares The Lord" (Is. 66:2). Rabbi Berehia objected: not with labor or wearying did the Holy One, blessed be He, create His world (His word was sufficient), yet you actually say, 'All these were made by My hand.' Rabbi Judah said: this means that *God created the world for the sake of the Torah*, which is referred to as *these* in the verse, '*These* are the statutes and ordinances and the *torot* (Lev. 26:46). Thus for the sake of all these things, i.e., the Torah, did God fashion the world.[56]

The implication: The world was created so that the Torah could fulfill its purpose, which is to help make the world a good place in which to live. Torah harbors the wisdom of the ages; it provides guidelines for man's living in the world. Indeed, it teaches human beings how and why to live a noble life.

## God Requires Justice and Righteousness

In our chapter *The Prophets and Monotheism* we concluded that these inspired men bequeathed the notion that social justice and the primacy of morality were at the essence of Monotheism. Religious practice was, of course, vital, but legitimate when accompanied by moral and ethical behavior. This is what the One God demanded of all people—Israelites and non-Israelites alike. The notion constitutes what has been called "Ethical Monotheism." The Rabbis inherited this perspective and proceeded to cultivate it in the context of their own time and clime. Indeed, justice and righteous behavior such as mercy and compassion, which, by definition, are at the core of morality, are constantly stressed in the records of their lives, and their teaching about these virtues was, in the words of George Foote Moore, "in the track of the Law (of Moses) and the Prophets."[57]

The basic guideline for the Rabbis in this sphere of morality was the concept that *God Himself possessed the various characteristics of morality and ethics, and it was thus man's responsibility to follow in His footsteps. It was man's chief purpose in life to be, in human measure, like God.* Julius Guttman put it this way:

> The passionate violence of the religious ethos of the Prophets had given place, in Talmudic times, to a quieter, more restrained, and in a way even sober, piety, bound to history and tradition. However, the activist character of Jewish religion was preserved. Religious life was still centered on the divine "commands" (i.e., observance of ritual and the law). However, piety is not so much the mere observance of the divine commandments as *the imitation of a Divine Model*. The biblical commandment to be holy even as The Lord is holy, and the injunction to walk in the ways of God, are interpreted by the Rabbis as *demands to imitate the divine qualities of love and mercy.*[58]

In essence, then, the spirit of rabbinic religion was clearly on the same track traversed by the Prophets.

## The Rabbis Speak

Justice and mercy are considered two of God's primary attributes. Thus Rabbi Meir interpreted Hosea 14:2 ("Return, Israel, to The Lord thy God") this way: Repent while God is starting with the attribute of mercy (Hebrew: *midat harahamim*); if you do not, He will be your God with the attribute of justice (Hebrew: *midat hadin*).[59] Similarly God created the earth and the heavens on the balanced basis of justice and mercy.[60]

Rabbi Samuel ben Nachman interpreted "The Lord is good to all" (Psalm 155:9) meaning that "it is God's nature to be compassionate." And Rabbi Joshua added that this means that "He inspires mankind with His compassion." And then Rabbi Abba said: "Should a year of famine commence tomorrow and men show compassion for each other, then the Holy One, blessed be He, will also be filled with compassion for them"[61]

In explaining the biblical scene wherein Abraham pleaded for mercy for the Sodomites saying, "Far be it from Thee! Shall not the judge of all the earth do justly! (Gen. 18:25), the Rabbis embellished the dialogue. Rabbi Aha pictures Abraham urging: You, God, swore not to bring a deluge upon the world. Would you evade your oath! Rabbi Levi sees Abraham pleading: You are a just God and if you want the world to endure, justice must be tempered with mercy. Unless you "forget a little" the world cannot endure. And so, "since Abraham loved righteousness," God anointed him with the oil of gladness."[62]

Rabbi Akiba interprets the words in Psalm 36:7, "Thy righteousness is like the mountain of God and like the great deep" to mean: God deals strictly with the righteous, calling them to account for the few wrongs which they commit in this world, in order to reward them in the world to come. He grants ease to the wicked (who did not accept the Torah that was revealed at Mount Sinai) and rewards them for the few good deeds which they performed in this world, in order to punish them in the future world. God has compassion even for those whose good deeds are few.[63] In this vein, in a touching anecdote about Rabbi Meir at the grave of his apostate teacher, Elisha ben Abuya, he finds in Ruth 3:13 and Psalm 145:9 a God, the absolutely good, who would deliver even such a sinner.[64]

From the foregoing it is apparent that the Rabbis well understood that what motivates humans to live in accordance with justice and righteousness was to view these virtues as God's virtues. Read on about the thirteen attributes of God enumerated in Exodus 34:5–7, which the Rabbis viewed as behaviors to be replicated by man in his regular encounters with his fellow man. They are appealed to in 4 Ezra in a moving plea for mankind.

> I know, Sir, that the Most High is called merciful (*rahum*) because he has mercy on those who have not yet come into the world; and gracious (*hanun*), because he is gracious to those who turn in repentance to his law; and longsuffering (*ereh apayim*) because he shows longsuffering toward those who have sinned, as to his own works; and liberal (*rav hesed*) because he had rather give than exact; and of abundant compassion (*notzayr hesed*) because he makes his compassions abound to those now living and to those who are gone and to those yet to come, for if he did not make them abound, the world and those who inhabit it could not live; and the giver (*nasay avon*), because if he did not give out of his goodness, that those who have done iniquities should be relieved of their iniquities, not the ten-thousandth part of men could survive; and the judge (*v'nakay*), because if he did not pardon those who were created by his word, and blot out the multitude of their sins, very few would be left of all the innumerable multitude.[65]

According to George Foot Moore,

> These illustrations from a single compilation of "sermon stuff" tell of the humanity of God written all over the revelation as it was read by philosophically unsophisticated men; the preachers at most did no more than seek to improve less obvious texts. Often they held up this side of God's character as an example of motivation for men to imitate it.[66]

*Chapter 5*

# Judaism and Christianity and Monotheism

## On God's Oneness: The Fork in the Road

"Hear O Israel, The Lord our God, The Lord is One" (Deuteronomy 6:4). It is concerning the absolute Oneness of God—the heart of the idea of Monotheism—wherein Judaism and Christianity part ways.

### THE DIVIDE

We now arrive at the period of history during which Christianity inherited the notion of Monotheism from its immediate predecessors. As noted, this notion included the absolute Oneness of the Deity and the tenets which flowed from it, viz. the Deity as the God of people, not place, Who uses His power to protect and care for people, Who is Creator of heaven and earth, and Who requires justice and righteousness.

In this chapter we discuss only the core principle of Monotheism—the Oneness of God, about which Judaism and Christianity differ. We do not deal with the tenets that flowed from the latter's notion of the Deity. This is a task for scholars of the New Testament and the church fathers. The divide between the two faiths has been described in historical terms by Robert Gordis as "the fork in the road," because the time when the ideological separation occurred—the turn of the millennium—was when Judaism and Christianity proceeded in different theological directions.

Before proceeding with discussion of this divide, we describe a non-normative notion of divinity that is embedded in scripture—what has been called a "minority view"—because it appears, in the view of some scholars, as having had a significant impact on the Christian idea. We include this theological thought-line here because it reflects the thesis of this Guide—the developmental character of the God idea. The full implications of this description are but briefly alluded to; this is for those who search for the Jewish root of Christianity.[1]

We then proceed to discussion of the basic content of this chapter—the dissonant theological relationship between Judaism and Christianity. This we do from the point of view of normative biblical and Judaic perspectives on the subject of the Deity. We will seek to locate the basic Christian notion, and then point to Judaism's divergent one.

## The Budding Notion of the Christian God Idea

As we have stressed throughout concerning the development of ideas, their evolution from era to era, such is the case with regard to the Christian God idea. Notions do not spring out of the blue, as new, fresh and original ones. Rather, what is usually viewed as "revolutionary" is, in reality, rooted, if faintly or in minor key, in previous periods' realms of thought. Now, Christianity's idea of God in its fundamental formulation views the Deity as a Trinity, as consisting of three distinct "persons," as God manifest in multiple forms yet united as one. Do some biblical texts harbor a similar notion, one that may well have served as the Christian notion in embryo?

Benjamin Sommer, in a recently published book, has traced this notion in scripture in great detail.[2] Before proceeding with Sommer's depiction, it must again be stressed that this was and is a non-normative notion, a minority position in the Hebrew Bible. The Bible itself, in its mainline priestly, Deuteronomic and prophetic material, has at its early authoritative beginning and long since distanced itself from the notion of divine multiplicity. Rather, it has put great emphasis on God's unity, insisting on the Deity's absolute singularity. And yet, try as the mainline ideologues did, this notion—what Benjamin Sommer calls the "fluidity tradition" and the "embodiment of God"—was not excluded from the biblical canon. Sommer contends that the final form of the Hebrew Bible tempers those notions, calls them into question, but allows them to remain in the sacred precincts.[3]

Sommer's basic thesis: God, as portrayed in a number of scriptural sections manifests Himself in different places and different times and evinces a number of concrete forms ("bodies") *while Himself remaining apart from these manifestations*, this all while the underlying unity of God prevails. This is *not* Polytheism, Sommer insists, but the *One God* who reveals Himself in multiple ways and forms *which appear to be independent entities*. He proceeds to document this thesis. To cite three biblical passages,

- In the Golden Calf episode (Exodus 33:1–3), God is still incensed by the people and announces that *He will not accompany them* on the journey lest He destroy them on the way. Rather, a *malakh* (an angel) will accompany them.

- And then there is the same angel in Exodus 23:20–23. The people were told that they must obey the angel who travels with them because it incorporates a manifestation of God's presence known as His *shem* ("name"); "I will send an angel in front of you. *Take care of him and obey him . . . for my name is within Him."* By stating that His name is in the angel, God appears to indicate that the angel carries something of God's own essence or self. And so, on the one hand, the angel is not an entirely separate entity, and on the other hand, it is not fully identical with God either, for, after all, God Himself declared that He will *not* travel with the people, but the angel *will*.

- In Genesis 18 God manifests Himself to Abraham in the form of three men. They speak to Abraham as human beings when one of the men, in verse 10, promises Sarah a son. But then another of the men (in verse 13) speaks as God: *"The Lord* said to Abraham, why did Sarah laugh," saying that she was too old to bear a child? Here it seems that The Lord appears in "bodily" form to Abraham.

In these cases, Sommer contends, the conception of an angel is something other than a messenger. He cites Richard Elliot Friedman explaining the theology behind these passages.

> These texts indicate that angels are conceived of as expressions of God's presence. God in this conception can make Himself known to humans by a sort of emanation of the Godhead *that is visible to human eyes*. It is a concrete expression of the Divine presence. In some ways, *an angel is an identifiable thing itself*, and on the other hand, merely a representation of Divine presence in human affairs.[4]

In a word, paradoxically, *multiplicity* of Divinity appears to characterize the *One God*.

If what has been delineated above has validity, it would seem apparent that a biblical notion of the Deity's multiplicity found expression in Christianity's doctrine of the Trinity. Indeed, the Trinity emerged as an example of the fragmentation of a deity into (three) distinct entities, concrete elements, "persons," yet which, it is claimed, do not undermine the notion of God's wholeness. As indicated, amplification of this theological phenomenon is not the task of this Guide, but rather that of those who seek to locate the Jewish roots of Christianity.

## The Christian God Idea

What follows is our analysis of Judaism and Christianity's theological differences based on what we have called "normative" biblical and Judaic perspectives (in contrast to the non-normative one depicted above), viz. God's absolute unity about which there can be no fragmentation of His essence. Moreover, we consider the historical setting and theological notions that prevailed at the time of the two faiths' "fork in the road."

During the nascent Christian period—the first and second centuries of the Common Era—many Jews had left the Holy Land and settled in Egypt and other locations around the Mediterranean Sea. In these places they were inevitably exposed to the pervasive religious mindset embedded in the atmosphere by the Greco-Roman overlords whose culture and religion were heavily influenced by the reigning paganism of the time.

In this early Christian setting, a prevailing religious mood was uneasiness with the traditional Jewish notion of a transcendent God to whom the ordinary person had no direct access. The regnant pagan religion at the time, weakened and unsatisfying as it was, provided seeds for a response to this apparently felt need for greater access to the Divinity. It is at this juncture in history when Jesus, as portrayed by the Apostle Paul and the other New Testament writers, enters the theological arena. What the early Christian leaders did was to morph the God of their Jewish heritage into that of a human being. Now, they averred, people had direct access to the deity. What follows seeks to show how, in this milieu, this notion of God came about. We discuss its three basic components: Jesus as "Messiah," as the "Logos," and the "Holy Spirit."

## Jesus: From Messianic Messenger to Messiah

When the New Testament's Mark pictures Jesus proclaiming that the kingdom of God was at hand, he was reflecting the prevalent Jewish doctrine of the coming of the messianic age.[5] The belief in such an age and the early appearance of a personal messiah who would lead in bringing it about was a longstanding notion both in Palestine and the diaspora. Indeed, the Hellenistic and Palestinian writings of the age are permeated with utopian thinking. Even the pharisaic leaders who reflected the restless mindset and difficult economic and social conditions of the ordinary folk in Palestine living under the oppressive yoke of their Roman overlords harbored Messianism as a strong propelling force.[6] In the minds of the early Christians, Jesus was seen as that messianic leader. Salo Baron points to Schelling's insight that "Jesus' biography had been written long before his birth." The age-old messianic hopes of the Jewish people furnished Palestinian believers in Jesus with the basic elements of that life as the embodiment and realization of their hopes.[7]

As Jesus and his band of followers proceeded to spread the word about this decidedly *this-wordly notion*, it provoked a sharp reaction on the part of the Roman administration.

> However pacific Jesus' aims may have been and however hard he may have tried to infuse purely spiritual meaning into the terms "messiah" and "king of Jews," these were fighting words of the first order. In the existing permanent state of tension any Roman administrator taught by the experience of other messianic commotions must have seen red at the mention of a new movement spreading in both the capitol and the provinces. The procurator must have considered it a matter of sheer prudence to suppress the agitation before it got out of hand. Such action took place in a fashion momentous to the history of mankind: Jesus' arrest, trial, and crucifixion.[8]

In any event, initially belief in Jesus as "messiah" on the part of the first Jewish Christians meant that he was a messenger appointed by God to help bring about a this-worldly cleansed age. He was a human leader with a human vocation much like being a "son of David" especially designated to fulfill God's purpose for Israel which was redemption from her oppressed condition.[9] In this way, Jesus was associated with the Divine realm which is to say: he was sent by God. It did not concern the essential nature of the messianic leader as himself divine. However, when early Christian teaching was carried from the core Jewish environment of Palestine to the Hellenistic gentile world, the this-worldly sense of messiahship lost its compelling thrust. Gentiles did not imbibe its traditional meaning and intent. The messiah (which is what "christ" means) as a human leader designated to bring about a better world was not easily intelligible to the Greek and Roman Christians either in language or mindset. For them a messianic leader had an altogether different connotation: "Christ (i.e., messiah) became a proper name, and Jesus—the Christ—became "Jesus Christ," the term "Christ" given a more exalted connotation, that of "The Lord." Thus "Jesus *is The Lord*."

How did this come about? Throughout Paul's letters Jesus is referred to as "The Lord, Jesus Christ." This name tended to overshadow "messiah"; rather he is "The Lord." The title also associated Jesus with the divine realm, but suggested another connotation coming from a different background. *"The Lord" was habitually used in the Greek cults as a title of a god*, the cult's supernatural head with whom the worshipper connected via his rituals. To the Jew "Lord" means the Creator, an omnipotent Being besides whom there is no other. To the Hellenist, however, *Theos* (the Greek word for "The Lord") is a generic title of a whole class of supernatural beings who are neither creators of the world nor omnipotent or omniscient. In this sense the lords of the various pagan cults were all gods—and it would be natural enough for the Greek-influenced early Christians to interpret Jesus as "The Lord."[10] And, finally, when the Hebrew name for God, "The Lord," was rendered into Greek, the same word, *Theos*, was used for Jesus. This clinched the matter for the early Christians. And so, what emerged in this period were categories of understanding about the deity familiar to the non-Jewish mind: "The Lord Jesus Christ" was preached to the gentiles as belonging to the superhuman realm.[11].

## Jesus as the "Logos"

This development was further anchored by the interpretation of Jesus as the "Logos," the Hellenistic idea widely current both among the Jews and pagans at the time. The Logos was the *word* of God, the instrument by which God, the transcendent, worked his will in the world. Philo, the Alexandrian philosophical theologian of Judaism, equated this Greek term with the biblical *dabar*, the "word," God's spoken word with which He created the world. At the same time, in the Hebrew Bible and later Apocryphal books, "wisdom" (Greek *sophia*) was beginning to play a mediating role between God and creation not unlike that of *logos* in Philo.[12] The point: the idea of God's relation to His creation was mediated through a subordinate element; some special mode of communication had developed in the living environment of Jesus' followers—including various degrees of *personification*. Thus from what might be considered a pure abstraction among most Jews was transformed by the early Christians into a physical co-worker with the Supreme Deity.[13]

Indeed, here was a pattern of thought ready for Christian use in interpreting Jesus as being identified with the divine realm. In the New Testament he is recorded as "the image of the invisible God, the First born of all creation";[14] as "the effulgence of God's glory and the very image of God's substance."[15] And then as the capstone of the notion: the Logos, the word of God, in the fourth gospel, which begins,

> In the beginning was the word, and the word was with God, and *the word was God . . . and the word became flesh* and dwelt among us, full of grace and truth. We have beheld his glory, as *the only son of the Father.*[16]

Here then was a gradual evolution of the God idea from a human being to a God. "At the beginning Jesus *as a man* commended to you by God with mighty deeds, wonders and signs which God worked through him in your midst, as you yourselves know."[17] By the time the New Testament writers were through interpreting Jesus, the human being, the most august religious categories of the ancient world of the first and second centuries had been employed. Jesus was the Messiah, The Lord, the Logos. He had been deified. Humans now had direct, physical access to their God.[18]

## The Holy Spirit

The term Trinity connotes the doctrine of God as a unity of three persons: the Father, the Son, and the Holy Spirit. The term itself does not occur in the New Testament. It is generally acknowledged that the church father Tertullian (345–320 BCE) either coined the term or was the first to use it.[19] However, though the explicit doctrine was formulated post-New Testament, the early stages of its development can be traced.

We have dealt with the subject of the close relationship between God and Jesus in which the former is incarnated in the latter and hence there is an organic unity between the two.[20] This may be understood as the first step in the evolution of the trinity doctrine. The next step was the development of the notion of a "Holy Spirit" which was joined with God and Jesus to constitute the trinity which Tertullian presumably later established as authoritative church doctrine.

There is, religionists assert, a mysterious power or presence of God in nature and with individuals and communities, inspiring or empowering them with qualities they might not otherwise possess. The term "spirit" translates the Hebrew *ruah* and the Greek *pneuma*, words denoting "wind," "breath," and by extension, a life-giving element with the adjective "holy." The reference is to the divine spirit, i.e., the Spirit of God (*Ruah Hakodesh* in Hebrew).[21] The early Christians inherited this notion from their Jewish forebears, and, as was the case with the Judaic notions of the messiah and the word of God, transmuted it in accordance with their own religious proclivities and objectives.

In the Hebrew Bible the Holy Spirit is God's power which created the world and all within it.[22] It is the inspiration of the Prophets who, because they possess (or are possessed by) the Holy Spirit, speak or act with an authority and power not their own. In this normative Hebraic context, the Holy Spirit is a wholly abstract notion with no concrete connotations. In the New Testament the notion is given a less abstract meaning by associating it with the godhood itself in human-like form. Here the Holy Spirit is endowed with independent personhood such as when "the Holy Spirit who God the Father will send and *he will teach you all* things."[23] Indeed, Jesus is understood to be the recipient of this spirit in a unique way such as when we hear the Holy Spirit descending *in bodily form* upon Jesus after his baptism.[24] It is with this Holy Spirit received from the Father that Jesus has taught.[25] And again, "the *spirit himself intercedes for us* with signs too deep for words" and teaches the faithful how to pray.[26] Moreover, the Holy Spirit is described as a *counselor* who is a guide to Jesus and his disciples.[27]

And so, as we have said, although the doctrine of the trinity as such was spelled out later than this early Christian period, the New Testament itself planted its seed, its basic three elements as expressed in Paul's blessing: "The grace of The Lord *Jesus Christ*, and the love of *God*, and the fellowship of the *Holy Spirit* be with you all."[28] And then, "Go, therefore, and make disciples of all nations, baptise them in the name of the *Father*, and the *Son*, and the *Holy Spirit*," declared Jesus to the disciples.[29]

## The Normative Jewish Reaction to the Christian God Idea

From the foregoing it is clear that Christian thinking about the Godhood went far beyond the original history concerning Jesus' life, teaching and ministry. It is evident, as well, that its teachings were contrary to Judaism's strongest leanings and at variance with its understanding of the core element of the doctrine of Monotheism. In short, fervently "spiritual" as the tradition was, strongly attached as it was to God, Judaism never forgot the chasm which separated the Infinite Deity from His creatures. Indeed, God is wholly other than a human person; as a separate and distinct power, He brought man to life as a separate and distinct human being.

The objections of Judaism to the Christian notion of the Godhood can be summarized under two rubrics: Jewish doctrine prior to Jesus, and the rabbinic reactions to subsequent early Christian formulations.

### *The Jewish Tradition before Jesus*

As we have pointed out, the messiah in Judaism is a human being charged by God to bring about a redeemed world. To consider such a messiah as a god himself in the person of Jesus who has actually arrived on the world scene is not only to contravene the absolute Oneness of the Godhood, but to ignore the conditions on the ground that fulfill the requirements of a messianic age. According to the Jewish tradition, the Messianic era will be one of global peace and harmony, an era free of warfare, strife and hardship (Isaiah 2:4). Indeed, the messianic notion at this early period envisioned the absence of the many ills that inflict personal and collective life. Such a condition hardly prevailed at the time.

More: The Logos in Jewish thought is, as was pointed out above, the *single* God's *word*, i.e., His *will*, the *force* with which He created the world and humans. To personify that word/will/force in the person of a human being is to fashion a concrete element independent of, subordinate to the One God, is to compromise the heart of the monotheistic notion—the absolute Oneness of the Deity. Such a view cannot help but be jettisoned by Judaism. Yet more: The Holy Spirit (*Ruah Hakodesh*) is the intangible yet very real power (another way of articulating God's will) in fashioning the world of nature and human beings. Here too, to personalize and concretize this notion and transmute it into yet another independent element of the Godhood is not only a questionable theological "stretch," but another dilution of Monotheism's core. Such is the view of normative Judaism.

Further, as we have sought to demonstrate throughout this book, the Jewish theological journey with regard to Monotheism had been to establish with undiminished fervor the unambiguous singularity of the Godhood. "Hear O Israel, The Lord our God, The Lord is one" asserts that there can be no other gods. "Revere only The Lord your God and worship Him alone, and swear only by His name" asserts that this dictum was to be acted out in the ongoing life of the people. "I, The Lord your God, brought you out of the land of Egypt, the house of bondage: You shall have no other gods besides me" heads the Ten Commandments. Such is the heritage of the Mosaic age.

And then there are the Prophets, who established the idea of God's Oneness as never before: "I am the first and I am the last, and there is no god but me" (Isaiah 44:6), "understand that I am He; before Me no god was formed, and after Me none shall exist" (43:10), "I am God. Ever since day was, I am He" (43:13). And, as indicated, the Rabbis strongly maintained the absolute soleness of the Deity via consistent ritual observance, study and prayer, as well as via ideational dicta.

## Direct Jewish Reaction to Early Christians

According to George Foote Moore, "It is evident that gentile Christianity, with its Supreme God, the Father, and its Son of God, creator and savior, was founded on a doctrine of two powers."[30] The Rabbis evinced great concern about this doctrine which they saw as a defection from strict monotheistic principle. There was the belief in Zoroastrianism that persisted in the early Christian era that there were *shtay reshuyot*, "two powers" at work in the world: God is the author of good only; as for the evil in the world another power must be assumed, for it is questioned: how can a good God allow so much evil to exist? Some other divine power must be responsible for such evil.

Much controversy and polemic about this subject prevailed among the Rabbis and Christian apologists. This was especially the case in Caesarea in the third century, an important Christian center of learning. As we have pointed out in our chapter 4, the midrashic tome, the Sifré, commented on Deuteronomy 32:39, "See then that I (*ani*), I (*ani*) am He; there is no God beside Me. I deal death and give life. I wound and I heal: none can deliver from my hand." Christians seized on the *double ani* in this text, claiming that it showed that two gods were at work in human affairs. To this the Midrash responds that the verse itself asserts that "there is no God beside Me" and that no other power can bring life or death, inflict injury or confer benefits. It then cites Isaiah 44:6, "Thus said The Lord, the King of Israel, their Redeemer, The Lord of Hosts: I am the first and I am the last, and there is no God like me."[31]

Other Midrashim counter the Christian argument that two powers gave the law and two powers created the world based on the apparent plural form *elohim* in Genesis 1:1. To this the answer given was that the *verb* of which *elohim* is the subject is in the singular form (*bara*).[32] And then, with specific reference to the Christian notion of God incarnated in Jesus, the Midrash comments on Exodus 20:2, "I am The Lord your God," says Rabbi Abbahu: A human king may be king though he has a father or a brother or a son. God says, I am not so. "I am first" for I have no father; "and I am last," for I have no brother; "and besides Me there is no god," for I have no son.[33] Finally, the Talmud asserts, "If a man says to you, 'I am a god,' he is lying; 'I am the Son of Man,' he will end by being sorry for it; 'I am going up to heaven,' he will not fulfill what he said."[34]

## CONCLUSION

We have come full circle regarding the basic fissure separating Judaism from Christianity concerning the God idea. For Christians the deity is composed of *three* elements—"*One God, the* Father from whom are all things and for whom we exist, and *one Lord, Jesus* Christ through whom are all things and through whom we exist" (I Corinthians 8:6), joined by *the Holy* Spirit. Judaism, by contrast, insists on the absolute *Oneness* of God. This represents the specific difference about the Godhood between Christianity as a religion distinct from polytheistic heathenism on the one hand, and strictly monotheistic Judaism on the other.[35]

Question: Did this basic theological condition hold up without alteration in any way in subsequent Jewish theological history? Our next chapter deals with this question.

*Chapter 6*

# Was Monotheism Compromised? The Divinity and the Human Being

## *The Breath of God*

The Lord God formed man from the dust of the earth, and He blew into his nostrils the breath of life, and man became a living being (Gen. 2:7).

Does this mean only that God created man, that He gave him life?

Or does it mean that God actually breathed something of Himself (of His own breath) into man?

If the latter meaning is the case, does that compromise the absolute Oneness of the Deity?

### THE THESIS OF THIS CHAPTER

The notion of God's transcendence—His total independence of the world and of humanity—and simultaneously of God's immanence—His abiding presence in the world and humanity—are, in essence, fundamentally the same basic notion. That is to say, God's immanence, important, of course, as the notion is in Jewish thought, means that we can know God only via His works, the manifestations of Him in the world, but never as He is in Himself. He, in His essential nature, is wholly apart from the world, which is another way of affirming His transcendence. This represents the normative Jewish notion about God and the world. The chasm between the Deity, as such, and humanity abides.

With the burgeoning of the mystical realm of thinking in Judaism and especially of the Kabbalah, God's relationship to the world and human beings is seen in a different light—a non-normative light. This points to the idea that *divinity does somehow inhabit the human being—a "Divine Spark" lodges in a person.* Thus, the chasm, the abyss, is bridged.

*The inclusion of this chapter here is because the notion it projects seems to hint at compromising the absolute singularity of the Deity that is limned and stressed throughout this book.*

## The Normative Notion: God's Transcendence and His Immanence

### Transcendence

According to normative Judaic thought, a fundamental principle about the relationship of God to man is that God is God and man is man, which is to say that they are totally separate of each other. The Bible states this: "The Lord formed man from the dust of the earth, and He blew into his nostrils the breath of life, and man became a living being" (JPS translation of the Hebrew, *nefesh*, soul, is: "being").[1] This means that God *created* man, that He gave life to a human being. God is God as He is in Himself and the "soul" (in this context another word for man, a human being) is His creation, an absolutely independent entity from the Godhood. The proverb has it this way: "The candle of The Lord is the soul of man."[2] This means that the soul of man was "kindled" by God. God made it possible for man to live. Ecclesiastes says this: "The dust returns to dust as it was and the spirit returns to God who gave it."[3] This means that God *gave* man his spirit, his life, and when man dies, God takes it back, as it were, which is to say that God acquiesced in man's demise.

Indeed, normative Judaism never forgot the chasm which separated the transcendent Deity from His creatures. The transcendence of God lies at the foundation of Jewish religion. The vital statement about this was made by the prophet Isaiah when he declared, "Holy, holy, holy is The Lord of hosts."[4] The term "holy" means *set apart*. God is radically apart or different from the reality we know. He is, to use a term suggested by the theologian Rudolf Otto, the *wholly other*. He is *sui generis*, incomparable. "To whom will you liken me, that I should be equal, says the Holy One?"[5] The High Holy Days version of the Kaddish prayer has it that "the Blessed Holy One is infinitely beyond all the praises, hymns, songs, adorations and consolations which human beings can utter." God transcends every worldly and human phenomenon. He is unconditioned by any outside forces, independent of all beside Himself. "Thus says The High and Lofty One who inhabits eternity whose name is Holy: 'I dwell in the high and holy place.'"[6] And when human beings seek to understand the essential nature of this God, Maimonides emphasizes that such knowledge of Him is beyond human grasp, that "in the contemplation of

His essence, our comprehension and knowledge prove insufficient; and in the endeavor to extol Him in words, all our efforts in speech are mere weakness and failure."[7]

*Immanence*

Alongside the notion of God's transcendence, the normative Jewish tradition affirms His immanence. The two notions tend in opposite directions yet stand side by side in Jewish religious thought. Thus the Prophet Jeremiah asserts, "Am I a God at hand, says The Lord, and not a God afar off? Can a man hide himself in secret places so that I cannot see him? says The Lord. Do I not fill heaven and earth?"[8] And then there is the full utterance of the Prophet Isaiah quoted above. After proclaiming, "Holy, Holy, Holy is the Lord of Hosts," he adds, "His glory fills the whole earth."[9] Yet more is the expanded context of Isaiah 57:15 quoted above, "For thus says The High and Lofty One . . . I dwell in the high and holy place, and also with him who is of a contrite and humble spirit." With these assertions the notion of God's immanence—His pervading presence in the world—is added to the belief in His transcendence, His definite apartness from the world and from humans. And, we need to emphasize, this notion of God's immanence was firmly maintained by the Rabbis as well: "As the soul fills the body, God fills the world."[10]

What prompted this emphasis the Jewish tradition places on God's immanence in addition to His transcendence? A God of absolute transcendence is an intolerable construct for the yearning human heart. His immanence, on the other hand, means that He is very much involved in the life of mankind. He is a *personal* God. He is not impervious to human prayer and supplication, so removed from the world of mankind as to be deemed inaccessible. Human beings yearn for personal, direct connections with the Deity, for response to their insistent needs and aspirations. Faith in God's immanence in the human world, His presence and availability, provide man with the conviction that God so responds. As the Psalmist expressed it,

> Whither shall I go from Thy spirit?
> Or whither shall I flee from Thy presence?
> If I ascend up to Heaven, Thou art there,
> If I make my bed in the nether-world, behold, Thou art there.
> If I take the wings of the morning,
> And dwell in the uttermost parts of the sea,
> Even there would Thy hand lead me
> And Thy right hand would hold me.[11]

The Rabbis proclaimed that though God is above the world, dwelling in remote exaltation, He is not inaccessible to humanity.

> Let a man go into the synagogue and take his place behind the pulpit and pray in an undertone, and God will give ear to his prayer, as it is said: Hannah was speaking within herself, only her lips moved, but her voice was not audible, and God gave ear to her prayer; and so he does to all his creatures, as it is said, A prayer of the afflicted when he covers his face and pours out his thought before The Lord, is as when a man utters his thought in the ear of his fellow, and he hears him. Can you have a God nearer than this who is as near to his creatures as mouth to ear?[12]

And so, according to normative Jewish thought, God is both wholly separate from, yet fully accessible to, man. Indeed, He is "transcendent" *and* "immanent" simultaneously.

## The Problem—And Efforts to Reconcile the Two Notions

It has always seemed to this writer that the mantra of the tradition about God being both transcendent and immanent simultaneously is problematic. That, on the one hand, God is totally apart, unknowable, beyond human imagination and, on the other hand and at the very same time, present and accessible to humans, seems to be a construct that is inherently self-contradictory. *How can that which is absolutely unknown be known?* The various passages quoted above about God being both out of and in the world in tandem seem to be mere assertions without any explanation about how they logically fit together as a compelling theological notion. It appears that the tradition simply was compelled to affirm both notions and has left it at that.

Efforts have been made to reconcile the two notions about God's nature by a number of contemporary thinkers. They have done so by claiming to discern *within* the Deity's transcendence His imminence. Which is to say that *though God is, indeed, transcendent, there is something about His nature which reveals His imminence—His "personality" and His pervasive presence in the world of the here and now*. It is this "human" characteristic and the wondrous character of the world God has created which is evidence of this. These efforts reveal a real struggle to grasp the relationship between the twin elements of the Deity's nature. They have proven to be difficult tasks indeed. What follows are some of the probes, and the problems they present.

1) *A personal God: Isadore Epstein* begins his effort by asserting that the whole Jewish religion revolves around the acceptance of the existence of a

"personal God." It is true, says Epstein, that the term "personality" is totally inadequate to describe the Deity, nonetheless, the notion must be maintained. Why? Epstein writes: "This must be insisted upon, as we could not, as persons, have any relationship, such as that which constitutes the essence of all religious belief, with an impersonal force."[13] An impersonal God who is too far away would have no relevance to human life. This argument goes something like this: *What would be the point of our prayers, for example, if we did not believe that God listens and responds to them? And so, God is personal and accessible. He is relevant to our lives because we humans need him to be!* Hardly a convincing argument.

Epstein continues with a more serious discussion about a personal God. He contends that those moderns who recoil from the thought of ascribing personality to God are mistaken because they confuse "personality" with "corporeality," the physical,

> What imparts to a mind personality is not the hands, the eyes, the brain, but the power to organize, direct and unify the various component parts of the body into one single purpose and goal. Personality is mind become autonomous—mind become emancipated from bondage to the body. If the universe has a mind, that mind would then be more, rather than less, personal than our own. For it would have more, rather than less, unity and organicity.[14]

What Epstein is saying here is that via human personality, we get a glimpse of the personality of God. This by analogy: even as humans evince personality by the way the mind brings together all the individual parts of the body, forging thereby an organic unit with one single purpose and goal, *so does God evince personality by virtue of how wondrously the world works—the world created and fashioned by God.* It is apparent that Epstein's argument for God as person is, in essence, no more than the traditional argument for God as the Designer of the world who we can know through His work, the manifestation of which is the world's wondrous organic nature. This tells us nothing about God as such, about His essential nature.

2) *The Personality of God: Louis Jacobs* takes his turn in seeking to grasp what is meant by the personality of God. Recognizing the inherent difficulty of the issue, he nonetheless writes,

> To describe God as a "Person" is to be sure totally inadequate in describing His true nature. *But there is personality in the universe, we are "persons," and it is very difficult to see how this can have emerged from the workings of a blind force.* Human personality is the highest thing we know in the universe. Man is greater than the most powerful force outside him in the universe in that he has an intellect and a moral sense. The beauty of Niagara Falls, for instance, is in

the eye of the human beholder. He can love and think and practice justice and they can do none of these. While learning the lesson taught by the proponents of the *via negativa* we are still obliged to describe God, if we speak of Him at all, in terms of the highest we know. This has been expressed by saying that God is not less than personal.[15]

Jacobs' point: via human personality we get a glimpse of the personality of God. Even as humans evince personality via their possession of intellect and a moral sense, by their capacity to love and think and practice justice, so is God personal in that these elements characterize the world He has created. Here again, the argument about God's character is derived from His works, the existence of manifestations of His activity in the world He has fashioned. It tells us nothing about God's essential nature.[16]

3) *God in History: Robert Gordis*, in his chapter "God and the Historic Process,"[17] points out how God has been discovered in history as revealed especially by the Prophets of Israel. This is similar to discovering God via the evidence of order and design in the universe fashioned by its Creator. The Deity as He is in Himself, His essential nature is not seen in Gordis' exposition. Rather it is manifestations of Him in the experience of people in historical time which is the way man can know God. Thus when, according to the ancient Hebrew historians and Prophets, "men found a pattern and a direction in the ebb and flow of events, a recognition that there was an underlying meaning to human events," they discerned in this the hand of God. When men detected the law of consequences rooted in the universe, compassion and mercy, justice and righteousness, grace and forgiveness inherent in the very structure of the world about them, they viewed this all as the handwork of a power, not human, who bestrides the world. Hence, in a word, man can and does know God, not as He is in Himself, but as He manifests Himself in the history of the world.

4) *The Limits of Knowledge of God*: *Ben Zion Bokser* cites the *Yigdal* hymn in the traditional Jewish prayer book as a summation of the limits of man's knowledge of God.

> O come, the living God adore,
> He is, He was, He will be ever more.
> His Oneness is a thing of mystery,
> No man can fathom His true unity;
> He is without a body's form or frame,
> *No mortal lips His essence can proclaim.*[18]

Indeed, Bokser contends that the only positive knowledge we may have of God is indirect. It is knowledge derived from His work. By understanding what God has planted into the world we can gain a certain knowledge of Him who has fashioned these, even as a person's art or writing is a reflection of his nature, a clue to his beliefs and values. Read the following Bokser statement which constitutes the core of this perspective.

> All the characterizations of God in our various religious writings must be understood in this sense—*they are really characterizations of His "work," not of His essence*. We say He is merciful because His work shows a concern for the preservation of each creature. We say He is gracious because His gifts are given us freely, without our necessarily deserving them. We say He is just because there is a principle of retribution at work in His world. Violations of the principles which govern existence, whether in the domain of the physical or in the domain of human relations, soon beget destructive consequences.[19]

And then Bokser concludes with this:

> Is *God a person? From all that we have said it is clear that God is not a person.* We speak of Him as though He were a person; we call Him "He," because the qualities of personality are the highest marks of perfection we know. In a figurative sense these qualities are applied to Him, but God is above personality as He is above everything else that is part of the world. A person functions through a physical self; he is finite, temporal, relative in his virtues and excellences. God is wholly other than all this.

This is well expressed in the Hymn of Glory, which is part of our liturgy for the Sabbath and the festivals:

> I will tell of Thy glory
> Though I have not seen Thee,
> I will speak of Thee in similes
> Though I cannot know Thy essence.
> Thou didst reveal a semblance of Thy splendor
> In the mystic visions of Thy servants, the Prophets:
> They envisioned Thy grandeur and Thy might
> From the stupendous work of Thy creation,
> *They speak of Thee not as Thou art*
> *But by inference drawn from Thy handiwork.*[20]

5) *An Upanishad Tale.* This Indian teaching amplifies in telling fashion the thought line of the Jewish Hymn of Glory.

> Bring me the fruit of that banyan tree. Here it is, venerable Sir. Break it. It is broken, venerable Sir. What do you see here? These seeds, exceedingly small. Break one of these, my son. It is broken, venerable Sir. What do you see there? Nothing at all, venerable Sir. The father said: that subtle essence—*that nothing at all*—my dear son, which you do not see there, from that essence this great banyan tree arises. Believe me, my dear son, now that which is the subtle essence in it is all that exists. That is the Truth. That is the Self, and that is you, Svetaketu, my son. Please, venerable Sir, give me further instruction, the son requested. So be it, my dear, the father replied.[21]

What the wise father is saying to his inquiring son is that from a "subtle substance," a "nothing at all," everything has come into being. Yes, you recognize something not human, a creative force at work—God—who is responsible for the tree, but about God Himself you know "nothing at all." He is but a highly elusive "subtle substance," invisible, beyond comprehension.

What emerges from all the above is that God can only be known via manifestations of Him in the world of nature and of humans. This is, of course, no small matter in the sphere of religion; but to claim on behalf of the normative Jewish tradition that such phenomena tells us much, if anything, about God's essential character, that His "immanence" reveals His essential transcendence, is to read into the tradition that which is not there.

*And so, in summary,*

The normative Jewish notion about God's nature is that whether viewed as "transcendent" or "immanent," He is wholly separate from the world and man, and we can never know God as He is in Himself. Indeed, the chasm between the Deity and humanity abides. This leads us to the following section of this chapter.

## The Divinity in Man Notion: What Prompted It?

There has always existed among people of faith a persistent effort to bridge the gap—what some have called the "yawning chasm," between the Creator and His creatures. This effort continued in the face of the traditional Jewish notion of God's transcendence combined with His immanence, which notion, no matter how parsed (as witnessed above), did not satisfy. Yes, "knowing" God via His tremendous works, the wondrous manifestations of Him everywhere in the universe of nature and humanity, was indeed compelling. However, for many spiritual seekers this was not enough to slake the thirst of their deepest yearnings. They sought richer experience with the Divine, more direct and tangible connection. Their tradition on this score, many felt, seemed weak, inchoate, oblique. They needed more. They sought answers to questions such as these: Can human beings truly communicate with a God whom they know only via His works—indirectly? When human beings speak to God in prayer with their hearts and souls, is it a *personal God* who responds to their needs, their yearnings and aspirations, to their continuous praise of Him?

It is to this condition that aspects of the recorded thought and experience of religionists of the past reacted in a variety of ways. We have detailed some of these reactions, to wit: Scripture itself appears to have projected the notion of God's multiplicity, of His concrete appearance to humans. Rabbinic literature has evinced the notion via God's *Shekhina* having, in some sense, concrete form and hence can be visibly grasped by people. Christianity, of course, has brought God down from heaven, as it were, and been incarnated in the man Jesus, who is thus directly accessible to humans. Even the quintessential Jewish rationalists (e.g., Maimonides) alluded to human beings possessing an "Active Intellect" which, in a sense, emanates from God's own "Divine Intellect."

This theological phenomenon morphed "full blown," as it were, in explicit and detailed fashion among the Jewish mystics, beginning with the Kabbalists of the thirteenth century. What they did was to establish a major, albeit non-normative, stream of thought that has endured—not without controversy—until this day. What follows is a depiction of one key facet of the basic notion of man's intimate connection with the Deity—the "Divine Spark" within man.[22]

## A "Divine Spark"—the Non-normative Notion

Note: The analysis that follows is based on the chapter "God and the Soul" in Louis Jacobs' *Religion and the Individual: A Jewish Perspective*, with extensive annotations by the writer of this book.[23]

As we have noted, according to the normative Jewish theological view, God is both transcendent and immanent, which, according to both notions, God as He is in Himself is wholly separate from human beings. There is, however, a significant stream of thought in the Jewish theological realm, *which points to the idea that divinity does somehow inhabit the human being.* Should this be so, then the "chasm" between God and humanity will have been bridged! This is the notion of a "Divine Spark" in man.

## Non-Jewish Sources

The analysis begins with the non-Jewish sources. The belief that there is a special mystical "spark" in man can be seen in western, eastern and Islamic mysticism. Bernard of Clairvaux (1090–1153), the French ecclesiastic, for example, speaks of a small spark of the soul and of God's nearness: "Angels and archangels are within us, but *He* is more truly our own who is not only *with us* but *in us.*" The German theologian and mystic Meister Eckhart (1255–1328) called this spark in man "the house in which God attires Himself." In eastern mysticism the identification of the mystical spark with the divine is frequent. For example, in the Hindu Upanishads we read this: "The All-working, All-wishing, All-smelling, All-tasting One who embraces the universe . . . is the spirit within my heart." Here the soul of man is identical with Brahma, the "absolute" or God, conceived as entirely personal. And in Islamic mysticism the idea appears in the works of the poet Hallaj, who proclaims: "The soul's love of God is God's love of the soul, and that *in loving the soul God loves Himself, for He draws home to Himself that which is in its essence Divine.*" In an ode the poet says: "O my soul, I searched from end to end: I saw in these nought but the Beloved: call me not infidel, O my soul, if I say that *thou thyself art He.*"[24]

## Philo of Alexandria (20 BCE–50 CE)

The notion of something of the Divinity in man in Jewish thought can be seen as early as the first century of the Common Era in the work of Philo, the Jewish philosopher who lived in Alexandria in Egypt, a major settlement of Jews living in the context of the dominant Hellenism of the time. This was the same era during which the New Testament's Paul functioned. One can therefore speculate about a convergence of thinking between the early Christians on this matter with that of Philo.

Philo writes this:

> For the essence or substance of that other soul is divine spirit, as truth vouched for by Moses especially, who in his story of the creation says that *God breathed a breath of life upon the first man* (Genesis 2:7), the founder of our race, into The Lordliest part of the body, the face, where the senses are stationed like bodyguards to the great king, the mind. *And clearly what was then thus breathed was ethereal spirit, even an effulgence of the blessed, thrice blessed nature of the Godhead.*[25]

In another of Philo's works[26] he expands on the idea of the soul being an "effulgence of the blessed nature of the Godhead" by interpreting Genesis 2:7 this way:

> "And God breathed into his (man's) nostrils the breath of life, and man became a living being." "Breathed into," we note, is equivalent to "inspired" or "besouled" the soulless (for God forbid that we should be infected with such

monstrous folly as to think that God employs for inbreathing organs such as mouth and nostrils; for God is not only not in the form of a man, but belongs to no class or kind.)

*Yet* the expression clearly brings out something that accords with nature. For it implies of necessity three things: that which inbreathes, that which receives, and that which is inbreathed. *That which inbreathes is God, that which receives is the mind,* and *that which is inbreathed is the spirit or breath. What, then, do we infer from these premises? A union of the three comes about, as God projects the power that proceeds from Himself through the median breath until it reaches the subject.*

And for what purpose is this but that we may obtain a conception of Him. *For how could the soul have conceived of God had He not inbreathed into it and mightily laid hold of it?* For the mind of man would never have ventured to soar so high as to grasp the nature of God had not God Himself drawn the mind unto Himself (so far as it was possible that the mind of man should be drawn up) and stamped it with the impress of the powers that are in the scope of the mind's understanding.

Thus, according to Philo, the human mind would be incapable of knowing God were it not that God had permitted the abyss between Him and His human creatures to be crossed by infusing the mind with something of Himself. Elsewhere Philo indicates that the gift of a divine part of the soul to Adam is shared by his descendants, although in fainter form. Indeed, *every man with regard to his mind is allied to the Divine Reason having come into being as a copy or fragment or ray of that Blessed Nature.*[27] In the later literature about the "Divine Spark," it, the spark, is frequently limited to Israel. In Philo, however, the more universalistic tendency prevails: *all* of Adam's descendants share in his (Adam's) nature having something of the Divine within man.

While researching further the works of Philo on this subject, this writer examined the volume by David Winston about Philo's theology. Winston expands somewhat on Jacobs' description above. He points to Philo's confidence in the "higher reaches of the human mind in that it rests on the self-assurance of the Platonist in him that the human intellect is intimately related to the Divine Logos, *being an imprint or fragment of that blessed nature. . . . God is the Archetype (the image) of rational existence, while man is a copy and representation.*" Indeed, says Philo, "The human mind is an inseparable portion of the divine and blessed soul for nothing is severed or detached from the divine but only extended."

Winston proceeds to point out that Philo's Greek contemporaries shared the same basic perspective. They too were followers of Plato (428–345 BCE) who posited the classic notion of divine archetypes. Thus, Plutarch, the historian and biographer (46–120 CE), writes, "*The soul of man is a portion or copy of the soul of the universe.*" And further, Plutarch speaks of the soul as not merely a work but also *a part of God* and as having come to be not by his (God's) agency (i.e., separate creative act) *but both from him as source and out of his substance.* Plotinus (205–270 CE) similarly conceives of the souls of humans as emanations from the One as images of that archetype: "Fire produces the heat which comes from it; snow keeps its cold inside itself."

Winston avers, "It is therefore clear that Philo's Platonic perspective allowed him to see the human mind/soul as an outreach of the divine Logos (an aspect of the divinity but also at one with it) which, although in some measure distinct from it, is at the same time a part of it."[28]

## The Rabbinic Literature (50–1290 CE)

According to Louis Jacobs, references to the purity of the soul and its identification with the Deity are to be found in the Rabbinic literature of the period between Philo (50 CE) and the Zohar (1290 CE), the latter to be discussed below. Thus, for example, the Talmud quotes Ecclesiastes 12:7. "The soul returns to God who bestowed it." From this it proceeds to teach that even as the soul was given to man in purity, so is man himself pure, and purity returns to purity.[29] Then there is the Midrash, which points to the soul's heavenly origin, and its returning to its source.[30] In the same vein is the famous Talmudic passage that reads as follows:

> Just as the Holy One, Blessed be He, fills the entire world, so too the soul fills the entire body.
>
> Just as the Holy One, Blessed be He, sees but is not seen, so too does the soul see, but is not seen.
>
> Just as the Holy One, Blessed be He, sustains the entire world, so too the soul sustains the entire boy.
>
> Just as the Holy One, Blessed be He, is pure, so too is the soul pure.
>
> Just as the Holy One, Blessed be He, resides in a chamber within a chamber, in His inner sanctum, so too the soul resides in a chamber within a chamber, in the innermost recesses of the body.
>
> Therefore, that which has these five characteristics, the soul, should come and praise He Who has these five characteristics.[31]

Here the Talmud is comparing the characteristics of man's soul to Divine characteristics. Thus, from this and the above passages, we can but infer identification of man's soul with God Himself.

There are, however, other rabbinic passages that might be so understood. For example, another Midrash says this: Just as a woman of royal lineage who marries a villager is never satisfied with all that her husband provides because she is accustomed to life in the royal palace, so the soul's longings are never satisfied *because it derives from ha-elyonim*, those above. Here we might discern a hint about a person's soul somehow being connected to heavenly-divine souls.[32] The idea that something of the divine (His *Shekhinah*) is manifest in human form and thus resides, as it were, in a human being can be discerned in Midrash *Mishle* to Proverbs 22:29. In this rabbinic text the *Shekhinah stands before God* and pleads successfully on behalf of King Solomon (who would otherwise have been denied a share in the world to come because of his transgressions). "Thus in depicting the *Shekhinah* as standing before God and speaking to Him, the Midrash goes very far in its dramatic and bold *personification*. It draws a clear distinction between God and His *Shekhinah*, which has become a 'persona' different and distinct from God."[33]

As to the classical medieval philosophers such as Abraham Ibn Daud, Maimonides, Gersonides, and Hasdai Crescas, a notion that hints at the connection of a human characteristic with Divinity is the doctrine of the *Active Intellect of man which emanates from* God (is fashioned by God?). With this intellectual capacity man can, through the exercise of his mind via study, grasp metaphysical truth.[34]

> And then there is Ibn Gabirol (11th century CE) who refers to the soul as a *pure radiance from God's glory* . . .
>
> Who can contain Thy might when from the abundance of Thy glory Thou didst create a pure radiance, hewn from the quarry of the Rock, and dug from the mine of Purity?
>
> And on it Thou didst set a spirit of wisdom, and Thou didst call it the Soul.
>
> Thou didst fashion it from the flames of fire of the Intelligence, and its spirit is as a fire burning in it.
>
> Thou didst send it into the body to serve it.[35]

While the above data is mixed as to the presence of divinity in human form (and by extension the notion of a divine spark hidden in the recesses of the human psyche), it does appear legitimate to claim that hints in that direction are to be found in some areas of rabbinic literature.

## The Zohar: The "Bible" of Jewish Mysticism (ca. 1290 CE)

Here the doctrine of the "Divine Spark" comes into full view in Jewish thought. The Zohar, generally considered to have been composed by the Spanish rabbi and Kabbalist, Moses de Leon (1250–1305), states clearly that the highest part of the soul—the *neshama*—comes from the world of the *sefirot* which emanates from the *Ein Sof* (God as He is in Himself).

> Rabbi Judah began his discourse by quoting the verse "Let every soul praise The Lord" (Psalm 150:6). We have been taught that all souls are derived from that Holy Body and they animate human beings. *From which place are they derived? From the place that* is called *Yah*. Which place is that? said Rabbi Judah. It is written: "How manifold are Thy works, O Lord. In wisdom hast Thou made them all" (Psalm 104:24). We have been taught that all things are contained in that wisdom the spring of which flows into thirty-two paths; all things above and below are contained within it.[36]

Now, in the Zoharic scheme, there are ten *sefirot* (i.e., Divine emanations, powers, often visualized as "rays"). The three highest of these are *Keter*, crown, i.e., the Divine Will; *Hokhma*, i.e., Divine Wisdom; and *Bina*, i.e., Divine Understanding. In the above passage man's soul is depicted as deriving ultimately from *Hokhma*, Divine Wisdom. This means much more than that God in His wisdom created man's soul. The sefira of wisdom is, in Zohar's thought, an integral aspect of the Deity. Although some Kabbalists view the sefirot as separate, distinct from God, *most classical Kabbalistic thinkers see them as an organic part of the Divine essence whose complex interactions with each other are merely indications of the One God's inner dynamism*. It is true that these ten sefirot relate to each other in ways that appear to disclose a degree of individual existence, yet they never attain the stature of independent entities. In fact, Kabbalistic texts warn against praying to them as if they were distinct gods.[37] In any event, since in this Zoharic construct the sefira *Hokhma* is viewed as an organic part of the *Ein Sof* (God's essence) and hence partakes of inherent divinity, and the soul is derived from *Hokhma*, the consequence is clear: *the soul of man is derived from God Himself*. Man harbors divinity within.

It should come as no surprise that some Kabbalists viewed this matter differently. The very fact that the mainline mystics acknowledged that the sefirot appeared to disclose a degree of individual existence and that they warned against praying to them shows that, for these religionists, something untraditional was afoot among Jews at the time. Indeed, the non-traditionalists *stressed the divide between the Deity and the sefirot*. They saw them not as wholly organic parts of the *Ein Sof*, the holy other, but rather as independent manifestations of God's essence. To be sure, for them, the sefirot partake of divinity as having emanated from the *Ein Sof*, but they were also, in significant measure, separate entities.

This is illustrated by a striking passage in the Zohar (*Teruma 135a*) in which the sefira *Shekhina,* who is feminine in gender, unites with the sefira *Yesod*, who is masculine by nature.[38] Furthermore, the sefirah *Binah* is pictured as the womb, the Divine Mother, who receives the seed, the point of the sefira *Hokhma*; she conceives and gives birth to the lower sefirot, including *Hesed*, *Gevurah*, and *Tiferet*. The light and power of these and the other sefirot are channeled through *Yesod* to the last sefira, *Malkhut*, also known as *Shekhina*. The latter, the daughter of *Binah*, the Divine Mother, becomes the bride of *Tiferet*. The union of *Shekhinah* and *Tiferet* constitutes the focus of religious life. Human righteous action stimulates *Yesod* and brings about the union of the divine couple. Human marriage symbolizes and actualizes divine marriage. Shabbat eve is the weekly celebration of the cosmic wedding, and the ideal time for human lovers to unite. *These kinds of interaction clearly imply distinct divine identities, independent of their Creator.*

Moreover, in the sixteenth century, the Kabbalist Isaac Luria and his school further emphasized the independence of the sefirot from their Source. Thus, for example, according to Luria, fragments of the Godhood were exiled into the physical world at the moment the world was created. These fragments constituted sparks of the Divine light that is God. The sparks are surrounded by *kelipot* (husks) and were embedded in the material world. The sparks can be reunited with their Creator as a result of the Jews' observance of the Torah.[39] Here, too, the *Shekhinah* represented by the sparks (as did the other sefirot, according to Luria) appear to have independent existence, were not always an integral part of their Creator. To be sure, the mainline Kabbalists, Matt writes, "continually insist that these sefirot were actually figures of speech and not to be taken literally; they are merely symbols of a spiritual reality beyond normal comprehension . . . nevertheless, the prominent mythological character of the (sefirotic) system cannot be denied."[40]

*From all that we have depicted above, we can say this about our "Divine Spark in Man" subject: whether the sephirot are integral to or independent of the Godhood, since they, in any case, partake of divinity (since they emanate from God Himself), and the soul derives from that divinity, a spark of God lodges in the human being. Such is the take of the Kabbalah, mainline and untraditional.*

Parenthetically, it is interesting to note the reading of the Luria passage above that "the sparks can be reunited within their Creator as a result of the Jews' observance of the Torah." Sommer adds to this: "The reason for the commandments is none other than to bring about redemption of the Divine." Daniel Matt put it this way: "The sparks became trapped in material existence. The human task is to liberate, or raise, these sparks to restore them to

Divinity. This process of *tikkun* (repair or mending) is accomplished through living a life of holiness. All human actions either promote or impede *tikkun olam* (repair of the world), thus hastening or delaying the arrival of the Messiah."[41]

This is the meaning of the various preliminary meditations of intent I personally recited throughout my youth and later prior to various ritual acts such as before the esrog blessing at sukkot, before the motzi blessing at the Passover seder, before the Kapparot (asking for forgiveness) ceremony on the eve of Yom Kippur. The meditation reads as follows:

> *L'shem yikhud Kudsha Brikh Hu ush'khintay al y'day ha-hu tamir v'ne-elam, b'shem kol Yisrael.*
>
> (The mitzvah I am about to perform) is for the purpose of *uniting the Holy One, Blessed be He, with His Shekhina,* because it (the *Shekhina)* has been hidden and out of sight. (And this is done) in the name of (or together with) all Israel.

This meditation is meant to remind its reciter that one's task in the world is to practice the mitzvot, to study Torah, to pray with focus, and to perform good for others. For these are ways to bring about the reunion of God's *Shekhina* with God himself—a true union of the Divine, affirming His Oneness.

## An Echo of Christianity

Another matter that should not come to us as a surprise: the sefirot concept as an adumbration of the Christian God idea. We have pointed to the contention that divinity seems to have appeared in multiple places and varied tangible forms—a phenomenon that has been found in scripture itself, in rabbinic literature, in Philo, in Christianity and in the Kabbalah. Indeed, the notion has moved about—back and forth—in many directions. So, too, do the Kabbalistic sefirot, as we have depicted them above, echo the Christian notion of the Trinity, the apparent multiplicity of the deity that Kabbalah implies and Christianity appears to accept.

Thus, Abraham Abulafia, the iconoclastic Sicilian Kabbalist born in Spain in 1240, who was considered a most important, albeit complex, figure in the history of Jewish mysticism, noted that some adherents of the sefirot have outdone Catholic adherents to the Trinity, turning God into ten![42] Kaufman Kohler pointed to Abulafia as the first to claim linkage between Kabbalah and the Trinity.[43] And a major seventeenth century Jewish intellectual, Leon de Modena, made a similar contention. According to Yaakov Dweck in a recent book about Modena's writings, with specific reference to the latter's opus, *Ari Nohem*,

> Kabbalists maintained that belief in the sefirot constituted a crucial element of Jewish faith and branded as heretics anyone who denied their centrality to Judaism. Modena repudiated this claim and leveled a severe countercharge of his own: after an examination of the sefirot as a concept, he concluded that it pointed to a plurality within God similar to the Christian doctrine of the Trinity.[44]

Another seventeenth-century figure, the highly regarded Kabbalist Shabbetai Sheftel Horowitz, noted the strong objections to his notion that viewed man's soul as being derived from God Himself. Horowitz' critics had accused him of implying, as did Modena, God being more than One.

And then there is Rabbi Shneur Zalman of Ladi, the 18th-century founder of the Habad movement within Hassidism, who posited that the soul of man "is an actual portion of God from above, *mamish*, literally" (*Tanya*, chapter 2). Though denied, of course, one can understand the claim of some that this envisions something of the Deity in human form moving about the human world. Indeed, Gershom Scholem, the master of Kabbalah studies in our time, asserts that despite the heroic efforts of various Kabbalistic ideologues to maintain the unity of God and avoid the danger of postulating Divine plurality, this has remained a problem for the doctrine of monotheism. Said Scholem,

> It is impossible to avoid the conclusion that this problem was from the beginning unsolvable. . . . The whole of theosophical (i.e., mystical theology) Kabbalism reflects a very ancient heritage of the soul, and it would be too much to say that this mythical heritage has everywhere been successfully integrated into the doctrine of monotheism (*Major Trends*, p. 225).

## Nahmanides (1195–1270 CE)

This highly influential Spanish rabbi, philosopher and Kabbalist, in his commentary to the Pentateuch, also articulated the notion of divinity in man. On the classic verse Genesis 2:7, "Then The Lord formed man of the dust of the ground, *and breathed into his nostrils the breath of life*, and man became a living soul," Nahmanides articulates an interpretation in the spirit of the Kabbalah that bears remarkable similarities with Philo's interpretation of the same verse.[45]

> This verse alludes to the exaltedness of the human soul, its essence and its mystical source. For it mentions God's full name (*The Lord Elohim*, The Lord God) in conjunction with it (i.e., the soul) and says: *Kee Hu nafah "b'apav nishmat*

*hayyim*," that "He (God) blew into his (man's) nostrils the soul (the breath) of life." This is to inform us that this soul did not come to man from the physical elements as in Genesis 1:26, nor from the angels as in Genesis 2:1. Rather, it is from *ruah Hashem Hagadol, mipiv daat utvunah (Proverbs 2:6)*, "The spirit of the Great God from whose mouth comes knowledge and understanding" (Proverbs 2:6). *Ki hanofayh b'apay aher mi-nishmato yitayno bo*," *"For when someone blows into someone else's nostrils, he gives him of his own breath."* This is what is said in Job 32:8, *v'nishmat shaddai t'vinaym*, "and it is the breath of the Almighty that gives them understanding."[46]

From this passage, says Jacob, it is clear that Nahmanides is stressing that man's soul comes from God Himself and is referring to the Kabbalistic doctrine that the soul comes from the Sefira *Binah*, divine understanding, as an emanation from God. Indeed, according to Nahmanides, there is a portion of the Divine in the soul of man.

## Bahya Ben Asher (1255–1340 CE)

This Bible commentator who lived in Saragossa, Spain, followed Nahmanides in interpreting scripture from the perspective of the Kabbalah. [47]

> That the soul, after its departure from the body, is immortal is stated in Genesis 2:7, which calls the *nishmat hayyim* "the soul of life," namely, a soul hewn out of the Source of life, *for the soul is hewn out of the Source of the Divine wisdom* (i.e., the Sefira *Hohma*, an emanation of God Himself). . . . Solomon in Ecclesiastes 3:19 says: "man's pre-eminence above the beast is nothing," and states that the pre-eminence of man over the beast is by virtue of that which is called *Nothing* (i.e., God), which is to say that by virtue of man's rational soul which derives from the Sefira *Hohma*.
>
> Hence, Genesis 2:7 speaks of God breathing into man's nostrils that we might understand the foundation (the root) of the soul and its most elevated state *since it emanates from the Holy Spirit*. It is for this reason that the soul is compared to The Holy One, Blessed be He, in five matters (*Berahot 10a*). A (Greek) sage observes: "Know yourselves and you will know God."

Indeed, Bahya understood scripture through the prism of Jewish mystical thought pointing to Divinity embedded in the soul of man.

## Menasseh ben Israel (1604–1657 CE)

Portuguese rabbi and Kabbalist, diplomat and publisher drew from the ideas of Nahmanides and Bahya in his treatise on the soul.[48] Referring to Genesis 2:7 he observes that this verse calls attention to *the spiritual and elevated nature of the soul which emanates from the Holy Spirit*—the very words used by Bahya. It is as if "The Holy One, blessed be He, as it were, touched the formless lump of Adam and blew the soul into it, thereby imparting to man some of the divine wisdom (the *Hohma* Sefira)." The souls of all other animals were created together with their bodies, but man's soul, being divine, was infused into him after his body had been created from the dust ... those who "prepare savouries" (i.e., rather fanciful comments to scripture) are quoted by Menasseh in pointing out that two of the letters of the word for soul, *neshama,* are the same as those in the word for heaven, *shamayim,* to hint at the divine origin of the soul.

## Hayyim Vital (1545–1620 CE)

Rabbi and Kabbalist in Safed and the foremost disciple of Isaac Luria, Vital recorded his master's teachings and following his (Vital's) death his writings spread and had a powerful impact on various circles throughout the Jewish world. Vital elaborated on the theme of the divine soul.[49] The true man, says Vital, is not the body for this is known in Scripture as the "flesh of man." The pure soul is the real man, using the body as its garment. As a result of Adam's sin there came about a mixture of good and evil in all things so that *even the divine soul, hewn from the four Divine elements represented by the four letters of the Tetragrammaton,* became surrounded by an evil soul deriving from the forces of impurity and known as the evil inclination.

Now the limbs of the physical body are garments for both the pure divine soul and for the impure evil soul. Thus when man uses his bodily limbs for sin he adds fuel to the forces of the impure soul. On the other hand, when he uses his limbs to perform good deeds, these nourish and sustain the pure divine soul enabling it to gain the upper hand over the unclean evil soul.

Vital proceeds to elaborate on the relationship of the soul, as described above, to the "upper world."[50]

> The greatness of man's soul has been described for it is *a great light born of the light of the sefirot themselves.* This is the meaning of "you are children of The Lord your God."[51] For *the children are in the category of a son who is completely attached to the father from whom he is descended.* This is the mystery behind the saying that the Patriarchs are the "Heavenly Chariot" carrying the light of the *sefirot* which ride above without the mediation of any other light. Yet more: this is the meaning of the verse, "As the girdle clings to the loins of a man, so have I, The Lord, caused to cleave to Me the whole house of Israel."[52]

And so, from this we see that Vital affirms the notion of the divine in the soul of man. More: as in the case of many of the Kabbalists, he sees Israel's role as central in the divine-human soul scheme based, as it is, on the notion that Israel on earth mirrors the heavenly pattern.

## Elijah de Vidas (1518–1592 CE)

This prominent Safed mystic was a disciple of both Moses Cordovero, the head of the mystic school of Safed and of his successor, the famed Ari, Rabbi Isaac Luria. De Vidas treats in elaborate detail the doctrine of the Divine Spark in man, and specifically that such an actual spark (*a nitzutz*) of the Deity is contained in the human being. De Vidas writes,

> Souls are flaming threads drawn down below from on high, their vitality stemming constantly from their sources. Death is caused by God drawing up to Himself the thread by which the soul is bound to Him, just as the scent of an apple is drawn away when one smells its fragrance. This is why Scripture (Deuteronomy 32:9) says, "For the portion of The Lord is His people, Jacob the lot of His inheritance." *The soul of an Israelite is an actual portion of the Deity*—taking the word "portion" not in the sense of a part *belonging* to God, but to mean a part *of* God.[53]

Jacobs proceeds to explain De Vidas. This does not mean, however, that there is any kind of separateness or division in God, but rather that *the source of the soul on high is a part of God. Souls inhabiting individual bodies are naturally separate entities, but in their source in God they are one with Him.* "For the portion of The Lord is with Him" (read *immo*—with Him—for *ammo*—His people) which means that God's portion of the soul which is Divine is with man; it is part of God's being with His "branches" here below. Hence this verse in Deuteronomy that speaks of Jacob as God's lot (*hevel*) can also mean "rope" of His inheritance, for *the soul and God are united like the strands of which a rope is constituted.*

Furthermore, the illustration of a rope is given to denote that the soul, even after its descent into the body, is still attached to God in that one end of the "rope" is in God's hands while the other inhabits the body. "The meaning of 'the love of God' and the 'cleaving' to Him is that man attaches himself to God by means of this link, *binding himself to the root of his soul which is attached to God.* Blessed be He." Just as man's soul loves his body to which it is joined and which is the body's source of life, so should man love God with whom his soul is united.

## Shabbetai Sheftel Horowitz (1561–1619 CE)

A native of Prague, a practicing physician and a highly regarded student of Kabbalah, Shabbetai Horowitz considered Moses Cordovera, the major Kabbalist, to be his chief teacher. Horowitz authored a famous book[54] at the beginning of which he writes this:

> It is known that the souls of the people of Israel are "a portion of God from above."[55] The verse, "For the portion of The Lord is His people"[56] hints at this. The term "portion" is to be taken literally. A portion separated from something is in every way like the thing from which it has been taken, the thing being the whole and the total which is naturally greater than the part separated thereof. But in essence the whole and the part are identical. In the same way *there is no difference or distinction between the soul of man and God*, except that God is the whole. He is the all-embracing light, the infinite, unending great light, whereas the soul is a portion and a spark separated from the great light. As King Solomon says, "the spirit of man is the candle of The Lord."[57] *He means to say that man's soul is a candle, a spark deriving from God's light.*

Clearly Horowitz follows in the footsteps of his Kabbalah predecessors: Cordovera, Vital, de Vidas and others. He is particularly noted for the special prominence he gives to the notion of the "Divine Spark," placing it, as he does, at the very beginning of his chief book.

Horowitz was quite conscious of the provocative character of his notion of Divinity residing in a human being as a compromise of God's total Oneness. And so he added a cautionary note to his readers warning them not to jump to conclusions about a complex and difficult theme. He wrote this:

> O student of this work, be not astonished at the idea; for my master teacher Rabbi Moses Cordovera has written even more than this in his holy *Pardes*[58] where he remarks, "The Patriarchs are more elevated than the *Sefirot* for they are not 'limbs' but are Divinity Itself in Its extension to creatures here below." *You see, that the master states explicitly that the Patriarchs are Divinity Itself.*

Horowitz then goes on to ask his readers to read through his entire work section by section in order to fully grasp his meaning on this matter.

As soon as the *Shefa Tal* was published it was widely acclaimed as a basic Kabbalistic textbook. However, the fears of the author himself about the notion of the divine character of man's soul were not unfounded. Soon fierce protests erupted which provoked Horowitz to write another book, *Nishmat Shabbetai Halevi*[59] designed to remove misconceptions about his earlier work.

In this new work the author reacts to the objections to his ideas emanating from many quarters involving his own sons, pupils, colleagues and teachers.

And then he himself states the objections: all Kabbalists agree that the infinite *Ein Sof*, the ultimate Deity, has no other parts or divisions; if then one says that every Jewish soul is a part of God, it must follow that God Himself has numerous parts, and this is as great an offense against the Oneness of God as is the Christian doctrine of the Trinity. Further every Jewish child is taught to praise God for *creating* his soul; thus if the soul is created, how can it be a portion of the Creator?

Horowitz proceeds to respond to these criticisms. At first, he does not acknowledge error on his part citing five great authorities for his contention about divinity in man—Moses himself, Rabbi Simeon ben Yohai, the traditionally reputed author of the Zohar, Nahmanides, Elijah de Vidas and Hayyim Vital. However, presumably the pressure of his critics induced Horowitz to alter his notion somewhat saying now that he never meant to assert that the Divine Spark in man is derived from the *Ein Sof*, from God Himself, but rather from one of the sefirot, one of God's emanations—the sefira of wisdom, an aspect of God's self-disclosure. Of course, Horowitz emphasizes, God is known to Himself alone; of Him nothing can be discerned or postulated. However, of the sefirot one can speak; the idea does not compromise God's Oneness, degenerate into a form of highly objectionable dualism. Indeed, there is a basic unity of the *Ein Sof* and the sefirot. It is like water poured into bottles of various colors which partakes of the color of the bottles without itself suffering change; or the human soul which is one and yet possesses various characteristics; or the multi-colored flames proceeding from one glowing coal. In this way Horowitz parried his critics.[60]

It is, nonetheless, fair to claim, Jacobs asserts, that the sefira doctrine Horowitz invokes here comes perilously close to compromising the absolute Oneness of God. This is because the very emphasis of the sefirot being at one with *En Sof* imparts to them inherent divinity. Thus to assert that the human soul's divinity stems from a sefira is asserting that it is rooted in the Godhead itself. Indeed, Gershom Scholem asserts, "The sefirot of Jewish mystical theology have an existence of their own; they form combinations, they illuminate each other, they ascend and descend. They are far from being static. What we have here is something like a real process of life in God." Hence, to posit the independent character of such phenomena and at the same time see them as being at one with the *En Sof*—the Divinity itself—is to posit independent phenomena as divine, and this appears to contravene the basic monotheistic doctrine. As we have indicated previously, Scholem sums up this perplexing issue: "The Zohar, indeed the whole of Kabbalistic mystical ideology, reflects a very ancient heritage of the soul, and it would be too much to say that this mystical heritage has everywhere been successfully integrated into the doctrine of Monotheism.[61]

And so, it appears that the contents of Horowitz' initial *Shefa Tal* might well claim "the last word" on this subject invoking, as he does, Moses, Simeon bar Yohai, Nahmanides, Hayyim Vital and Elijah de Vidas: A Divine soul does indeed inhabit the human being. With regard to Horowitz' claim of support by Moses in citing the shema as proof-test. "Hear O Israel, The Lord our God, The Lord is One,[62] Jacobs interprets Horowitz in the spirit of his *Shefa Tal*. He reads Horowitz interpreting the verse with a boldness his critics would surely say does border on blasphemy in this way: *"Hear! Israel and The Lord our God are one Lord."* Thus Shabbetai Sheftel Horowitz, prominent Kabbalist, can be seen as having observed that the human Israel is organically united with God. Such is Jacobs' conclusion.

## Shneur Zalman of Ladi (1745–1812 CE)

Founder of the Habad movement within Hassidic Judaism, in Shneur Zalman we encounter a highly developed theological system based on the notion of a "Divine Spark" in man. He relied especially on Hayyim Vital, the chief expounder of the Lurianic Kabbalah school. In his magnum opus, the Tanya,[63] Shneur Zalman speaks of the two souls which every Jew possesses: the "animal soul" which is the vital source of his desires and appetites. This soul is constantly at war with *the divine soul, the portion of God within man.*[64] Here is how he describes the divine soul:

> The second soul in Israel is *an actual portion of God from above* (*haylek Eloha mi-maal mammesh*), as it is said, "And He (God) breathed into his (man's) nostrils the soul (neshama) of life; and man became a living being."[65] As the Zohar comments, "When one blows, it is from himself that he blows," that is to say, from his most inward essence for man ejects his most inward vitality when he blows powerfully. In the same way the souls of Israel "ascended in God's thought" (i.e., were fashioned by God), as it is written "'Israel is my son, my first born,"[66] and "You are children of The Lord your God."[67] This means that as the child derives from the "brain" (i.e., the semen) of the father so, as it were, the soul of every Jew is derived from God's thought and wisdom. *D'ihu hahim*, "For God is wise," and *Hu v'hahmato ehad*, "He and His wisdom are one," as Maimonides says: *Hu Hamada v'hu Hayodaya*. "He is the knowledge and the knower."[68]

This Tanya passage is referring to Maimonides' Mishna Torah 2:10 concerning the *Hilchot Yesoday Hatorah*, "The Laws Concerning the Fundamentals of the Torah." In the case of man, Maimonides asserts, what he knows is external to him; his knowledge and his life are separate elements. In the case of God, however, "He, His knowledge and His life are one from all sides and corners, in all manners of unity. . . . Thus you could say: *Hu Hayodaya v'Hu Hayadua v'Hu Hadaya atzmah, hakol ehad*, "He is the knower, He is the subject of knowledge, and *He is the knowledge itself*, all is one. Now, Maimonides' purpose here was only to emphasize the total Oneness of the Deity in contrast to the plurality of man. *The Tanya, however, uses this passage for its own purposes, which is to stress that "wisdom" and "God" are one and the same. Thus when Schneur Zalman asserts that the soul stems from "wisdom" he is asserting that the soul stems from God Himself.*[69]

A well-known phenomenon in religion is the equation of wisdom with God, in which a property of the Deity such as His cultic presence or *wisdom* is considered an entity in itself. For example, in Proverbs 9:1–4, the *hokhma*, the wisdom of God, is presented in personified form.

> Wisdom has built her house, she has hewn her seven pillars,
> She has slaughtered her animals, mixed her wine
> Yes, she has set her table.
> She has sent out her young women, she calls from the rooftops of the city, "Whoever is foolish, turn aside here!"

God's wisdom is similarly personified in *Ben Sira* 24, who portrays herself as bestriding heaven and earth and as authority over people and Zion. In the *Wisdom* of *Solomon* 10:1–10, wisdom is portrayed as a guard of the first father of the human race, who saved him after his fall, who gave him strength to master all things, and who helped her people Israel throughout the vicissitudes of her collective life.[70]

Shneur Zalman continues his thought-line about the nature of wisdom. Such knowledge about God is difficult to comprehend. There are many gradations of souls.

> Nevertheless, *the root of every soul, from the highest of all ranks to the lowest, all derive, as it were, from the Supreme Mind which is Heavenly wisdom.* As in the illustration (if it is permitted to say this) of the child who stems from the brain (semen) of his father. Even the child's finger and the nails are formed from the actual drop of brain (semen) which remains in the mother's womb for nine months, then descends from stage to stage until it changes so much that nails are formed, and yet it is still bound to and united with, in marvelous fashion, its first essence when it was part of the brain (semen) of the father . . . *so it is with the root of men's souls: they remain bound and united with a wonderful and essential unity with their original essence and entity, namely the Hohma Ila-ah, the Heavenly Wisdom (God).*[71]

Indeed, according to the Shneur Zalman of Ladi, there is an actual portion of God in every Jewish soul.

Dov Ber of Lubavitch (1775–1827), Schneur Zalman's son and successor, articulates the "Divine Spark" in man notion in the spirit of his father and imparts to it practical application. Thus in depicting the "Divine Soul" in the context of prayer, Dov Ber asserts that when man is in true prayer his Divine Soul is the authentic link with the Supreme Divinity. This means that *an experience of the "Divine Soul," though it is expressed through the normal channels of human will, thought and emotions is, in reality, an experience of the Divine with the Divine, as it were. It is an "essential" experience—Divine essence responding to Divine essence, the spark drawing near to the flame.*[72] (Our analysis of Jacobs ends here.)

**Conscience.** A non-mystical reading of the human psyche might well be understood as a Divine spark inhabiting the human being: viewing "conscience" from a religious perspective.

There appears that there is something, some factor *inside* man, that affects his attitudes sand actions. Its concern is decisions about values, chiefly good and evil. It is generally thought of in a negative sense—a faculty that reminds us, by stimulating feelings of guilt and shame, that we are doing wrong. The troubled heart is a sign of conscience.

The term has been articulated in numerous ways by religionists of all persuasions. Thomas Aquinas: "Conscience is that which witnesses or binds, incites and accuses, stings and rebukes." Immanuel Kant: "There exists in the human psyche an *innate sense* of what is right or wrong." Martin Buber: "Conscience is *that court within the soul* which concerns itself with the distinction between what is good and what is not good." Milton Konvitz: "The heart of conscience is not a voice that speaks outside of man; rather, *it is an internal hearing agency so that man may listen to the voice of God*."

Indeed, this is what the prophet Elijah experienced at Mount Horeb as the *Kol d'mama dakah*, "the still small voice" speaking to him when all alone, the silent voice reminding Elijah that he was in the presence of the Deity. It was not "the whirlwind, the earthquake, the fire"—external factors—that riveted the prophet's attention, but the voice of God within him telling him what he must do.[73] So, too, in the Unetaneh Tokef prayer in the High Holy Days liturgy, the shofar awakens the worshipper and urges him to "listen" to the "still small voice" urging him to change his ways.

And so, conscience is the Divine voice within a person which, when cultivated by religious action and focused thought, acts as a deterrent when, for example, one has the resources to escape the wrath of someone one has victimized. It works when one has the power to get away with stealing someone else's money. George Santayana articulated this well when he said that a person's true self is revealed when he is all alone: would he/she be honest and aboveboard? How would one behave when he knows that no one is *watching*? This is what Jacob's father-in-law, Laban, had in mind when he said to Jacob, "May the Lord *watch* between you and me when we are out of sight of each other. If you ill treat my daughters or take other wives besides my daughters—*though no one else is about, remember, God Himself will be witness between you and me.*"[74]

Why does conscience work to nurture ethical behavior? Because *the matter in the end is between a person and his Maker. He stands ever in the presence of the Divine who is watching.* "For not a man sees (does God see); a man sees only what is visible, but *the Lord sees into the heart.*[75]

Here, then, is a phenomenon pointing in the direction of the Divine-in-human idea.

We have sought to trace the idea of a Divine Spark in man from its beginnings in Philo, through the Kabbalists, to its place in the Chabad system, as well as the implications of it in the human characteristic of "conscience." Admittedly, the notion is highly unconventional in Jewish religious thought, but for all the emphasis in normative Judaism on the impassable gulf between the individual soul and God, the daring idea did emerge in some circles that the abyss had been bridged."[76]

## The Divine Image

There is a major biblical concept that appears to parallel the Divine Spark in man we have depicted. In Genesis 1:27 we hear, "And God created man in His image, in the image of God He created him; male and female He created them." Now, the two notions—the Divine Spark (*nitzutz*) and the Divine Image (*zelem*)—are manifestly different. The former denotes Divinity intrinsic to man, that it is inherent in the human being regardless of his actions (though, to be sure, it can be diminished by man's evil behavior). *The latter—the Divine Image—is conferred on man by man himself via his own actions*. Gershom Scholem stressed the point of their dissimilarity. He indicates that unlike the Divine Spark, the *zelem* is developed by the practical efforts of man. Scholem quotes the mystical way Moses de Leon, the author of the Zohar, makes this point: "The purpose of the *zelem* in man is to exhibit its powers and abilities in the world. When it descends into this world it receives, via man's own actions, power to guide this vile world and to undergo a *tikun* of "the above and the below," for it is of high rank. *And when it is in this world, it perfects itself, which was not the case in the beginning before its descent.*[77]

However, despite the dissimilarities of the two notions, the implications of both are fundamentally in tandem, as we shall see. We have discussed the Divine Spark idea up to this point. We now examine the Divine Image in some detail.

The Rabbis amplify the biblical assertion about the Divine Image. Thus Rabbi Joshua ben Levi tells of a procession of angels who pass before a man when he is traveling, and the heralds proclaim before him, saying, "Make room for the image (*eikonion*) of God."[78] A seminary student once recorded Dr. Abraham Joshua Heschel in class criticizing the popular idea that Judaism prohibited images of God inside synagogues. In fact, he said, if you look around during a Shabbat service, you will see that God's image fills each occupied seat. The assembled worshippers are themselves potential images of God.

*How* does one become an "image of God"? By imitating His ways. This is the import of the regnant dictum Moses was instructed to convey to the people: "You shall be holy for I, The Lord your God, am holy."[79] This means that man's holiness is acquired via imitation of God's ways. Thus when the Midrash speaks of "walking in God's ways," it is averring that just as God is called merciful so are you to be merciful; and just as God is compassionate, so are you to be compassionate.[80] To act as God acts in mercy and love, Dr. Heschel observes, is the way to reflect God's likeness within the human actor.[81] *Man becomes what he worships*: "Says the Holy One, Blessed be He, he who acts like Me shall be like Me." Says Rabbi Levi ben Hama, "Idolators resemble their idols (Psalm 115:8); how much more must the servants of The Lord resemble Him."[82] Maimonides in his Code, the Mishna Torah, observes that the reason God is called by the Prophets "long suffering," "merciful," "righteous," "upright," etc. (Exodus 34:5–7) is so that man is to replicate these qualities in his life with the result that *he becomes actually God-like*.[83]

And yet, Heschel observes,[84] God's likeness may be—alas, very often is—defiled and distorted. Man must recognize and preserve this likeness but he fails. The consequence: "I have placed the likeness of My image in them and through their sins I have upset it," God declares.[85] But there is hope. The Midrash interprets the verse in Deuteronomy 1:10 as if it were written, "Lo, today you are like the stars of heaven, but in the future you will resemble the Master."[86] *The likeness is broken, but it is not utterly destroyed.*

*When* does one become an image of God? Scripture relates that the patriarch Abraham and his household had just undergone circumcision. This was a sign of the covenant between him and his descendants and God for all time. It was a bond made between the Hebrews with the Power that governs the universe, along with a pledge later undertaken by Abraham's descendants to live a life of faith, a life characterized by morality and justice. It was a bond that affirmed the one God who was the Source of these values. Immediately after Abraham performed the circumcision rite, Genesis 18:1 tells us: "And the Lord appeared to him by the oaks of Mamre as he sat by the opening of the tent in the heat of day." Both Rashi and Nahmanides link God's appearances to Abraham with the patriarch's act of circumcision. Nahmanides put it this way:

> The Torah narrates that the Lord appeared to Abraham while he was still recovering from his circumcision in order to inform us that no prophetic revelation was here involved. Abraham did not fall on his face or pray. Nevertheless this vision was vouchsafed to him purely as a mark of honor to him. (*Commentary to Genesis 18:1*)

Take note: the sage is telling us that God usually appears to a person in the Bible with a message, a blessing, a promise, a demand. Not here. He just appears at this particular juncture. God appeared in Abraham's midst *when the effort and sacrifice involved in carrying out the rite of circumcision took place. The Divine is activated when human beings themselves perform acts of high purpose.* Indeed, Abraham had just connected his people to an exalted cause; he committed them to a life of exemplary living via the deed of circumcision *and it was at that point* that God appeared to him. And it is at that point that Abraham reflected God's image.

Nahmanides cites additional examples of this phenomenon.

- Moses and Aaron had led the Israelites through much difficulty and turmoil, instructed them in the appropriate rites of their faith with patience and precision, whereupon Leviticus 9:23 tells us: "And Moses and Aaron went into the tent of meeting; and when they came out they blessed the people, and the glory of the Lord appeared to all the people." God's revelation is here accompanied by no message or command; *His presence is felt because of the quality of behavior on the part of Israel's leaders.*

- Genesis 32:2 tells how Jacob had just made peace with his father-in-law, Laban. Then as they were about to part we're told: "And the angel of God appeared to him (Jacob)." No message, no promise is delivered. *God met a person here because that person made peace with another.*

- In the Genesis passage cited, we hear of Abraham sitting at the door of his tent, extending warm hospitality to three strangers who appeared nearby. At this point we read: "And the Lord appeared to him (Abraham) by the oaks of Mamre, as he sat at the opening of his tent in the heat of day." Again, God appeared with no message, no demand, no blessing, no promise. *In this setting He appears because a man reached out to help his fellow man.*

Martin Buber confirms this perspective inherent in the Bible. According to Buber, it is in the earnest intention and high quality of a person's worldly deeds that he experiences communion with God. God is an unknown being beyond the world only for the indolent, the decisionless, the lethargic, the man enmeshed in his own designs.

> For the man who chooses, who decides, who is aflame with his goal, God is the closest, the most familiar being, *who man through his own action* realizes ever anew, experiencing thereby the mystery of mysteries.

## What are the Implications of the Divinity in the Human Being Notion?

We have depicted a highly charged idea found in a significant stream of Jewish thought concerning the place of the Deity in human life—the Divine Spark in man. We have also limned the more conventional notion on the matter—the Image of God in man. Here we venture to explicate the implications of these notions, *which together project the idea that Divinity somehow is harbored in a human being.* Indeed, what is implied by the idea that man harbors Divinity within his being?

The implications can be discerned in the life of the individual as such, as the individual relates to others.

*The significance of self.* When one is aware that Divinity is present within his self, this inevitably confers on that person a sense of extraordinary self-worth. A person of faith sees God as possessing surpassing characteristics: He is merciful, compassionate, long-suffering, but also just and judgmental, stern and creative.[87] This means that these very characteristics lodge within him, thus making him a persona of enormous quality and capacity.

Gershom Scholem points to the notion that if man is a "microcosm" of the Divinity—"a doctrine which found universal acceptance among the kabbalists"—then man is obviously capable of exerting influence on the world. "Indeed, it is this which bestows on him the enormous importance and dignity that the kabbalists went to great lengths to describe." It is because man alone was granted free will that he has the power to either advance or disrupt through his actions the enhancement of the unity of the world. "Man's essence is unfathomably profound." Even his physical structure is precious because it harbors God's likeness. This is why the body of a criminal condemned to death must be treated with reverence (Deuteronomy 21:23), and Hillel taught that keeping one's own physical body clean is an act of reverence for its Creator.[88] These affirmations about man's profound self-worth constitute the grounds for his role in the world. As Scholem articulates this mystical thought line, "Man's principle mission remained to bring about a *tikun* or restoration of this world, and to connect the lower with the upper, thereby 'crowning' creation by setting the Creator upon His throne and perfecting His reign over all His handiwork."[89]

Moreover, the awareness of Divinity within is the source of great inner satisfaction. An individual contemplating this phenomenon becomes profoundly conscious of the blessings Divinity lodged in him confers. Thus, Abraham Isaac Kook avers,

> The greater you are, the more you need to search for your self. Your deep soul hides itself from consciousness. So you need to increase aloneness, elevation of thinking, penetration of thought, liberation of mind—until finally your soul reveals itself to you, *spangling a few sparkles of her light.* There you find bliss, transcending all humiliations or anything that happens. Then you gather everything, without hatred, jealousy, or rivalry. The light of peace and a fierce boldness manifest in you. The splendor of compassion and the glory of love shine through you. The desire to act and work, the passion to create and to restore yourself, the yearning for silence and for the inner shout of joy—these all band together in your spirit, and you become holy.[90]

Indeed, Rav Kook echoed Isaac of Akko, the thirteenth century mystic, who wrote, "Whoever attains the mystery of cleaving to God will attain the mystery of equanimity."[91] And Abraham Abulafia, another influential mystic, similarly spoke about the deep personal satisfaction that awareness of Divinity within confers.

> You feel an extra spirit—arousing you, flowing over your entire body, bringing pleasure. It seems as if fine balsam oil has been poured over you from your head to your feet—once, maybe more. You are overjoyed, in delight and trembling: the soul in delight, the body in trembling.[92]

*The significance of others.* If a person is aware that Divinity abides within a human being as such—within *all* human beings—as a fundamental aspect of their nature, it follows that he must treat with honor the Divinity both he and others harbor. Why? Because he is obliged to honor Divinity as such—a basic obligation for a man of faith. Thus the principle: man must treat his fellow man with reverence and respect.

This is a conception of far-reaching importance in Jewish thought. *Reverence for God is shown via reverence for man.* The fear one must feel of offending or hurting another must be as of ultimate importance as one's fear of God for Divinity inheres in that other. An act of violence against an innocent other is a desecration of the Divinity within the violated. To be arrogant toward another person is to be blasphemous toward God: "He who oppresses the poor blasphemes his Maker. He who is gracious to the needy honors Him."[93] The Midrash stresses: "You must not say, since I have been put to shame, let my neighbor be put to shame, for in the likeness of God He (God) made that neighbor.[94] The Rabbis teach that he who sheds the blood of another human being is considered as though he diminished the Divinity.[95] Martin Buber illustrates this dictum via two examples in scripture. Cain and David both murdered (David—indirectly—"slew Uriah the Hittite via the sword"—2 Samuel 12:9), and both are called to account by God. Cain attempts evasion: "Am I my brother's keeper?" He is a man who shuns the dialogue with God. Not so David, who answers, "*I have sinned against The Lord.*"[96] This is the true answer, says Buber; whomever one becomes guilty against, in truth, one becomes guilty against God.[97]

## In Summary

And so, in response to our question about the implications of the notion of the Divinity in man, we can say this: such Divinity stimulates human beings' profound self-worth and deep respect for fellow humans. Taken together, these constitute the motivating force for personal ethical behavior and for collective moral action in general.

*Chapter 7*

# Why Is the Notion of the Oneness of God—the Cornerstone of Monotheism—of Such Great Importance?

### ANI MAAMIN... ANI MAAMIN...
### I BELIEVE WITH COMPLETE FAITH...

The second of the thirteen principles of the Jewish faith according to Maimonides—*Mishne Torah, Yesodai Hatorah 1:2*

I believe with complete faith that the Creator, blessed be His name, is a unity, and that there is then no unity in any manner like His, and that He alone is our God, who was, is, and will be.

The Basic Declaration:

"Hear, O Israel! The Lord our God, The Lord is One" (Deuteronomy 6:4). This, the *Shema* ("Hear"), is the great text of Monotheism. For over two thousand years it has been recited twice daily by devout Jews. The Jewish child is taught the verse as soon as he can learn to speak. The Jew repeats it on his deathbed if he is able to utter any sound at all. The Jewish martyrs recited it as they made ready to give their lives for their faith. Throughout the ages it has been the most powerful single declaration of the significance of the Jewish religion. So, too, at the conclusion of every religious service Zechariah 14:9 is chanted: "And The Lord shall be King over all the earth; in that day shall The Lord be One, and His name One."[1]

I have posed the question dealt with in this chapter—"Why is the notion of Monotheism, the stress on the Oneness of God, so important?"—to many Jews on many occasions and rarely have received coherent answers.

In one specific instance, for example, I asked a PhD psychologist, observant Jew, regular Shabbat service attendee, how many times in his lifetime had he recited the Shema, which proclaims the Oneness of the Deity. His response: "Probably about five thousand times." I then queried, what does the Oneness of God mean? Why is it so important? To which he stammered something about God overseeing the world. This truly accomplished man did not know what the Oneness of God connoted even though he has recited the Shema in synagogue, at home, at table, at bedtime some 5,000 times! Though I have no statistical data to prove it, I venture to say that such is the condition among most Jews in our time.

The content of this book about the notion of Monotheism contains many an answer to our question about the importance of the Oneness of God idea. Here I want to offer a succinct summary of the idea's fundamental significance.

When juxtaposed with the paganism of the past (and of the present!), the notion of the absolute Oneness of the Deity harbors three fundamental principles for all time.

### One God Means One Humanity

> Have we not all one Father? Did not one God create us? Why do we break faith with one another, profaning the covenant of our ancestors? (*Malachi 2:10*)

One God created all human beings. He is our "Father," as it were, and we are all brothers and sisters. Hence, all men and women are, in the nature of things, members of one "family." The many "fathers" of paganism, by contrast, renders many different families unconnected with each other.

The One God's people, members of *one* family, share the same "blood," as it were, are made of the same basic stuff that gives them life, and it is this which binds them together. This bond creates a sense of solidary among all members of the family. It is a deep-rooted feeling that prompts responsibility for one another, which motivates protection of the family's weak and oppressed members, which gives rise to a decided drive for justice, and for love and compassion for kinsmen. According to biblical dicta, such behavior is mandatory because it is God, the Father's, will: "You shall love your neighbor as yourself. I am The Lord."[2] Further, humane behavior is called for because all humans were created "in God's [the Father's] image,"[3] which is to say that even as *the One Father* evinces love and mercy, justice and compassion for His human creatures, so must these attributes be replicated by members of the human family. This is what the Prophet Malachi and the Deuteronomist viewed as behavior that flows from the notion of God as "Father" and people as God's "children." Malachi here speaks the prophetic voice which articulates the definitive idea of monotheism. He designates "Father" as being the Creator of *all* human beings; He is a universal God, the one and only God.

The very nature of paganism did not allow for consistent practice of the above humane characteristics. Paganism posited the existence of multiple "father" gods who governed different facets of the world. These were authoritative deities of separate and different families of people. Each god had its own followers, and since the god of one people was considered superior to the god of another people, their respective followers felt themselves justifiably superior to the others. Moreover, since in paganism the gods were constantly at war with each other, their respective followers felt themselves legitimately at war with each other. Conversely, when everyone recognizes the one and only God, there must not be, as a matter of principle, more wars—this is a logical notion if wars are wars between different gods. It is evident that this logic does not regularly govern the behavior of Jews, Christians and Moslems in practice, but it is enough for a vision of forging swords into plowshares.

## One God Means One Morality

> Monotheism was reached through the belief that the will of God for righteousness is supreme in the history of the world; *one* will rules for all to *one* end—the world as it ought to be. In this way a national God became the universal God, whose essence was thus, to put it in a word, moral. —George Foote Moore, *Judaism*

One God means that there is one standard for moral and ethical living—one moral code whose source and authority is the One God. By contrast, multiple gods means multiple divine wills espousing multiple and contradictory obligatory moral codes.

Hence, the pursuit of justice, for example, is applicable to *all* of God's children whose "Father" is the One Universal God. It is applicable at *all* times and in *all* places, to *all* tongues and cultures. Deuteronomy 16:20 demands, "Justice, justice shall you pursue," which Bakhya Ibn Pakudah explains as meaning to emphasize that the double use of the word "justice" applies under all circumstances, whether to one's profit or loss, whether in one's own words or actions, whether dealing with a fellow Jew or a non-Jew.[4] Regarding this principle—a single standard for moral behavior—there can be no competing god or gods to teach otherwise. This is what One God means as it pertains to human moral living according to basic Jewish teaching.

To illustrate the radical contrast between this scriptural teaching vis-à-vis pagan teaching, note the following passage that states in God's name: "You shall not render an unfair decision; *do not favor the poor or show deference to the rich*; judge your neighbor fairly.[5] Further: "Hear out your fellow men and decide justly between any man and a fellow Israelite or a stranger. You shall not be partial in judgment. *Hear out low and high alike.* Fear no man for judgment is God's."[6]

On the other hand, the Babylonian Code of Hammurabi, commissioned by the pagan god of justice, the sun-god *Shamash*, had a different take on this subject. The law of justice was applied differently to a nobleman than to a commoner (a member of the lower class including such as an ox driver or a slave). Thus the law of "an eye for an eye, a tooth for a tooth" (*lex talionis*) was a scaled punishment: penalty for its infraction was based on social status.

> If a man has destroyed the eye of a member of the aristocracy, *they (the court) shall destroy his (the perpetrator's) eye*. If he has destroyed the eye of a commoner, *he (the perpetrator) shall pay one mina of silver*. If a *seignior* (a man of high rank) knocked out the tooth of a seignior of his own rank, they (the court) shall knock out his (the perpetrator's) tooth. If the seignior knocked out a commoner's tooth he (the perpetrator) shall pay one-third mina of silver"[7] Indeed, Hammurabi's god hardly advocated fair justice, although he did place greater value on an eye over a tooth!

Especially significant is the fact that King Hammurabi claims that the sun-god, Shamash, commissioned him to write his code; later he says that it was the god Marduk, the head god of Babylon, who did so. Now, these two gods played different roles in the lives of the people. Shamash was the promoter of justice, and Marduk was the director of the land—and they had different, often clashing, requirements for the people's lives, as the code's content demonstrates.[8] This was a system of law inherently unstable, inconsistent and ultimately unsustainable.

## One God Means One Design

- *Jeremiah:* Their gods *who did not make* the heavens and the earth. . . . It is The Lord who . . . established the world by *His wisdom*, and by *His understanding* stretched out the heavens.[9]

- *Second Isaiah:* It is The Lord who formed the earth. . . . *He did not create it in chaos. He formed it to be inhabited.* . . . I [God] did not say to the offspring of Jacob: "Seek Me in chaos."[10]

- *Genesis:* God's creation of the earth and the heavens and all within them is accomplished according to a carefully pre-determined plan and design.[11]

The One God which Monotheism embraces means there is *one* design of the natural world which is the work of One *Designer* we call God. Paganism, by contrast, posits many designers with varied designs.

The natural world has wondrous order and system, a basic dependability and stability. Discernible rules are embedded in it which make possible (scientific) study of the world based on the ability to rationally analyze and predict probable outcomes.

On the other hand, a world divided among various gods—one of sun and another of moon, one of fire and another of water, one of flood which destroys and another of beneficent rain which nourishes the earth, one of scorching desert and another of frigid tundra, one of earthquake and another of sturdy terrain—such a world is confusing, tension-full for different followers of the different gods, rendering the astonishing unity of the natural globe beyond human capacity to explicate.

A wise observer of the natural world described it this way:

> Night falls on one hemisphere, only that a new day may fall upon another. The bee steals its sweetness from the flower but at the same time, fertilizes it with the pollen she has unconsciously carried away on her body from some other flower. The sun draws up the water from the ocean in the form of vapor; the vapor becomes a cloud; the cloud empties itself as rain; the rain replenishes the river, which empties into the ocean. Light and darkness, sunshine and storm, growth and decay *all point to a mysterious unity in the universe, to a world that has been planned and is controlled by One Mind.*

This enables us to say that the unity of nature is the result of a unitary will, a single Designer, One God . . . and this enables the human mind to discern universal laws applicable everywhere. Thus,

- The ecological chain that keeps the natural world in constant balance.

- The law of gravity that makes it possible to rationally study the world and fashion plans for it.

- The stability of the cosmos that made possible Einstein's historic studies, which relied on exact mathematical formulae governing time and space. The extraordinary ability of scientists to predict the exact times—to the minute—when the moon eclipses the sun is a striking example of this phenomenon.

- The design of the human body is the same everywhere. Thus the body can be studied and cures prescribed in one place and era and applied everywhere and at all times.

# Notes

## INTRODUCTION

1. *The Religions of Ancient Israel*, p. 29 and 80. Zevit uses the term for this methodology, *Historiography*, which Webster's Collegiate Dictionary defines as "the writing of history based on the critical examination of sources, the selection of particulars from the authentic materials, and the synthesis of particulars into a narrative that will stand the test of critical methods."
2. JPS Torah Commentary: Exodus, p. xiii.
3. *Zakhor: Jewish History and Jewish Memory*, p. 11.
4. *A Faith for Moderns*, pp. 106–111.
5. *The Faith of Judaism*, pp. 261–262.
6. Eichrodt, *Theology of the Old Testament*, Vol. 1, p. 227.
7. In his *Theology of the Old Testament*, Edmond Jacob articulates this central notion about the God of history, to wit: "The coming of God into the world represents the main power line of Israel's religion" (p. 201). He also writes:

The special characteristic of biblical revelation is that God binds Himself to historical events to make them the vehicle of His purposes. . . . God's presence in history is that of the hidden God whose intentions always remain full of mystery in men's eyes (Isaiah 45:15; 55:8), but the hidden God is also the One who comes at certain moments in time to demonstrate through certain events the totality of His being and His action. This coming of God into history—we prefer the term "coming" as being more dynamic than "presence"—is on God's side an action and at the same time an interpretation (pp. 188–189).

8. *A Social and Religious History of the Jews*, Vol. 1, p. 14 and 53.
9. In Michael Meyer's *Ideas in Jewish History*, p. 169.
10. Sack's *Makhzor*, p. xii. For a similar perspective, see *The Tanya* by Shneur Zalman of Ladi, chapter 2.

# CHAPTER 1

1. See note about chronology in the Introduction, p. 6.
2. The Tetragrammaton, Greek "four letters," *the sacred*. The designation for the four Hebrew consonants YHWH, that compose the name of Israel's God (Exodus 3:15).
3. Genesis 12:1.
4. Exodus 6:2–3. The divine name is traditionally not pronounced; instead, *Adonai*, "[the] Lord," is regularly substituted for it, this because of the great sanctity the divine name represents; this practice helps avoid inappropriate usage of the name.
5. Genesis 17:3–8; Exodus 22:7–8.
6. For these dates, see Otto Eissfeldt, *The Old Testament: An Introduction*, p. 200, and Artur Weiser, *The Old Testament: Its Formation and Development*, p. 108.
7. Bright, *A History of Israel*, p. 97.
8. See *How to Read the Bible*, "The Call to Abraham," p. 103, and note #22, p. 707.
9. Alt, *Essays on Old Testament History and Religion*, pp. 3–86, especially pp. 13–38.
10. Genesis 17:1–2.
11. Exodus 6:3.
12. *HarperCollins Bible Dictionary*, p. 685.
13. Genesis 49:25; see also Sarna in *JPS Torah Commentary*, Excursus 4: *El Shaddai*.
14. Genesis 31:42 and 53.
15. *HarperCollins*, ibid., p. 687.
16. Genesis 49:24.
17. *HarperCollins*, ibid.
18. Frank Moore Cross, *Canaanite Myth and Hebrew* Epic, pp. 10–12.
19. Cross, ibid., p. 6.
20. Baron, *A Social and Religious History of the Jews*, Volume One, p. 44. For Alt's fuller articulation of this thought, see his *Essays*, ibid., pp. 81–82.
21. Roland DeVaux, *Ancient Israel*, pp. 4–11.
22. Ibid., p. 11.
23. Ibid., p. 10.
24. Genesis 18:1–8.
25. Genesis 24:28–32.
26. Genesis 19:1–8.
27. Judges 19:16–24.
28. Genesis 19:8 and Judges 19:23.
29. Leviticus 25:25 and 25:47–49.
30. II Samuel 3:22–27 and 2:22–23.
31. DeVaux, ibid., p. 11.
32. The early patriarchal period, i.e., Abraham, Isaac and Jacob: approximately 1800–1700 BCE. The later patriarchal period, i.e., Joseph and his

descendants: approximately 1700–1300 BCE, at which point the Mosaic era begins, approximately 1300 BCE. See Introduction, p. 6.

33. Cross, ibid., pp. 43–54, and *HarperCollins*, ibid., p. 686.
34. Genesis 14:18–20.
35. Genesis 16:13–14.
36. Genesis 21:33.
37. Genesis 35:6–7.
38. Exodus 6:3.
39. See Sarna, *JPS Torah Commentary*, ibid., p. 19, concerning the term used for the early Israelites (Exodus 3:18), which term like "the God of the Fathers" belongs to a pre-Mosaic stage in the history of Israelite religion and probably widely used among the pastoral nomads of the region.
40. Genesis 14:17–20.
41. Genesis 18:20–32
42. See Joshua, chapter 10, in which Adonizedek is portrayed as helping his besieged brethren in Gibeon.
43. *HarperCollins*, ibid., p. 252.
44. Genesis 18:19.
45. *HarperCollins*, p. 252 and p. 686.
46. Genesis 14:19–20.
47. *HarperCollins*, ibid., p. 252.
48. Genesis 33:20.
49. Genesis 31:19.
50. Bright, ibid., p. 102. For a convenient summary of this patriarchal period in which the nascent notion of God was developing, see Gerhardt Von Rad, "A History of Yahwism and of the Sacred Institutions in Israel in Outline," in *Old Testament Theology*, Volume I, pp. 3–14. For a full and authoritative depiction of Canaanite religion in the patriarchal period, see William Foxwell Albright, "Canaanite Religion in the Bronze Age (approximately 2000 to 1500 BCE)," in *YHWH and the Gods of Canaan: An Historical Analysis of Two Contrasting Faiths*.
51. Alt, *Essays*, p. 86.

## CHAPTER 2

1. John Bright, *A History of Israel*, p. 158.
2. Michael Grant, *The History of Ancient Israel*, p. 44.
3. Mark Smith, *The Early History of Israel*, pp. 184–185.
4. David N. Freedman, "Who is Like Thee Among the Nations?" in *Ancient Israelite Religion*, p. 328. See Salo Baron's similar assertion about the impact of the Exodus experience in Meyer's *Ideas of Jewish History*, p. 321.
5. G. Ernest Wright, *The Old Testament Against Its Environment*, pp. 46–54; Sanders, *The Monotheizing Process*, pp. 12–19.
6. Exodus 3:13–15.
7. Nahum Sarna, *JPS Torah Commentary*, p. 31.

8. Nahum Sarna, *Exploring Exodus*, pp. 51–52.
9. Grant, ibid., p. 44.
10. *HarperCollins Bible Dictionary*, pp. 736–737; see also Frank Moore Cross in his *Canaanite Myth and Hebrew Epic*, pp. 60–75, for a detailed analysis of the term "YHWH."
11. *HarperCollins*, ibid. p. 252 and 686.
12. Exodus 20:2 and Deuteronomy 5:6–7.
13. Sarna, *JPS Torah Commentary*, p. 109.
14. Deuteronomy 6:4.
15. Deuteronomy 6:4–9.
16. Deuteronomy 6:13–15.
17. For a full depiction of Egyptian influence on Israel in the period between 1500–1300 BCE, see Donald Redford in his *Egypt, Canaan and Israel in Ancient Times*, chapter 13. Also Nahum Sarna, *Exploring Exodus*, pp. 151–155. For the texts of the Egyptian hymns to the monotheistic-leaning gods, Re, Amun, and Aten, see Prichard, *Ancient Near Eastern Texts (ANET)*, pp. 365–372.
18. Sarna, ibid., pp. 156–157.
19. See Redford, ibid., 377–382.
20. Baron, *A Social and Religious History of the Jews*, Vol. 1, pp. 45–46.
21. Deuteronomy 4:19 and 17:2–5.
22. Sarna, ibid., p. 144.
23. Exodus 20:4–6 and repeated in Deuteronomy 5:7–9.
24. Baron, ibid., p. 13.
25. Sommer, *The Bodies of God*, pp. 66–67.
26. Zevit, *Religions of Ancient Israel*, pp. 259–261.
27. Sarna, ibid., p. 145.
28. Sommer, ibid., pp. 66–67.
29. Exodus 33:20, "and live"; this perhaps means that a person who fashions an image of God "takes his life in his own hands."
30. Genesis 17:1–8.
31. Genesis 31:42, 53.
32. Genesis 49:24.
33. Exodus 3:14.
34. See "The Meaning of YHWH" on p. 24 in this chapter.
35. Genesis 14:19–20.
36. *HarperCollins*, ibid., p. 252.
37. Exodus 20:8–11.
38. *From the Stone Age to Christianity*, p. 319.
39. Deuteronomy 4:32.
40. Deuteronomy 10:14.
41. I Samuel 2:8.
42. 2 Kings 19:15.
43. Halpern, *The Development of Israelite Monotheism*, p. 97.
44. Eichrodt, *Theology of the Old Testament*, p. 220.
45. Genesis 3:22.

46. Genesis 11:7.
47. Exodus 23:20–21
48. Sommer, *The Bodies of God*, p. 42.
49. Deuteronomy 4:19.
50. Exodus 18:11.
51. Deuteronomy 6:4 and 6:14.
52. Exodus 20:3.
53. Exodus 18:11.
54. Deuteronomy 4:19.
55. Exodus 15:11.
56. Judges 11:24.
57. I Samuel 26:19.
58. See Halpern, "The Development of Israelite Monotheism," in *Judaic Perspectives on Ancient Israel*, pp. 82–84. Also Dever, "Folk Religion in Early Israel," pp. 47–56, and McCarter, "The Religious Reforms of Hezekiah and Jeremiah," pp. 67–80, both the latter in *Aspects of Monotheism—How God is One*.
59. Bright, ibid., p. 159.
60. Eichrodt, ibid., p. 222.

# CHAPTER 3

1. For this basic thought line, see Kaufmann, *The Religion of Israel*, pp. 343–347. Also for a lucid depiction of the work of the Prophets in this regard, see Gordis, *A Faith for Moderns*, pp. 106–112. Note especially the updated and more detailed depiction of this perspective, which includes the historical factors that animated this developmental process, the trenchant analysis of Mark Smith in *The Early History of God*, pp. 182–194.
2. McCarter, *Aspects of the Religion*, p. 143.
3. Mark Smith, *The Early History of Israel*, pp. 187–188. See also Baruch Halpern, "The Development of Israelite Monotheism," p. 85ff, for additional nascent notions of biblical universalism in the pre-exile period.
4. Sommer, *The Bodies of God*, pp. 165–172. Concerning Kaufmann's claim about the originality of Monotheism stemming from biblical Israel on the basis of mythic symbols having lost their power in Israel, see Jon Levenson in his *Sinai and Zion*, pp. 102–111. Here Levenson disputes this claim, documenting the vitality of myth in biblical Israel.
5. Isaiah 2:8, 18.
6. Jeremiah 2:10–16; also Hosea 8:4–6.
7. Ibid. in Jeremiah.
8. Ezekiel 18:12; 20:24; 20:39.
9. Deuteronomy 4:28.
10. Deuteronomy 4:35.
11. Deuteronomy 4:39.
12. See Deuteronomy chapter 4 as a whole, especially verses 15–20.

13. *The Book of Isaiah* (Expositors Bible), Vol. 2, p. 44.
14. John Bright, *A History of Israel*, p. 355.
15. *The Origins of Biblical Monotheism*, p. 165.
16. Isaiah 10:5.
17. Habakkuk 1:5–6, 10. Quote of Wright is in *The Evolution of God*, p. 171.
18. Second Isaiah 45:5–7.
19. Second Isaiah 41:21–24.
20. Second Isaiah 44:6–8.
21. Second Isaiah 48:12–16.
22. *The Religious Ideas of the Old Testament*, p. 60. An aside: Mark Smith makes intriguing comment concerning an element that reinforced the notion of a single God due to the exilic experience. "With the rise of *the individual* along with the family as significant units of social identity (Deuteronomy 24:16; Jeremiah 31:29–30; and Ezekiel 18) came the corresponding notion on the divine level, namely, of a *single God* responsible for the cosmos." *The Early History of God*, ibid., p. 194. For a lucid depiction of how the exile facilitated the breakthrough to consistent Monotheism, which denies the existence of other gods, see Gerd Theissen in his *Biblical Faith: An Evolutionary Approach*, pp. 58–59.
23. Smith, *The Early History of God*, p. 187.
24. Amos 9:7.
25. Micah 4:1–3; also Isaiah 2:2–3.
26. Isaiah 19:18–22.
27. Zephaniah 3:9–10
28. Jeremiah 29:12–13.
29. Jeremiah 16:19.
30. Zechariah 2:15.
31. Second Isaiah 45:20–25.
32. Second Isaiah 45:1–7.
33. Second Isaiah 49:6.
34. N. Sarna, *Studies in Biblical Interpretation*, pp. 153–154.
35. Sarna, ibid., pp. 152–153.
36. *Tzafnas Paneyakh*, edited by David Herzog, #5.
37. Ibn Ezra's introduction to his commentary on Genesis, where he surveys four different approaches to Bible commentary. In the third approach, he also says, "The Torah was not given to the unintelligent; the intellect must be the intermediary between man and God."
38. Thomas Aquinas, *Summa Theologica*, Question 2: The Existence of God, Article 2: Whether it can be demonstrated that God exists.
39. B. Halpern, "The Development of Israelite Monotheism," pp. 102–103.
40. Amos 5:25–27.
41. Hosea 4:11–14.
42. Hosea 9:10.
43. Hosea 10:1–2; 11:1–2; 13:1–2.
44. Isaiah 2:8, 20–21.
45. Isaiah 17:7; 30:21f; 31:7; 17:7–8.

46. Micah 1:6–7.
47. Micah 5:12–14.
48. Jeremiah 1:16; 10:1–10.
49. Jeremiah 2:23, 28; 11:9–13.
50. Jeremiah 19:4–5.
51. Jeremiah 3:9; 7:16–20; 7:32; 8:1–2.
52. Ezekiel 6:3–4.
53. Ezekiel 7:20.
54. See especially the searing passage in Ezekiel 8:5–18, as well as 20:5–8.
55. Ezekiel 14:5–8.
56. Second Isaiah 42:17.
57. Second Isaiah 44:9–15.
58. Second Isaiah 45:20.
59. Second Isaiah 46:1–9. Bel is the chief god of Babylon and Nebo is another of its gods.
60. Baron, *A Social and Religious History*, Vol. 1, p. 48.
61. Jeremiah 29:12–14.
62. Ezekiel 11:16–17.
63. Baron, ibid., Vol. 1, p. 164. See also, "Emancipation from State and Territory," pp. 16–25.
64. *Ideas of Jewish History* (Meyer), p. 201.
65. Ibid., p. 231.
66. Ibid., p. 257.
67. Ibid., p. 279.
68. G. E. Wright, *The Old Testament Against Its Environment*, p. 47.
69. See Eichrodt quote, p. 2 in this book.
70. Baron in *Ideas of Jewish History* (Meyer), p. 329.
71. See Graetz, ibid., pp. 236–237.
72. *Ideas of Jewish History*, p. 282.
73. Baeck in his last major work, *The People Israel*, in *Ideas*, ibid., p. 347.
74. For the term *berit* see Deuteronomy 7:9 and I Kings 8:23.
75. Levenson, *The Love of God*, p. 19.
76. Second Isaiah 54:5–6.
77. Isaiah continues: God's affirmation of His people, His love for them as His children, is good news. This is good news, not just for Israel, but for everyone: "Foreigners will join them and unite with the descendants of Jacob" (*14:1*). "Let no foreigner who is bound to The Lord say, 'The Lord will surely exclude me from his people'" (*56:3*). "The Lord Almighty will prepare a feast of rich food for all peoples" (*25:6*). They will say, "This is our God . . . let us rejoice and be glad in His salvation" (*25:9*).
78. More Prophets tell the story:

> Hosea also described a break in the relationship: "You are not my people, and I am not your God" (*1:9*). Instead of giving the words of a wedding, he states the words of a divorce: "She is not my wife, and I am not her husband (*2:2*). But as with Isaiah and Jeremiah, this was an exaggeration. Hosea quickly adds that the relationship is not

over: "'In that day,' declares The Lord, 'you will call me "my husband" . . . I will betroth you to me forever'" (*2:16, 19*). "I will show my love to the one I called 'Not my loved one.' I will say to those called. 'Not my people,' 'You are my people'; and they will say, 'You are my God'" (*2:23*). "I will heal their waywardness and love them freely, for my anger has turned away from them" (*14:4*). "You do not stay angry forever," says Micah. "You will be faithful to Jacob, and show love to Abraham, as you pledged on oath to our ancestors in days long ago (*7:30*). Zechariah gives a good summary: "'Shout and be glad, Daughter Zion. For I am coming, and I will live among you,' declares The Lord" (*2:10*). "I will save my people from the countries of the east and the west. I will bring them back to live in Jerusalem: they will be my people, and I will be faithful and righteous to them as their God" (*8:7–8*). Finally, Malachi says: "On the day when I act," God says, "they will be my treasured possession. I will spare them, just as a father has compassion and spares his son who serves him" (*3:17*).

79. See item #1 in this chapter, "The Deity is a Supreme God."
80. Amos 4:13.
81. Amos 5:8. Pleiades and Orion are two star-filled constellations in the heavens which in ancient times were seen as evidence of God's overwhelming creativity. See *HarperCollins Bible Dictionary*, p. 735 and 803.
82. Isaiah 29:15–16.
83. Isaiah 37:16.
84. Jeremiah 10:11–13; 51:15–16.
85. Jeremiah 27:4–7; See also 32:16–17.
86. Second Isaiah 42:6–8.
87. Zechariah 12:1–2.
88. The Genesis story of creation is considered by scholarly consensus to have originated somewhere between 550–450 BCE, being the work of priests in exile. It was thus composed in the same era of Second Isaiah, ca. 530 BCE, and Zechariah and Malachi, ca. 520–475 BCE. Clearly, then, Genesis' theological views had much in common with regard to the subject at hand.

For Genesis 1–2:3 considered the Priestly (P) story of creation and hence its time of origin, see *The New Oxford Annotated Bible*, p. 1. For the consensus among recognized authorities on this, see Otto Eissefeldt, *The Old Testament*, p. 188; George Fohrer, *Introduction to the Old Testament*, p. 179; and Artur Weiser, *The Old Testament*, p. 136. For the dating of P, see Eissefeldt, ibid., p. 207; Fohrer, ibid., p. 185; and Weiser, ibid., p. 138. For the dating of Second Isaiah, see Oxford, ibid., p. 822. For Zechariah, ibid., p. 1148, and for Malachi, ibid., p. 1160.
In Genesis 1–2:3, the priestly author depicts God's creation of the *earth and the heavens and all within them as accomplished with plan and purpose*. This was to demythologize the origin of the cosmos depicted in the current accounts of the ancient Near East. Instead of divine combat and struggle with a willful primordial matter (a struggle men on earth replicated vis-à-vis each other), we find here in the prophetic era order (cosmos) out of chaos. This is the work of a sole Sovereign Master of the universe directing the work of creation according to a carefully determined plan. In summary,

On the first day God created light and darkness, night and day; on the second, the firmament separating earthly and heavenly waters; on the third day, dry land and vegetation; on the fourth, the heavenly luminaries—the sun ("greater luminary") for ruling the day, and the moon (chief "lesser luminary") for ruling the night; on the fifth, sea creatures and birds; and on the sixth, land creatures—and finally, humans. The first three days present frameworks of the created cosmos with the last three days their respective inhabitants. God names the works of the first three days and humans, as per 2:19–20, and then,
God is shown fashioning the world in six days and resting on the seventh day as recorded in the fourth commandment (Exod. 20:11). And so, out of the original chaos God created an orderly world in which he assigned a preeminent place to man. (See *HarperCollins*, ibid., pp. 192–193 for further analysis of this creation account. See also *The New Oxford Annotated Bible*, p. 1.)

89. Exodus 20:12–17.
90. Exodus, ch. 21.
91. *A Social and Religious History of the Jews*, p. 84. See also William Foxwell Albright, *YHWH and Gods of Canaan*, pp. 312–313, and Yehezkel Kaufmann, *The Religion of Israel*, p. 345.
92. Amos 2:6.
93. Isaiah 1:17.
94. Zechariah 7:9–10.
95. Jeremiah 2:2–3.
96. Ezekiel 16:49–50. For additional sources in this social justice realm, see Micah 6:6–8; Amos 5:11–15; 5:21–24; Second Isaiah 58:6–12; Jeremiah 22:13–17; Ezekiel 22:29; First Isaiah 10:1–2; Mal. 3:5.
97. Kaufmann, ibid., p. 345.
98. Amos 5:21–24.
99. Micah 6:8.
100. Isaiah 1:11–17.
101. Jeremiah 6:30. See Jacob Chinitz on this subject, "Were the Prophets Opposed to Sacrifices?" in *Jewish Bible Quarterly*, Vol. 36, No. 2 (2008).
102. Jeremiah 7:9–11.
103. Zechariah 7:9–10.
104. Second Isaiah 56:7.
105. *The Faith of Judaism*, p. 262.

# CHAPTER 4

1. Yosef Yerushalmi, *Zakhor: Jewish History and Jewish Memory*, p. 21.
2. See article "Zoroastrian" in Hasting's *Encyclopedia of Religion and Ethics*, Volume XII, pp. 862–869, and George Foote Moore, *History of Religions*, Volume I, pp. 357–405.
3. Sifre #329.
4. Berakhot 5:3; Megilla 4:9.

5. Deuteronomy Rabbah 2:31.
6. Sanhedrin 30a.
7. For more about the struggle against dualism in rabbinic literature, see George Foote Moore, *Judaism*, Volume I, pp. 364–367, and Volume II, pp. 115–116.
8. Moore, ibid. pp. 366–67.
9. Midrash Tanhuma, Naso #19 on 1 Kings 8:27.
10. Barukh 3:24–25.
11. Song of Songs Rabbah 3:10; Pesikta D'rav Kahana 1:3.
12. Leviticus Rabbah 4:8; Berakhot 10a.
13. Exodus Rabbah 2:5.
14. *Siddur Sim Shalom*, p. 282.
15. Hartman, *A Living Covenant*, pp. 57–58.
16. Fishbane, *Sacred Attunement*, p. 123.
17. Pesakhim 113a.
18. Taanit 23a.
19. Genesis 17:11.
20. Genesis 1:2.
21. Mireae Eliade, *The Sacred and the Profane*, chapter 1.
22. Fishbane, ibid., p. 149.
23. See Psalm 19 used in the Shabbat morning service as an example of this; also Hartman, ibid. p. 224, and Jack Shechter, "The Amen Specialist and the Fourteen Morning Blessings" in *Journey of a Rabbi*, University Press of America, Vol. Two, pp. 25–31.
24. Leviticus Rabbah 24:3.
25. Genesis 43:23.
26. Proverbs 14:31.
27. Genesis Rabbah 24:7.
28. Mekhilta to Exodus 20:16.
29. *Journey of a Rabbi*, Volume 2, p. 28.
30. Fishbane, ibid., pp. 116–119.
31. Levenson, *The Love of God*, pp. 68–72.
32. Siphre Deuteronomy 32.
33. *Hisquini* to Deuteronomy 6:5.
34. Lieberman, *Hellenism in Jewish Palestine*, p. 121.
35. Josephus, *Antiquities*, Vol. 18, ch. 3, #1.
36. Avoda Zarah, Mishnayot 1, 2, 4, 6, 7.
37. Wisdom of Solomon 14:22–31.
38. Avoda Zarah 54b, emphasis added.
39. Hartman, ibid, p. 210.
40. Moore, *Judaism: The Age of the* Tannaim, Vol. 1, p. 397. See also p. 60ff. in this book.
41. Genesis 1:27.
42. Ethics of the Fathers 3:18.
43. Moore, ibid, p. 398.
44. Koren Siddur, p. 337, 369.

45. Koren Rosh Hashana Mahzor, p. 440.
46. For these statements, see Louis Finkelstein, editor, Sifre on Deuteronomy, chapter 50.
47. Genesis Rabbah 1:3.
48. Genesis Rabbah, 1:9.
49. Genesis Rabbah 3:7.
50. Tankhuma, Buber, Vayara, #24.
51. This analysis based on Moore, *Judaism*, Volume 1, p. 375, 384.
52. Syriac Barukh 14:18 (early Second Century CE).
53. 4 Esdras 8:44 (late First Century CE); also Barukh 14:18.
54. Barukh, ibid., 3:7.
55. Isaiah 49:6; 42:6; 60:3.
56. Genesis Rabbah 12:2.
57. Moore, ibid, p. 391. Instructive, as well, is Moore's observation that the continuity of thought regarding the God idea in general, its "essential unity of conception," its "real consensus in substance," also existed within the classical rabbinic literature itself. Ibid., pp. 357–358.
58. "The Religious Ideas of Talmudic Judaism" in *Philosophies of Judaism* (New York: Holt, Rinehart, 1964), p. 41. See also Solomon Schechter's illuminating essay on this subject of *Imitatio Dei* in *Some Aspects of Rabbinic Theology*, chapter XIII (Behrman House).
59. Pesikta 164a.
60. Genesis Rabbah 15.
61. Ibid., 33:3.
62. Ibid., 39:6, Leviticus Rabbah 10:1.
63. Leviticus Rabbah 27:1.
64. Jerusalem Talmud, Hagiga 77c.
65. This passage is in *The Old Testament Pseudepigrapha*, edited by James Charlesworth, No. 62 (123), (New Haven, CT: Yale University Press). For the Hebrew of the passage, see *Sifre Deuteronomy*, No. 39 (edited by Louis Finkelstein, JTS, N.Y. 5729 (1969)).
66. Moore, *Judaism*, pp. 393–394.

## CHAPTER 5

1. See Sommer, *The Bodies of God*, pp. 132–136, for the apparent Jewish roots of the Christian notion of the Deity.
2. Sommer, Ibid., pp. 38–57.
3. Ibid., p. 125.
4. For the Friedman quote, see his *Disappearance of God: A Divine Mystery*, pp. 12–13.
5. Mark 1:1–3.
6. Salo Baron, *A Social and Religious History of the Jews*, Vol. 2, p. 58.
7. Ibid., p. 65.

8. Ibid., p. 70.

9. See Talmud, Sukkah 52a: "The Messiah Son of David, who will be revealed soon in our day." This is based on Psalm 18:51: "Great triumphs He gives to the king, and shows steadfast love for His anointed (*meshikho*), *to David* and to his descendants forever."

10. Kirsopp Lake, *An Introduction to the New Testament*, p. 238.

11. Harry Emerson Fosdick, *A Guide to Understanding the Bible*, p. 45.

12. Proverbs 8:22–31; Wisdom of Solomon 9:1–2.

13. For this analysis see *HarperCollins Bible Dictionary*, p. 619, and Abba Hillel Silver in Where *Judaism Differed*, p. 98.

14. Colossians 1:15.

15. Hebrews 1:3.

16. John 1:1 and 14.

17. Acts 2:22.

18. For Jesus as God in the New Testament, see 2 Corinthians 1:3, 4:4–6. See also John Collins in his article "Jewish Monotheism and Christian Theology" in *Aspects of Monotheism: How God is One* points to data in late biblical and Jewish apocryphal literature, which appears to serve as precedent for Jesus as divine. He points to angelic figures in the book of Daniel, the Dead Sea Scrolls and the book of Enoch, which appear to portray them, in some sense, as divine, and in Philo's *Life of Moses*, who is seen, also in some sense, as divine. Then also there is Proverbs 8:12–22, where *wisdom* is personified ("I, wisdom, live with prudence; I attain knowledge and foresight.... The Lord created me at the beginning of His course"). Also in Ben Sira 24:3 ("I am the *word* which was spoken by the Most High; it was I who covered the earth like a mist"). About all these figures Collins says this:

> Each of these figures, to be sure, can be understood as God's agent or representative, so that homage given to them is ultimately given to God. But these passages also show that the idea of venerating God's agent, at least in the eschatological future, was not unthinkable in a Jewish context.... Hence, the veneration of Jesus by his first-century CE Jewish followers should be somewhat less surprising in light of the foregoing evidence.

Collins' observation is similar to that of Sommer (pp. 114–115 in our text), both of which are illustrative of the developmental process in biblical ideas (our thesis) here in the context of Christianity's notion of the Deity.

19. *HarperCollins*, ibid, p. 1178.

20. Matthew 11:27; John 10:30, 14:9–11, 20:28; Colossians 2:9.

21. *HarperCollins*, ibid., p. 432.

22. Genesis 1:2; Ps. 33:6; Ezekiel 37:1–10.

23. John 14:26.

24. Luke 3:21–22.

25. Acts 3:33.

26. Romans 8:26–27.

27. John 14:16–17. *Paraclete* is the Greek word for counselor. Its root meaning refers to an advocate, someone called alongside to strengthen and fight on behalf of another.

28. 2 Corinthians 13:14.
29. Matthew 28:19. For a lucid detailed depiction of the Holy Spirit notion and the doctrine of the Trinity, see Millar Burrows in his *Outline of Biblical Theology*, pp. 74–82. For a "dogmatic" explication of the Trinity, see Karl Barth in his *Dogmatics in Outline* (New York: Harper and Row, 1959), pp. 42–45.
30. Moore, *Judaism: The Age of the Tannaim*, p. 364.
31. *Sifré* #329, edited by Louis Finkelstein.
32. Genesis Rabbah 8:9.
33. Exodus Rabbah 29:4, also Isaiah 44:6.
34. Jerusalem Talmud, *Taanit*, 65b. Note: "Son of Man" is often used in the New Testament for Jesus as a divine figure. See *HarperCollins*, p. 1053.
35. Moore, ibid, notes, p. 116 in his notes.

# CHAPTER 6

1. Genesis 2:7.
2. Proverbs. 20:27.
3. Ecclesiastes 12:7.
4. Isaiah 6:3.
5. Isaiah 46:5.
6. Isaiah 57:15. See Epstein, *The Faith of Judaism*, p. 141.
7. *Guide to the Perplexed*, I.58.
8. Jeremiah 23:23–24.
9. Isaiah 6:3.
10. Leviticus Rabbah 4:8.
11. Psalm 139:7–10.
12. Jerusalem Talmud, Berakhot, 13a.
13. Epstein, ibid., p. 137.
14. Ibid., p. 145.
15. Jacobs, *A Jewish Theology*, p. 50.
16. For a more carefully reasoned argument about God as *personal*, see Louis Jacobs in his *God, Torah, Israel: Traditionalism Without Fundamentalism*, "Belief in a Personal God: The Position of Liberal Supernaturalism," pp. 3–19.
17. Gordis, *A Faith for Moderns*, p. 104ff.
18. Siddur Sim Shalom, p. 327. For Bokser's version in poetic form, see his *Judaism: Profile of a Faith*, p. 46.
19. Bokser, ibid., p. 46. For the rest of this trenchant analysis, see the full chapter, pp. 47–54.
20. See Hebrew text and translation, *The Koren Siddur*, pp. 570–571. This is the *Shir Hakavod*, "The Song (Hymn) of Glory," attributed to Rabbi Judah Hahasid (d. 1217).
21. *The Chandogya Upanishads*, VI.13, 1–31 (ca. 400 BCE).
22. For a detailed discussion of the impact of God's presumable "concreteness" in the Kabbalah, see Sommer, *The Bodies of God*, pp. 129–182.

23. Jacobs, *Religion and the Individual*, pp. 42–58.
24. Jacobs, ibid., pp. 42–43.
25. *On the Special Laws*, Loeb Classical Library, Vol. 8, p. 85. For Philo's views about the soul, see Harry A. Wolfson, *Philo*, Cambridge, Mass., 1948, Vol. I, pp. 389–395.
26. *Allegorical Interpretation*, ibid., Vol. 1, p. 171.
27. *On the Creation*, ibid., Vol. 1, p. 115.
28. Winston, *Logos and Mystical Theology in Philo of Alexandria*, pp. 28–30.
29. Shabbat 152b.
30. Sifre Deuteronomy, Piska 306.
31. Berakhot 10a.
32. Ecclesiastes Rabbah to Ecclesiastes 6:6.
33. Sommer, *The Bodies of God*, p. 127. Quote is Peter Shafer's in his *Mirrors of His Beauty*, p. 96.
34. See Isaac Husik, *A History of Medieval Jewish Philosophy*. New York, 1958, pp. 45–47. A good popular account of medieval thought on the soul is *Ahad Ha-Am*'s essay on Maimonides entitled *Shilton Ha-sekhel, Collected Works*," Berlin, 1921, vol. 4, pp. 2–11.
35. *Keter Malkhut*, XXIX, translated by Bernard Lewis, London, 1961, 9. 49.
36. Zohar II, 174a.
37. Sommer, ibid., p. 129. The parallel to the Indian idea of the avatar suggests itself, especially because several of the ten avatars of the god Vishnu were, in fact, worshipped on their own—indeed, some devotees of Krishna came to see them as deities in their own right, and Vishnu as no more than an avatar of Krishna (rather than the other way around).
38. Ibid., p. 129–131.
39. Matt, *The Essential Kabbalah*, pp. 8–9; Zohar 3:65b.
40. Ibid., pp. 10–11.
41. Ibid., p. 15.
42. Ibid., p. 10.
43. Jewish Encyclopedia entry: Abulafia, Abraham ben Samuel.
44. Introduction to *The Scandal of Kabbalah: Leon Modena, Jewish Mysticism and Early Modern Venice* (Princeton, NJ: Princeton University Press, 2011).
45. See Hebrew and English translation and commentary in *Mesorah* Publications, pp. 93–96.
46. The term *neshama* means both "breath" and "soul." For further elaboration of the concept of man's soul originating in God's "breath," see Nahmanides' *Nefesh Hahayyim*, I, chapter 15.
47. Commentary to the Pentateuch, Jerusalem, 1970, p. 61.
48. *Sefer Nishmat Hayyim*, Stettin, 1851, Maamar I, p. 2b.
49. Shaare Kedusha, "Gates of Holiness," Sulzbach, 1758, Part 1, Shaar I, pp. 3a–4a.
50. Ibid., part III, Shaar II and III, pp. 25b–29a.
51. Deuteronomy 14:1.
52. Jeremiah 13:11.

53. *Reshit Hohmah*, Amsterdam, 1717. Shaar Ha-Avodah, Ch. III, pp. 67–69.
54. *Shefa Tal*, Hanover, 1612.
55. Job 31:2.
56. Deuteronomy 32:9.
57. Proverbs 20:27.
58. *Pardes Rimmonim*, Karetz, 1786, Shaar I, Ch. 7, p. 8a.
59. Prague, 1616 during Horowitz' lifetime and Jerusalem, 1850.
60. See Moses Cordovero's depiction of the process by which the essential nature of the Deity remains unknown and unchanged while appearing to be known and change in man's eyes. This in Cordovera's *Pardes Rimmon*, "Water, Light, and Colors," as translated by David Matt in *The Essential Kabbalah*, p. 38.
61. Gershom Scholem, *Major Trends in Jewish Mysticism*, pp. 224–225.
62. Deuteronomy 6:4.
63. (Brooklyn, NY: Kehot Publication Society, 2012), ch. 2.
64. About the soul in the Jewish morning liturgy, see Berakhot 60b.
65. Genesis 2:7.
66. Exodus 4:22.
67. Deuteronomy 14:1.
68. This passage is at the very beginning of chapter 2 in the Tanya.
69. See Mishna Torah, ch. 2, Law #10. This idea is also in Maimonides' *Guide for the Perplexed*, Vol. one, ch. 68. See Gershom Scholem's *Kabbalah*, "The Kabbalah and Pantheism," pp. 144–152, for a valuable survey of this subject—God in and out of the world and of mankind.
70. See Kyle McCarter, "The Religious Reforms of Hezekiah and Josiah," in *Aspects of Monotheism: How God is One*, p. 69.
71. Jonathan Sacks in his Koren Rosh Hashana Makhzor, p. xii, has articulated this notion of Shneur Zalman in striking modern terms (see p. 4 in the introduction to this book).
72. *Kunteros* Hahitpalut, "Tract of Ecstasy," translated by Louis Jacobs, London, 1963.
73. I Kings 19:11–12.
74. Genesis 31:49–50.
75. I Samuel 16:7.
76. Jacobs, *Religion and the Individual*, p. 58.
77. Gershom Scholem, *Kabbalah*, p. 159.
78. Deuteronomy Rabbah 4:4.
79. Leviticus 19:2.
80. Sifre to Deuteronomy 11:22.
81. Abraham Joshua Heschel, *Man's Quest for God*, p. 126.
82. Deuteronomy Rabbah 1:10.
83. Hilkhot Deot 1:16.
84. Heschel, ibid., p. 127.
85. Talmud, Moed Katan, 15b.
86. Deuteronomy Rabbah 1:10.
87. Exodus 34:6–7.

88. Leviticus Rabbah 34:3.
89. Scholem, *Kabbalah*, ibid., p. 153.
90. Orot Hakodesh 3:270 as per Daniel Matt, *The Essential Kabbalah*, p. 124.
91. *Meirat Einayim*, p. 218; Matt, ibid., p. 118.
92. *Otsar Eden Ganuz*; see Idel, *The Mystical Experience in Abraham Abulafia*, p. 188, as per Matt, ibid., p. 111.
93. Proverbs 14:31.
94. Genesis Rabbah 24:7.
95. Mekhilta to Exodus 20:16.
96. Cain: Genesis 4:9; David: 2 Samuel 12:13.
97. Buber, *On Judaism*, p. 220.

# CHAPTER 7

1. There is an apparent contradiction between the concept "Our God" and that of "The Lord is One" contained in the Shema. "Our God" denotes the God of Israel. "The Lord is One" denotes that God is the Father of all people. The tension between particularism and universalism is characteristic of scripture. For the Rabbis, this issue was of immediate concern because in their time they were in close contact with Roman society and its sensitivities with regard to the nature of the Godhood: was Israel's God not the gentile's God as well? The *Siphre*, the midrash on Deuteronomy 6:4 seeks to soften the tension. God is indeed The Lord of the universe, the midrash states, but also "His name rests upon Israel in particular, which signifies that it is Israel which keeps the God idea alive; she is especially devoted to the One God." What the Rabbis are stressing here is that, although God is the God of all people everywhere on earth, His Presence is embedded with Israel in particular in that it is her task to harbor God's Oneness with special tenacity by being wholeheartedly devoted to His singularity in word and deed. In this way, the notion and the highly consequential tenets that flow from it will long endure for *all* people.
2. Leviticus 19:18.
3. Genesis 1:27.
4. Bahya Ibn Pakudah, Commentary to Deuteronomy 16:20.
5. Leviticus 19:15.
6. Deuteronomy 1:16–17.
7. *Ancient Near Eastern Texts Relating to the Old Testament*, edited by James B. Prichard, p. 175, #196–201.
8. Prichard, Ibid., p. 163, 165.
9. Jeremiah 10:11–13; 51: 15–16.
10. Second Isaiah 45:11–12, 18–19.
11. For the design of the world in summary form as per Genesis 1–2:3, see chapter 3, "The Prophets and Monotheism," note #88.

# Selected Bibliography

Albright, William Foxwell. *From the Stone Age to Christianity: Monotheism and the Historical Process*. Second Edition. Baltimore: Johns Hopkins University Press, 1957.

———. *YHWH and the Gods of Canaan*. New York: Doubleday & Co., 1968.

Alt, Albrecht. *Essays in Old Testament History and Religion*. New York: Doubleday Anchor Book, 1968.

Armstrong, Karen. *A History of God*. New York: Gramercy Books, 1993.

Baron, Salo W. *A Social and Religious History of the Jews*, Vol. 1. New York: Columbia University Press, 1952.

Bokser, Ben Zion. *Judaism: Profile of a Faith*. New York: Alfred A. Knopf, 1963.

———. *The Jewish Mystical Tradition*. New York: The Pilgrim Press, 1981.

Bright, John. *A History of Israel*. Third edition. Philadelphia: Westminster Press, 1981.

Buber, Martin. *The Prophetic Faith*. New York: Macmillan, 1949.

Burrows, Millar. *An Outline of Biblical Theology*. Philadelphia: Westminster Press, 1946.

Childs, Brevard. *Myth and Reality in the Old Testament*. Naperville, IL: A. R. Ellenson, 1960.

Clements, Roland. *God and Temple: The Idea of Divine Presence in Ancient Israel*. Oxford: Basil Blackwell, 1965.

Collins, John. "Jewish Monotheism and Christian Theology." In *Aspects of Monotheism—How God is One*. Washington, DC: Biblical Archaeological Society, 1996.

Cross, Frank Moore. *Canaanite Myth and Hebrew Epic: Essays in the History of the Religion of Israel*. Cambridge, MA: Harvard University Press, 1973.

De Vaux, Roland. *Ancient Israel: Its Life and Institutions*. New York: McGraw-Hill, 1961.

Dever, William. "The Contribution of Archaeology to the Study of Canaanite and Early Israelite Religion." In *Ancient Israelite Religion: Essays in Honor of Frank Moore Cross*. Philadelphia: Fortress Press, 1987.

———. *The Lives of Ordinary People in Ancient Israel.* Grand Rapids, MI: Eerdmans, 2012.
Eichrodt, Walther. *Theology of the Old Testament*, Vol. I. Philadelphia: Westminster Press, 1967.
Eissfeldt, Otto. *The Old Testament: An Introduction.* New York: Harper and Row, 1966.
Eliade, Mircae. *The Sacred and the Profane.* London: Harcourt Brace, 1959.
Epstein, Isidore. *The Faith of Judaism.* London: The Soncino Press, 1954.
Finklestein, Israel, and Neil Asher Silberman. *The Bible Unearthed.* New York: The Free Press, 2001.
Finklestein, Louis. *The Pharisees: The Sociological Background of Their Faith.* Philadelphia: Jewish Publication Society, 1946.
Fishbane, Michael. *Sacred Attunement.* Chicago: The University of Chicago Press, 2008.
Fosdick, Harry Emerson. *A Guide to Understanding the Bible.* New York: Harper and Row, 1956.
———. *The Modern Use of the Bible.* New York: Macmillan, 1958.
Friedman, David Noel. "Who is Like Thee Among the Gods?" In *Ancient Israelite Religion.* Philadelphia: Fortress Press, 1987.
Friedman, Richard Elliot. *The Hidden Face of God.* New York: HarperCollins, 1997.
Gordis, Robert. *A Faith for Moderns.* New York: Bloch, 1960.
Grant, Michael. *The History of Ancient Israel.* New York: Charles Scribner's Sons, 1984.
Halpern, Baruch. "The Development of Israelite Monotheism." In *Judaic Perspectives on Ancient Israel.* Philadelphia: Fortress Press, 1987.
———. *The Emergence of Israel in Canaan.* Chico, CA: Scholars, 1987.
*HarperCollins Bible Dictionary.* San Francisco: Society of Biblical Literature, 1996.
Hartman, David. *A Living Covenant.* New York: The Free Press, 1985.
Heschel, Abraham Joshua. *Man's Quest for God.* New York: Charles Scribner's Sons, 1954.
———. *The Prophets.* New York: Harper Torchbooks, 1962.
Jacob, Edmond. *Theology of the Old Testament.* New York: Harper & Brothers Publishers, 1958.
Jacobs, Louis. *Principles of the Jewish Faith.* New York: Basic Books, 1964.
———. *God, Torah, Israel: Traditionalism Without Supernaturalism.* Cincinnati: Hebrew Union College Press, 1990.
———. *Religion and the Individual.* Cambridge: Cambridge University Press, 1992.
Kaufmann, Yehezkel. *The Religion of Israel.* Chicago: The University of Chicago Press, 1960.
Kugel, James. *How to Read the Bible.* New York: Free Press, 2007.
Lapp, Paul. *Biblical Archaeology and History.* New York: World Publishing Company, 1970.
Levenson, Jon. *The God of Love.* Princeton, NJ: Princeton University Press, 2016.
Lieberman, Saul. *Greek in Jewish Palestine.* New York: Jewish Theological Seminary, 1942.

Matt, Daniel. *The Essential Kabbalah: The Heart of Jewish Mysticism*. San Francisco: Harper, 1995.

McCarter, P. Kyle. "Aspects of the Religion of the Israelite Monarchy." In *Ancient Israelite Religion*. Minneapolis: Fortress Press, 1987.

Meyer, Michael A. *Ideas in Jewish History*. New York: Behrman House, 1974.

Moore, George Foot. *Judaism in the First Centuries of the Christian Era: The Age of the Tannaim*. Volume I. Cambridge, MA: Harvard University Press, 1954.

Noth, Martin. *The History of Israel*. Second Edition. New York: Harper and Row, 1960.

———. *A History of Pentateuchal Traditions*. Englewood, NJ: Prentice Hall, 1972.

Prichard, James B. *Ancient Near Eastern Texts: Relating to the Old Testament*. Third edition. Princeton, NJ: Princeton University Press, 1969.

Rad, Gerhardt von. *Old Testament Theology*, Vols. I and II. New York: Harper and Row, 1962.

Redford, Donald. *Akhenaten: The Heretic King*. Princeton, NJ: Princeton University Press, 1984.

———. *Egypt, Canaan, and Israel in Ancient Times*. Princeton, NJ: Princeton University Press, 1992.

Sanders, James. *The Monotheizing Process*. Eugene, OR: Cascade Books/Wiph and Stock, 2014.

Sarna, Nahum. *Exploring Exodus*. New York: Schocken Books, 1986.

———. *Genesis*. Philadelphia: Jewish Publication Society, 1989.

———. *The JPS Torah Commentary: Exodus*. Philadelphia: Jewish Publication Society, 1991.

———. *Studies in Biblical Interpretation*. Philadelphia: Jewish Publications Society, 2000.

Schechter, Solomon. *Some Aspects of Rabbinic Theology*. Springfield Township, NJ: Behrman House.

———. *Studies in Judaism: Second Series*. Philadelphia: Jewish Publication Society, 1938.

Scholem, Gershom. *Major Trends in Jewish Mysticism*. New York: Schocken Books, 1946.

———. *Kabbalah*. New York: A Meridian Book, 1974.

Shanks, Herschel, ed. *Aspects of Monotheism—How God is One*. Washington, DC: Biblical Archaeological Society, 1996.

Silver, Abba Hillel. *Where Judaism Differed: An Inquiry Into the Distinctiveness of Judaism*. New York: Macmillan Company, 1957.

Smith, Mark. *The Early History of Israel*. Grand Rapids, MI: William Eerdsmans Publishing Company, 2002.

———. *The Origins of Biblical Monotheism*. Oxford: Oxford University Press, 2001.

———. *The Memoirs of God*. Minneapolis: Fortress Press.

Sommer, Benjamin. *The Bodies of God and the World of Ancient Israel*. Cambridge: Cambridge University Press, 2011.

Theissen, Gerd. *Biblical Faith: An Evolutionary Approach*. Philadelphia: Fortress Press, 1985.

Tigay, Jeffrey. *You Shall Have No Other Gods: Israelite Religion in Light of Hebrew Inscriptions*. Atlanta: Scholars Press, 1980.

Weiser, Artur. *The Old Testament: Its Formation and Development*. New York: Association Press, 1968.

Winston, David. *Logos and Mystical Theology in Philo of Alexandria*. Cincinnati: Hebrew Union College Press, 1985.

Wright, George Ernest. *The Old Testament Against Its Environment*. London: SCM Press, 1966.

Yerushalmi, Yosef Hayim. *Zakhor: Jewish History and Jewish Memory*. Seattle: University of Washington Press, 1983.

Zevit, Ziony. *The Religions of Ancient Israel*. London: Continuum, 2001.

# Index

Abba, Rabbi, 93
Abbahu, Rabbi, 90, 104
Abraham, 29, 46; exalted cause of, 131–32; hospitality of, 14; Melkizedek blessing, 17–19, 30; patriarchal era launched by, 9, 144n32, 149n78; Sodomites and, 17, 19, 93; YHWH and, 9–12, 23, 75, 97
Abulafia, Abraham, 120, 134, 156n43, 158n92
*Adonai*, 71, 144n4
Aha, Rabbi, 93
Ahriman, 68, 70
Akhenaten, 26–27
Akiba, Rabbi, 88, 93
Albright, William Foxwell, 6, 30, 145n50, 151n91
Alt, Albrecht, 9, 11, 13, 19
Amos, 23, 37, 43, 48, 49, 65, 89, 148n24, 148n40, 150n80, 150n81, 151n92, 151n96, 151n98; communication with, 78; on creator of heaven and earth, 60–61; on social justice, 63; on morality and ethics, 64
Anat, 16
angels, 34, 48, 122, 154n18; appearing to Jacob, 132; creation of, 89; as God's presence, 33, 97, 114; sent by God, 47, 131
Aquinas, Thomas, 47, 129
Asherah, 16
Asherah (goddess), 28
Astarte, 16
Aten, 26, 146n17
Aton of Amenophis IV, 2
Avodah, 74
*Avodah Zarah*, 86

Baeck, Leo, 56–57, 149n73
Bahya Ben Asher, 122
Baron, Salo, 3, 13, 27–28, 63, 98, 153n6; on detachment from land, 52–53, 57, 145n4; on peoplehood, 55
ben Eliezer, Yosef, 46–47
ben Hama, Rabbi Levi, 131
ben Hasdai, Rabbi Avraham, 47
ben Jacob, Eliezer, 88
ben Korkha, Rabbi Joshua, 73
ben Nachman, Rabbi Samuel, 93
ben Yohai, Rabbi Simeon, 126
Berehia, Rabbi, 91
Bernard of Clairvaux, 114
Bible, 3, 38, 67, 144n8, 144n12, 146n10, 148n37, 150n88, 154n11; authors of, 58; on creation of man, 89, 106; on *El*, 16; God of, 55,

132–33; God's unity in, 96–97;
Hebrew, 38–39, 96, 100–101;
Monotheism as central idea, 5; on
nomads, 14, 22–23; revelation in,
143n7; teaching, 4–5, 90; on YHWH,
10. *See also* Torah; *specific books of*
blood vengeance law, 15
Bokser, Ben Zion, 110–11, 155n18–19
Book of the Covenant, 55, 62
Brahman, 2
Bright, John, 6, 10, 40, 45, 145n1
Buber, Martin, 129, 133, 135, 158n97

Caesarea, 103
Canaan, 14, 45–46, 52, 81; *El* worship,
16–19, 25, 47; gods in, 35, 38;
Hebrews in, 6–7, 13, 21; Mosaic
period settlement, 7, 27; patriarchal
era settlement, 6–7, 12–13, 15,
145n50; Polytheism in, 16, 19
Catholic Mass, 85
Chemosh, 34–35
Christian God idea, 96–98, 102–104
Christianity, 68, 70, 95, 96, 154n18;
bringing God from heaven, 113;
in divinity and humanity, 120–21;
Godhood in, 102–104. *See also*
classical rabbinic/early Christian era;
Judaism, Christianity and
circumcision, 74–76, 131–32
clans, 11, 14, 15
classical rabbinic/early Christian era,
1, 5; chronology of, 6; creator of
heaven and earth in, 89–92; justice
in, 92–94; learning in, 77–79;
mitzvot and, 74–81; morality in, 92;
one God everywhere in the world
affirmation in, 72–73; Oneness of
God in, 73–74, 83; overview, 67–68;
people deity in, 86–88; Polytheism
negated in, 86–88; prayer in, 79–81;
protective deity in, 88–89; ritual in,
74, 75–76, 77, 84–85; rote practice,
spiritual intention in, 83–85; supreme

deity in, 68–74; Zoroastrian dualism
and, 68–72. *See also specific rabbis*
conscience, 129–30
Cordovera, Moses, 125, 157n60
creator of heaven and earth, 5, 17, 18,
95; Amos on, 60–61; in classical
rabbinic/early Christian era, 89–91;
creating for Israel, 91; creating for
man, 90; creating for righteous,
90–91; creating for Torah, 91;
Isaiah on, 61; Jeremiah on, 61–62;
in Midrash, 89; in Mosaic period,
30–31; in patriarchal era, 18–19; in
prophetic period, 60–62
Crescas, Hasdai, 117
Cross, Frank Moore, 12–13, 144n18
cults, 12, 19, 21, 26, 48, 49, 52, 99–100
Cyrus, 40, 44

*dahil*, 14
David, 35, 57, 99, 135, 154n9, 158n96
Day of the Lord doctrine, 2
De Leon, Moses, 118, 130
Designer and Sustainer, 87, 89, 109, 141
Deuteronomy, 14, 23, 29–31, 48, 69,
95, 103, 137, 146n12, 148n22,
149n74, 158n1; on bowing down,
33; interpreting, 131; on Jacob, 124;
on justice, 133, 139; on Moses, 45;
on mother bird, 55; on Oneness of
God, 83
Dever, William, 35
De Vidas, Elijah, 124, 125–27
Divine Image, 81, 130–33
Divine Mother, 118–19
Divine Spark, 105–106, 113, 115, 117,
118–19, 124–26, 127–30, 133
divinity: access to, 98; desecration of,
81–82; divine causality, 2–3; Divine
Intellect, 113; divine self-disclosure,
3; divine supremacy, 25–26; Divine
Understanding, will, wisdom, 118;
multiplicity of, 96, 97. *See also*

creator of heaven and earth; people deity; protective deity; supreme deity
divinity and humanity, 80; Bahya Ben Asher on, 122; conscience and, 129–30; De Vidas on, 124; Divine Image, 81, 130–33; Divine Spark, 105–106, 113, 115, 117, 118–19, 124–26, 127–30, 133; echo of Christianity in, 120–21; God's transcendence and immanence in, 106–108, 112–13; Horowitz on, 125–27; implications of, 130–35; Menasseh ben Israel on, 122–23; Midrash on, 117; Nahmanides on, 121–22; non-Jewish sources on, 113–14; overview, 105–106; Philo of Alexandria on, 114–16; prompting of divinity in man, 112–13; Rabbinic literature on, 116–17; reconciling two notions of, 108–12; Shneur Zalman of Ladi on, 127–29; significance of self and others in, 131–32; Vital on, 123–24; Zohar on, 118–20
Dov Ber of Lubavitch, 129
Dubnow, Simon, 54
Dweck, Yaakov, 120–21

Eckhart, Meister, 113–14
ecological chain, 141
Egypt, 32, 34, 43, 61, 67, 73, 81, 98, 114; exodus from, 21–22, 24–25, 78, 103; justice in, 23; sun god, 26–27
Eichrodt, Walter, 2, 36, 55, 143n6
Einstein, Albert, 141–42
*El*: Bible on, 16; *El Bethel*, 16; *El Elyon*, 16, 17, 18, 30, 31; *El Roi*, 16; El Shaddai, 10, 11, 16, 23, 144n13; Hebrews and, 15–19; in patriarchal era, 15–19; as supreme god, 18; worship in Canaan, 47
Eliade, Mircea, 77, 152n21
Elijah, 43, 129
*En Sof*, 126
Epstein, Isadore, 2, 66, 108–109, 155n6

Ethical Monotheism, 65–66, 92
Exodus: book, 30, 32, 33, 55, 69, 73, 75, 93, 96–97, 104; from Egypt, 21–22, 24–25, 27–28, 78; as Israel's defining story, 23, 145n4; in Mosaic period, 22–23
Ezekiel, 37, 39, 50; communication with, 78, 148n22; covenant and, 57–58; on justice, 63; on land, 52–53; on protective deity, 60

Fishbane, Michael, 74, 82, 152n16
food, 74–75
Friedman, David Noel, 22
Friedman, Richard Elliot, 97, 153n4
*From the Stone Age to Christianity* (Albright), 6

Gabriel, 89
Gamliel, Rabban, 89
Geiger, Abraham, 4, 11
*gemilat hasadim*, 74, 81. *See also* good deeds
Genesis, 10–11, 19, 23, 46–47, 62, 81, 97, 104, 114–15, 121–22, 130, 131–32, 135, 141, 148n37, 150n88, 158n11
Gersonides, 117
al-Ghazali, Abu Hamid, 47
God: allowance for idolatry, 87–88; angels as presence, 33, 48, 97; angels sent by, 47; character of, 2–3; Christian God idea, 96–98, 102–104; Christianity bringing from heaven, 113; of the Fathers, 15–19; Hebrew pact with, 75–76, 131; in history, 110; humanity of, 94; impersonal God, 109; involvement with humanity, 1, 24, 55, 60, 71–72, 89, 105, 108, 112–13; of Israel, 9, 10, 19, 23, 26, 37, 43, 55, 78, 158n1; Jesus as, 154n18; in Judaism, 3, 65; limits of knowledge of, 110–11; love

for people, 58–59; nature of, 2–3, 115; one God everywhere in world affirmation, 72–73; one God means one humanity, 138–39; personal God, 107–109, 112–13; personality of, 109–10; single God, 30, 31–32, 102–103, 148n22; as social and political idea, 55–56; spiritual development and, 2–4; transcendence and immanence of, 106–108, 112–13; unity of in the Bible, 96–98, 101, 121, 137; universality of, 2, 42–44, 66. *See also El*; YHWH

Godhead, 36, 57, 97, 114, 126

Godhood, 101, 106; Christian thinking on, 102–104; dualism in, 70; as fundamental to Jewish Monotheism, 89; local manifestations of, 38; in Mosaic period, 30; nature of, 158n1; in physical world, 119; singularity of, 68

*The God of the Fathers* (Alt), 9, 11–13

Golden Calf, 96–97

good deeds, 73–74, 81–82, 93, 123

Gordis, Robert, 2, 95, 110, 147n1

Graetz, Heinrich, 54, 55

gravity, 141

Guttman, Julius, 92

Habad movement, 121, 127

Hallaj, 114

Halpern, Baruch, 33–35, 48, 147n58

Hammurabi Code, 140

Havdalah, 76–77

Hebrews: in Canaan, 6–7, 15, 21; *El* and, 15–19; as nomads, 6, 13–16, 18; pact with God, 75, 131. *See also* Israel; Judaism

Henotheism, 35

Heschel, Abraham Joshua, 131

Hillel, 80, 133

*A History of Israel* (Bright), 6

Holy Spirit, 98, 101–104, 122

Horowitz, Shabbetai Sheftel, 121, 125–27

Hosea, 37, 49, 59, 60, 78, 93, 149n78

humanity, 82; collective and individual, 24; creator of, 60; faith and, 47; of God, 94; God's involvement with, 1, 55, 71–72; one God means one humanity, 138–39. *See also* divinity and humanity

Hymn of Glory, 111, 155n20

Ibn Daud, Abraham, 117

Ibn Ezra, Abraham, 45–47, 148n37

Ibn Gabirol, 117

idolatry, 27, 50–51, 65, 131; gentile, 86; God's allowance for, 87–88; in paganism, 62; punishment for, 64

immanence, 105, 106–108, 112–13

impersonal God, 109

intensive learning, 73–74, 83

Isaac, 9, 10, 12, 19, 23, 29, 46, 144n32

Isaiah, 49, 89, 91, 143n7, 149n77; communication with, 78; on creator of heaven and earth, 61–62; on immanence, 107; on justice, 63; Monotheism and, 44–47; on morality and ethics, 64–65; on Oneness of God, 42; on protective deity, 59; Second Isaiah, 27, 39–41, 43–44, 50, 62, 65, 140, 150n88; on transcendence, 106; on two powers, 104

Israel: commemorations in religion, 2; early religion in, 33, 36; Exodus as defining story, 22–23, 145n4; heaven and earth created for, 91; history of religion, 1–2; nomads and, 6, 17, 27, 52, 145n39; people of, 34, 43, 53, 54, 60, 88, 125; prophets of, 11, 44, 51, 110; YHWH as God of, 23

Jacob, 9, 10, 12, 19, 23, 28, 29, 42, 81, 124, 130, 144n32, 149n77; angel appearing to, 132
Jacobs, Louis, 109–10, 113, 116, 124, 126–27, 155n16
*jar*, 14
Jeremiah, 27, 37, 39, 44, 48–50, 52–53, 148n22, 149n78; communication with, 78; on creator of heaven and earth, 61; on immanence, 107; on justice, 63; on morality and ethics, 64–65; on one design, 140; on protective deity, 59–60
Jesus: as God, 154n18; Jewish tradition before, 102–103; as Logos, 100–101; from messenger to Messiah, 98–100; Oneness of God compromised by, 102–103
Jethro, 34
Jewish survival: peoplehood, in absence of land, 54–57; in prophetic period, 52–57; religion, in absence of land, 52–54
Joab, 15
Joseph, 12, 81, 144n32
Joshua, Rabbi, 93
Judah, Rabbi, 90, 91–92, 118, 155n20
Judaism: authentic, 56–57; doctrine of, 55; Godhood as fundamental to Monotheism, 89; God in, 3, 65; material in, 80; Monotheism as cornerstone, 68, 73, 102; normative thought, 72, 98, 108, 112; origins of, 4; true, 54. *See also* Talmud
Judaism, Christianity and: Christian God idea in, 96–98, 102–104; fissure between, 104; fork in the road, 95–96, 98; Holy Spirit in, 101–102; Jesus, from messenger to Messiah in, 98–100; Jesus as Logos in, 100–101; Jewish tradition before Jesus, 102–103
justice: in classical rabbinic/early Christian era, 92–94; Deuteronomy on, 139; in Egypt, 23; in Mosaic period, 31–33; in patriarchal era, 15, 17, 19; in prophetic period, 62–66; social justice, 63, 92, 151n96. *See also* morality

Kabbalah: Lurianic Kabbalah school, 127; mainline and traditional, 119; thinking in, 105; Trinity and, 120–21
Kaddish prayer, 106
Kant, Immanuel, 129
Kaufmann, Yehezkel, 38–39, 54, 147n1, 147n4; on morality and ethics, 64; on peoplehood, 56–57
Kohler, Kaufman, 120
Konvitz, Milton, 129
Kook, Abraham Isaac, 134
*Koren Rosh Hashana Makhzor* (Sacks), 4, 157n71
Krishna, 156n37
Krochmal, Nahman, 53–54
Kugel, James, 10–11
*kvodo malay ha-olam*, 72

Laban, 12, 14, 29, 130, 132
learning: in Caesarea, 103; in classical rabbinic/early Christian era, 78; intensive, 73–74, 83
Levenson, Jon, 58, 83–84
Levi, Rabbi, 72, 93
Lieberman, Saul, 86
Logos, 98, 100–101, 102, 115–16
*Los Angeles Jewish Journal*, 70–71
Luliani, Rabbi, 89
Luria, Rabbi Isaac, 119, 123, 124
Lurianic Kabbalah school, 127

Maimonides, Moses, 47, 69, 106, 117, 127–28, 131, 137, 156n34, 157n69
Malachi, 60, 138–39, 150n78, 150n88
Marduk, 140
Mark, 98
Matt, Daniel, 119–20

*matzeva*, 28
McCarter, Kyle, 35
McCarter, P. K., 38
Meir, Rabbi, 71, 88–89, 93
Melkizedek, 17–19, 30
Menasseh Ben Israel, 122–23
Messianism, 98–100
Micah, 43, 48, 49–50, 60, 150n78; communication with, 78; on morality and ethics, 64
Michael, 89
Midrash, 73, 79, 82, 88, 131, 135, 158n1; creator of heaven and earth in, 89–90; on divinity and humanity, 117; on heart, 83; on might, 84; on Shema, 69; on soul, 83–84, 116; on two powers, 103–104
mitzvoth, 73, 83, 88, 120; for circumcision, 75–76; classical rabbinic/early Christian era and, 74–77; for food, 74–75; for Havdalah, 77; for *Seudah Shleesheet*, 76; for Shabbat, 75
Modena, Leon de, 120–21
Monotheism, 14, 17, 60, 137, 139, 148n22; as Bible's central idea, 5; chronology, 6; as cornerstone of Judaism, 68, 70, 102–103; doctrine, 121, 126; Egyptian sun god and, 26–27; emergence of, 2; ethical, 65–66, 92; Godhood as fundamental to, 89; incipient or implicit, 35; Isaiah and, 44–47; in Mosaic period, 21, 25, 31–32, 33–36; normative thought on, 5, 11; in patriarchal era, 9–11, 15, 19; in prophetic period, 37–44, 51; tracing of, 1. *See also* Oneness of God; Oneness of God, as Monotheism cornerstone
Moore, George Foote, 68, 70, 88, 92, 94, 103, 139, 153n57
morality, 66, 131; Amos on, 64; in classical rabbinic/early Christian era, 92; Isaiah on, 64; Jeremiah on, 64–65; Kaufmann on, 64; Micah on, 64; in Mosaic period, 31; one God means one morality, 139–40; in patriarchal era, 17; in prophetic period, 54, 62–65; Zechariah on, 65
Mosaic period, 1, 9–10, 144n32, 145n39; Canaan settlement in, 7, 27, 46; chronology of, 6; creator of heaven and earth in, 30–31; divine supremacy in, 25–27; Exodus, 22–23; Godhood in, 30; justice requirement in, 31–33; morality in, 31; overview, 21–22; people deity in, 27–29; protective deity in, 29–30; question of pure Monotheism, 33–36; root principles of, 3–4; YHWH in, 2, 22–25
mystics, 1, 6, 76, 80, 105, 111, 113–14, 118–20, 124, 134

Nahmanides, 121–22, 126–27, 132
natural world, 141
*Nishmat Shabbetai Halevi* (Horowitz), 125
nomads: Bible on, 14; Hebrews as, 6, 13–16, 18; Israel and, 17, 21, 27, 145n39; Semitic, 12; solidarity amongst, 15; view of, 22
normative thought: on Christian God idea, 102–104; on God's transcendence and immanence, 106–108, 112–13; on Holy Spirit, 101; Jewish theology, 72, 95, 96, 98, 105, 130; on Monotheism, 5, 9, 11; on soul, 129; on Yahwism, 10

Oneness of God, 39–40, 86, 95, 104, 126; abiding presence of, 3; in classical rabbinic/early Christian era, 73–74, 83; Deuteronomy on, 83–84; flow from, 5; Isaiah on, 42; Jesus compromising, 102–103; multiplicity of divinity and, 97; one God everywhere in world affirmation,

72–73; properties of, 4; in prophetic period, 47–50, 66. *See also* Shema

Oneness of God, as Monotheism cornerstone: one God means one design, 140–42; one God means one humanity, 138–39; one God means one morality, 139–40; overview, 137–38

Ormuzd, 68, 70

paganism, 98; attachment to, 29; cults of, 100; designers of, 141; fathers of, 138; gods in, 39–40, 50–51, 139–40; idols in, 62; nature of, 139; practices, 27–28, 48–49, 86

*Pahad*, 10, 12, 29, 30

patriarchal era, 1, 145n50; Abraham launching, 9; Canaan settlement in, 6–7, 15; chronology of, 6; creator of heaven and earth in, 18–19; Hebrew tenacity in, 15–19; justice requirement in, 15, 17; Monotheism origination and, 9–11, 19; morality in, 17; people deity in, 11–13; protective deity in, 13–14, 17; religious notions in, 18–19; seeds planted in, 11, 15; YHWH found in, 9–10, 24–25. *See also* Abraham; Isaac; Jacob

Paul, 98–99, 102, 114

people deity: in classical rabbinic/early Christian era, 86–87; in Mosaic period, 27–29; in patriarchal era, 11–13; in prophetic period, 47–52

peoplehood: Baeck on, 56–57; Baron on, 55; circumcision and, 75–76; Jewish survival in absence of land, 54–57; Kaufmann on, 56

personal God, 107–109, 113

Philo of Alexandria, 100, 120, 121, 131, 154n18, 156n25; on divinity and humanity, 114–16; on soul, 114

Plato, 115–16

Plotinus, 116

Plutarch, 115–16

Polytheism, 21, 35, 73, 96; in Canaan, 16, 19; negated, in classical rabbinic/early Christian era, 86–87; in prophetic period, 51; war on, 28, 48, 51

prayer: Amida, 78, 85; Blessing of New Mood, 79; in classical rabbinic/early Christian era, 79–81; good deeds and, 81–82; Kaddish, 106; for well-being, 80–81. *See also* ritual

prophetic period, 1, 9; chronology of, 6; creator of heaven and earth in, 60–62; insights during, 2; Isaiah and Monotheism, 44–47; Jewish survival in, 52–57; justice in, 62–66; Monotheism development in, 37–44; morality in, 54, 62–65; Oneness of God in, 47–50, 66; people deity in, 47–52; polytheism in, 51; protective deity in, 57–60; ritual in, 48, 63–66; supreme deity in, 37–44. *See also* Amos; Ezekiel; Hosea; Isaiah; Jeremiah

protective deity: in classical rabbinic/early Christian era, 88–89; Ezekiel on, 60; Isaiah on, 59; Jeremiah on, 59–60; in Mosaic period, 29–30; in patriarchal era, 13–14, 17; in prophetic period, 57–60

Proton Kinoun, 2

Proverbs, 73, 88, 89, 117, 122, 127–28, 154n18

Psalms, 33, 45, 76, 79, 93, 107, 118, 131, 152n23, 154n9

Rabbis. *See* classical rabbinic/early Christian era; *specific Rabbis*

Rav Kahana, 75

Redford, Donald, 26–27, 146n17

*Religion and the Individual: A Jewish Perspective* (Jacobs), 113

Responsa, 79

ritual, 120; in classical rabbinic/early Christian era, 74, 75–77, 84–85; consistent, 103; in prophetic period, 48, 64–66
Robinson, H. W., 42, 45
rote practice, 83–85

Sacks, Rabbi Jonathan, 4, 11, 157n71
*Sacred and the Profane* (Eliade), 77
Sanders, James, 22–23
Santayana, George, 129
Sarna, Nahum, 2, 26, 28, 145n39; on Ibn Ezra, 45–46
Saving Remnant doctrine, 2
Scholem, Gershom, 121, 126, 130, 133, 157n69
Schulweis, Rabbi Harold, 70–71
*Seudah Shleesheet*, 76
Shabbat, 23, 75, 79, 82, 90, 119, 131, 152n23
Shaddai, 11–12, 29–30
shalom, 81
Shamash, 140
*Shefa Tal* (Horowitz), 125–26, 127
Shema, 25, 34, 83, 88, 127, 158n1; Midrash on, 69; recitation of, 137–38
Shneur Zalman of Ladi, 6, 121, 127–30, 157n71
Simeon the Righteous, 74
single God, 30, 31–32, 102, 148n22
Smith, Mark, 22, 40–41, 43, 147n1, 148n22
Sodomites, 17, 19, 93
Sommer, Benjamin, 28–29, 33–34, 38, 96–97, 119, 153n1, 154n18
soul: Midrash on, 83–84, 116; normative thought on, 130; Philo of Alexandria on, 114–15; Talmud on, 116; Zohar on, 126–27
spiritual development, 2–4
spiritual intention, 83–85
Suffering Servant doctrine, 2
supreme deity: in classical rabbinic/early Christian era, 68–74; non-existence of other gods and, 37–42; in prophetic period, 37–44; universality of God and, 42–44
syncretism, 15–19

Talmud, 4, 70, 79; requirements in, 82; on son of God, 104; on soul, 116–17
Ten Commandments, 25, 28–29, 34, 62, 103
Tertullian, 101
Tigay, Jeffrey, 51–52
Torah, 74, 76, 78–79, 93, 119–20, 148n37; heaven and earth created for, 91–92; love flowing from, 88; Mishna, 4, 69, 86, 127, 131
transcendence, 105, 106–108, 112–13
tribes, 13–15
Trinity, 96–97, 101–102, 120–21, 126, 155n29. *See also* Holy Spirit; Jesus
*Tzafnas Paneyakh*, 46

universality of God, 42–44
Upanishads, 111–12, 114

Vishnu, 156n37
Vital, Hayyim, 123–24

"Where Was God in the Earthquake?" (Schulweis), 70–71
Winston, David, 115–16
Wright, G. Ernest, 22, 54–55
Wright, Robert, 40

Yerushalmi, Yosef, 2, 67
YHWH: Abraham and, 9–11; Bible on, 10; Bright on, 10; as God of Israel, 23; meanings of, 24–25, 144n2; in Mosaic period, 2, 22–25; in patriarchal era, 9–10; as standard, 6; worship of, 38, 51; Yahwism, 10, 13
Yigdal hymn, 110

*Ze-ayr Anpin*, 76
Zechariah, 44, 60, 62, 137, 150n78, 150n88; on justice, 63; on morality and ethics, 65
Zedekiah, 61
Zephaniah, 43
Zevit, Ziony, 1–3, 28, 143n1

Zohar, 6, 116, 130; on divinity and humanity, 118–20; on soul, 126–27
Zoroastrian dualism, 103; classical rabbinic/early Christian era and, 68–72; contemporary version of, 70–72; opposition to, 68–70

# About the Author

For two decades, **Jack Shechter** served as Associate Professor of Biblical Studies and Dean of the Department of Continuing Education—renamed *The Whizen Center for Continuing Education*—at the University of Judaism (now the American Jewish University). Prior to his tenure at the University of Judaism, he served as Executive Director of the New England Region of the United Synagogue of America, followed by a decade as the Rabbi of Congregation B'nai Israel in Pittsburgh. He was ordained at the Jewish Theological Seminary and received his PhD in Biblical Studies from the University of Pittsburgh. He is also the author of *The Land of Israel: Its Theological Dimensions* (2010) and *Journey of a Rabbi* (2014), both published by the University Press of America.

www.ingramcontent.com/pod-product-compliance
Lightning Source LLC
Chambersburg PA
CBHW022013300426
44117CB00005B/174